FINANCIAL ACCOUNTING

STUDY GUIDE

THIRD EDITION

RICHARD F. KOCHANEK
A. DOUGLAS HILLMAN
CORINE T. NORGAARD

FINANCIAL ACCOUNTING

STUDY GUIDE

THIRD EDITION

RICHARD F. KOCHANEK

UNIVERSITY of CONNECTICUT

A. DOUGLAS HILLMAN

DRAKE UNIVERSITY

CORINE T. NORGAARD

SUNY—BINGHAMTON UNIVERSITY

1997

DAME
PUBLICATIONS, INC.
HOUSTON, TX.

© HARCOURT BRACE JOVANOVICH, INC.—1992, 1989
© DAME PUBLICATIONS, INC.—1997

All rights reserved. No part of this publication may be reproduced, stored in a retrieval system, or transmitted, in any form or by any means, electronic, mechanical, photocopying, recording, or otherwise, without the prior written permission of the publisher.

Permission is hereby granted to reproduce Part 3, "Learning Goals Achievement Test" in this publication in complete pages, with the copyright notice, for instructional use and not for resale by any teacher using classroom quantities of the related student textbook.

Requests for permission to make copies of any part of the work should be mailed to: **Dame Publications, Inc.**, 7800 Bissonnet—Suite 415, Houston, TX 70074.

ISBN 0-87393-557-8

Printed in the United States of America.

Contents

To the Student		vii
Chapter 1	Introduction to Using Accounting Information	1
Chapter 1	An Accounting Information System	11
Chapter 2	Processing Business Transactions	29
Chapter 3	Adjusting Entries	67
Chapter 4	Completion of the Accounting Cycle	85
Chapter 5	Accounting for a Merchandising Business	113
Chapter 6	Internal Control and Cash	137
Chapter 7	Accounts Receivable and Bad Debts Expense	159
Chapter 8	Short-term Financing	177
Chapter 9	Inventories and Cost of Goods Sold	195
Chapter 10	Long-term Assets	219
Chapter 11	Corporations: Paid-in Capital	241
Chapter 12	Additional Stockholders' Equity Transactions and Income Disclosures	255
Chapter 13	Long-term Liabilities	279
Chapter 14	Investments in Stocks and Bonds	299
Chapter 15	Statement of Cash Flows	321
Chapter 16	Analysis and Interpretation of Financial Statements	347
Chapter 17	Business Consolidations and International Accounting	367
Chapter 18	Financial Reporting Issues	379
Appendix A	Federal Income Taxes	387
Appendix B	Understanding Published Annual Financial Reports	399
Appendix C	Application of Compound Interest and Tables	401
Appendix D	Special Journals and Accounting Systems	415
Appendix E	Payroll System	431
Appendix F	Partnership Accounting	447

To the Student

This **Study Guide** is especially for use with **Financial Accounting,** Third Edition by Hillman, Kochanek, and Norgaard. The **Study Guide** provides you with the tools to become an active learner and take direct responsibility for your learning. The format of the "Guided Study of This Chapter" section is unique to the Hillman, Kochanek, and Norgaard learning package. We have designed it to direct you in the learning process. To develop your learning skills, try to look beyond the correct answer to how we are guiding your study. The design will help you in learning how to learn accounting. Mastering the ability to learn is a skill that will benefit you through your entire career.

The chapter titles in the **Study Guide** are the same as those in the textbook. All references in the **Study Guide** are to the textbook's exhibits and illustrations. Each chapter in the **Study Guide** has four sections:

1. EXPLANATION OF MAJOR CONCEPTS
2. GUIDED STUDY OF THIS CHAPTER
3. LEARNING GOALS ACHIEVEMENT TEST
4. ANSWERS TO LEARNING GOALS ACHIEVEMENT TEST

Section 1, "Explanation of Major Concepts," contains a short summary (and simple illustrations) of important concepts covered in the corresponding textbook chapter. Section 2, "Guided Study of This Chapter," uses a progressive question-and-answer format. Careful use will help you understand the principles behind the accounting methods described in the corresponding textbook chapter. Keyed directly to specific textbook illustrations, the Guided Study questions are a step-by-step explanation of textbook ideas.

You should feel comfortable with each learning goal when you have finished studying a chapter in the textbook and study guide. Use section 3, "Learning Goals Achievement Test," and section 4, "Answer to Learning Goals Achievement Test," to help you test your competence in each learning goal. Sections 3 and 4 provide a set of short achievement tests with solutions. If you take these tests on a "closed book" basis, they will either confirm your competence in mastering the learning goals or point to specific topics where you need more study.

How to Use This Study Guide

Students have found this **Study Guide** to be useful in various ways. Most students report that they receive the greatest benefits from the following procedure:

1. Study the entire textbook chapter before turning to the ***Study Guide.***
2. Read section 1 of the ***Study Guide*** chapter, referring to the textbook as necessary to refresh your memory.
3. Turn to section 2 of the ***Study Guide*** and use it in the following manner:
    a. The right-hand side of each page contains questions with spaces to write in the answers. The left-hand side of each page contains answers to the questions. The format positions each answer one frame lower on the page than the question. Place a sheet of paper over the page so that you can see the first question but not the answer below and to the left of it.
    b. Write the answer to the question in the space provided. Refer to the textbook if necessary. This helps you recall the material you have studied in the chapter.
    c. Move the paper covering the page down one frame and compare the answer given with the one you have just written. If you are correct, go to the next question. If you are wrong, restudy that portion of the textbook. Figure out why your answer did not agree with the answer given in the Guided Study section.
    d. If you cannot figure out why your answer differs, mark that frame for discussion with your instructor.
4. After you have completed study of the textbook chapter and have done the assigned exercises, problems, and cases, take the Learning Goals Achievement Test in section 3. Do not refer to the textbook or notes when you take this test. Then use section 4 to check your answers. Use the learning goals numbers on each problem to identify the section of the textbook that you need to study more.

In addition to the above method, some students find it helpful to go back for a quick review before quizzes and tests.

There is no best method to study that applies to all students. Experience shows that **the most successful students have a definite study plan and follow it strictly**. To achieve the highest possible level of competence in ***Financial Accounting***, Third Edition, be sure to adopt and follow carefully a self-study plan.

The routines you set and follow today will serve you well as a student and in your future career. Rapid changes in technology and knowledge lie ahead. Those students who *learn to learn* will stand the best chance of dealing with the changes. Your career will be one of continual learning. Developing the skill of learning will be of great benefit to you.

Richard F. Kochanek
University of Connecticut
Storrs, Connecticut
June 1996

Introduction to Using Accounting Information

EXPLANATION OF MAJOR CONCEPTS

Business Planning Activities

Management must plan and control the business activities. Planning is the process that includes: developing assumptions about the future, establishing goals, making decisions, developing and putting plans into action, and evaluating results. Budgeting and controlling are part of the planning process. A budget is a financial plan for a future period. Controlling is the process of measuring and evaluating actual performance and taking corrective action.

Management must periodically ask questions. One question is, "How much cash will the business generate from operations?" Another questions is, "How much cash will the business need for investments in new assets?" A third question is, "How will the business obtain the cash that is necessary for operating and investing needs?"

The Accounting Information System and Its Users LG 1,2

Accounting is an information system. It generates information about an economic unit for decision makers inside and outside the business. The first step is gathering financial and other economic data. Once we gather the data we must measure and interpret it. We put together accounting measurements in reports for planning, controlling, and decision making.

An accounting information system is the resources and procedures within a business that transform effects of economic events into financial information.

We categorize users of accounting information into two groups: external users and internal users. External users are persons outside an organization who need and use accounting information about that organization. They do not have access to the accounting records, but rely on reports prepared by the accountant for that organization. They include creditors, investors, tax authorities, regulators, contributors to charitable organizations, government agencies, and others.

Internal users are persons within the organization who make decisions affecting the operations of the organization. They rely on the reports of the accountant for *planning* and *controlling* operations. Exhibit I-1 diagrams the accounting information system and its relationships to users. Exhibit I-2 lists the external user interest groups for a business.

The Entity Concept LG3

Each set of accounting records focuses on a specific organization. We record transactions from the viewpoint of that specific unit only. Each unit or organization that we maintain accounting records for is a separate accounting entity. A bank is an accounting entity. A pizza parlor that has borrowed money from that bank is another accounting entity. Both entities record the loan in their accounts, but from differing points of view. To the bank, the loan is a receivable. To the pizza parlor, it is a payable. It is even possible that the same person could own the bank and pizza parlor. But for accounting purposes, they are separate entities and have separate sets of accounting records.

Businesses organize in one of three ways: as single proprietorships, partnerships, or corporations. A single proprietorship is an unincorporated business with a single owner. These are the most numerous types of business organizations. A partnership is an unincorporated business with more than one owner. Persons in professional practice such as doctors and accountants frequently use this type of organization. In a proprietorship or partnership, the owners are personally responsible for the business debts. The corporation is a business recognized by the state as a legal entity. Most corporations have multiple owners, known as stockholders. A corporation is accountable for its own acts and its own debts. Most large businesses organize as corporations. In the United States, corporations do the largest volume of business. Exhibit I-4 shows the proportion of types of businesses. It also shows the proportion of total revenue generated by the various types of business organizations.

Financial Statements LG4

The primary financial statements are the balance sheet, the income statement, and the statement of cash flows. The balance sheet summarizes assets, liabilities, and owner's equity as of a point in time. Assets are economic resources a business owns. Liabilities are claims against assets by creditors. Owner's equity is the sum of claims to assets by the owners. For a balance sheet, total assets must equal total liabilities plus total owner's equity. This is the basic accounting equation.

$$\text{Assets}(A) = \text{Liabilities}(L) + \text{Owner's Equity}(OE)$$
(Economic Resources)   (Claims on assets)

The income statement presents the results of operations for a period of time. Inflows of assets that occur when a business performs services or sells goods are revenues. The use of assets when earning revenues we call expenses. Net income is the difference between revenues and expenses.

The statement of cash flows shows all the reasons why cash on the balance sheet changes during a period of time. The statement of cash flows presents the cash flows from three categories of activities: operating, investing, and financing. Operating activities shows the cash received from revenues and cash paid for expenses. Investing activities show the cash flows from buying and selling long-term assets.

Introduction to Using Accounting Information 3

Financing activities shows the cash flows from activities such as issuing stock or debt, or retiring debt.

Analyzing Information LG 5

The goal of this text is to show you how to use accounting information to make decisions. Often, it is easier to see relationships if we show financial statement items as percents instead of dollars. This creates a common-size statement. In a balance sheet, total assets, or total liabilities plus total owner's equity is 100%. In an income statement, total revenue is 100%. We begin developing our ability to analyze financial statements by asking questions about changes in financial statement items.

GUIDED STUDY OF THIS CHAPTER

A. Business Planning Activities
Cover the questions that follow with a piece of paper. Slide the paper down to reveal the first question. Use the text to find the answer to the question. Then slide the paper down to show the answer and the next question. Continue in this manner through the Guided Study.

1. Business leaders need to establish and continually review organizational ___Goals___ and ___Objectives___.

A1. goals, objectives

2. The process that includes establishing goals and objectives for the business is ___Planning___.

A2. planning

3. A financial plan for a future period is a ___Budget___.

A3. budget

4. The process of measuring and evaluating actual performance and taking corrective action is ___Controlling___.

A4. controlling

5. Management of Toys "R" Us must periodically make three types of decisions. They are ___operating___ decisions, ___investing___ decisions, and ___financing___ decisions.

Introduction

A5. operating, investing, financing

B1. information system

B2. collect, process, communicate

B3. resources and procedures in a business that change economic data into financial information

B4. management accounting

B5. financial accounting

B6. What is the current and long-term profitability? How does an investment in this business compare with other alternatives?

B. Business Reporting and Assessment Activities

1. Accounting is an _Information System_.

2. The three steps in the flow of data in a typical accounting information system are _Collect_, _Process_, _Communicate_.

3. An accounting information system is the _Resources + procedures in a business that changes economic data into Financial information_.

4. The part of accounting that provides information to internal users is _management accounting_.

5. The part of accounting that provides information to external users is _Financial accounting_.

6. Questions that owners might ask include _what is the current + long term profitability of the business_.

7. Questions that lenders might ask include _whether a business seeking a loan has the ability to make interest payments + to repay the loan_.

Introduction to Using Accounting Information 5

B7. What is the current and long-term profitability? What is the ability of the company to pay amounts owed on time?

B8. Does the business have responsible business practices? Does management have high ethical standards?

B9. balance sheet, income statement, statement of cash flows

B10. organization unit for which we gather and process financial and economic data for the purpose of decision making

B11. single proprietorship, partnership, corporation

B12. assets, liabilities, owner's equity, specific moment in time

B13. assets

B14. liabilities

B15. owner's equity

8. Questions that society groups might ask include __are the business leaders ethical + environ-mentally responsible__

9. The three primary financial statements are __B/S Balance sheet__, __Income sheet Statement__, and __Statement of cash flows__.

10. An accounting entity is any __is an organization unit for which we gather + process financial + economic data for the purpose of decision making__

11. The three types of business organization are __Proprietorship, Partner-__, __ship__, and __Corporations__.

12. The balance sheet summarizes __assets__, __Liabilities__, and __Owners equity__ as of a __specific moment in time__.

13. Economic resources or items of value a business owns are __assets__.

14. Claims against the assets by creditors are __Liability__.

15. The sum of all claims against the assets by owners are __Equities (Owners)__.

16. For a balance sheet, total assets must __equal__ total liabilities __plus__ total owner's equity.

6 Introduction

B16. equal, plus

17. We refer to this equality as the _Basic accounting equation_.

B17. basic accounting equation

18. The _Income Statement_ presents the results _operations_ for a _period of time_.

B18. income statement, operations, period of time

19. The inflows of assets from performing services or selling goods are _Revenues_.

B19. revenues

20. The use of assets or incurrence of liabilities when earning revenues are _Expenses_.

B20. expenses

21. Net income is the _when Total Revenues exceed Total expenses_.

B21. difference between revenues and expenses

22. The reasons why cash on the balance sheet changed is shown on the _Statement of the cash flows_.

B22. statement of cash flows

23. Net cash from _operating activities_ activities shows the difference between cash received from revenues and cash paid for expenses.

B23. operating

24. Net cash from _investing activities_ activities show the cash outflows from buying long-term assets and the cash inflows from selling long-term assets.

B24. investing

25. Net cash from _Financing_ activities shows the net cash inflow or outflow from additional financing a business needs.

B25. financing

C. Analyzing Information

1. It is easier to see relationships if we show financial statement items in _Percentages instead of $_.

Introduction to Using Accounting Information 7

C1. percentages instead of dollars

2. In a _common-size statement_, we express each item in the statement as a percent of the total for that statement.

C2. common-size statement

3. In a common-size balance sheet, we set _both total assets_ and _total liabilities + owners' equity_ each at 100%.

C3. total assets, total liabilities plus total owner's equity

4. In a common-size income statement, we set _total revenues_ at 100%.

C4. total revenues

5. In analyzing the balance sheet for Toys "R" Us, what is the percentage change in total assets _6.9_ %.

C5. 6.9

6. The numerator in this calculation is the _dollar amount of change_ which is $ _6,571,193_ minus $ _6,149,608_ .

C6. dollar amount of change, 6,571,193,000, 6,149,609,000

7. The denominator in this calculation is the _dollar amount for prior year_ which is $ _6,149,608_ .

C7. dollar amount for prior year, 6,149,609,000

8. Is the percent of total liabilities for Toys "R" Us increasing or decreasing? _✓_ Is this favorable or unfavorable _Favorable_ .

C8. decreasing, favorable

9. In analyzing the income statement for Toys "R" Us, what is the percentage change in total revenues? _10.1_ %

C9. 10.1

10. The dollar amount of change in total revenues is $ _799,519,000_ = $ _8,745,586,000_ – $ _7,946,067,000_ .

C10. 799,519,000, 8,745,586,000 7,946,067,000

11. The total asset turnover for Toys "R" Us for 1994 was _1.39_ times.

C11. 1.38

12. We found this by dividing _total revenues_ by _average total assets_ .

8   Introduction

C12. total revenues, total average assets

13. Total asset turnover measures the _ratio – Operating efficiency_

C13. operating efficiency

LEARNING GOALS ACHIEVEMENT TEST

1. (LG 1-2, 4) Indicate whether each of the following statements is true or false:

   _T_ a. A financial plan for a future period of time is a budget.
   _F_ b. The process of measuring and evaluating actual performance and taking corrective action is planning.
   _T_ c. Accounting has many purposes, but the primary purpose is to provide information that is useful to people in decision making.
   _F_ d. The part of accounting that provides information for internal users is financial accounting.
   _F_ e. The only people who would give careful study to financial reports of General Motors Corporation are its board of directors, officers, managers, and employees.
   _T_ f. Even though you are not responsible for operations of the American Cancer Society, you could use its accounting reports to form an opinion of how much of its contribution receipts actually get through to persons intended to receive help under its charitable relief programs.
   _T_ g. Federal and state governments have a legitimate reason to be interested in a business' financial reports.
   _T_ h. There is a natural relationship between the study of accounting and the study of management because all managers use accounting information in some way.
   _F_ i. As a student, it is unlikely that you are using actual accounting information today.
   _F_ j. Businesses are organized as either single proprietorships or corporations.
   _F_ k. Economic resources or items of value a business owns are liabilities.
   _F_ l. An inflow of assets from delivering services is an expense.
   _T_ m. Net cash from operating activities shows the difference between cash received from revenue and cash paid for expenses.
   _T_ n. In a common-size balance sheet, total assets are equal to 100%.
   _F_ o. In a common-size income statement, total expenses are equal to 100%.

2. (LG 3) Of the following listed organizations, circle those that are accounting entities:

   a. (A grocery store) owned by Mollie Newton.
   b. (A dry cleaning shop) owned by Mollie Newton.
   c. (Feinberg's), a large department store.

d. The Appliances Department of Feinberg's.
e. The Newton Reporter, a business forecasting service owned and operated by Mollie Newton.
f. The Loan Department of the First National Bank.

3. (LG 4) Write out in words the basic accounting equation.

Total assets are equal to liabilities + equity

ANSWERS TO LEARNING GOAL ACHIEVEMENT TEST

1. a. T   f. T   k. F
    b. F   g. T   l. F
    c. T   h. T   m. T
    d. F   i. F   n. T
    e. F   j. F   o. F

2. a, b, c, and e.

3. Assets = Liabilities + Owner's Equity.

Chapter 1

AN ACCOUNTING INFORMATION SYSTEM

EXPLANATION OF MAJOR CONCEPTS

Generally Accepted Accounting Principles LG 1

Generally accepted accounting principles are the standards used by accountants to make financial information meaningful. They come about either when practices are so widely used that they have gained general acceptance or through pronouncements of authoritative bodies. There are three primary authoritative accounting bodies: the American Institute of Certified Public Accountants (AICPA), the Financial Accounting Standards Board (FASB), and the Securities and Exchange Commission (SEC). The FASB is the independent nongovernmental body that develops and issues standards for external reporting. Pronouncements of the FASB are called *Statements of Financial Accounting Standards.*

Fields of Modern Accounting LG 2

We divide accounting practice into three major categories: public accounting, private accounting, and governmental accounting. Public accounting offers auditing, tax and management advisory services to the public for a fee. Accountants practicing in private accounting work for a single business. They measure and interpret the economic information for that organization. Private accountants work as management accountants, cost accountants, or internal auditors. Governmental accountants work for governmental bodies collecting the information used by administrators, regulators, and legislators.

Ethics and Accounting LG 3

Ethics is the process which individuals use to evaluate their conduct in light of moral principles and values. Ethical conduct is fair and socially acceptable. Ethical issues arise from competing interests. In order to give guidance in these situations, many professions and companies have developed written codes of conduct. Each chapter in the textbook includes an ethics case that allows discussion of the ethical issues.

The Accounting Equation LG 4

Every accounting entity has three basic elements: assets, liabilities, and owner's equity. Assets are things of value found in the organization--for example, money, supplies, tools, land, buildings, or equipment. Each asset has a monetary valuation (usually its cost). We can add the value of assets together and determine the dollar amount of total assets in an entity. Assets have one of two types of claims against them. Assets are either owed to someone (creditor claims) or they are owned by someone (ownership claims). Creditor claims are known as liabilities. Ownership claims are known as owner's equity.

Four types of events may cause ownership claims to change: investment by owners, withdrawals by owners, revenues, and expenses. Investments occur when the owner contributes assets to the business entity. If the owner removes assets from the business for personal use, this is a withdrawal. Revenues occur when there is an increase in assets from performing services or selling goods. A business incurs expenses when there is an outflow of assets or increase in liabilities as a result of generating revenues.

The fact that all assets are subject to these two types of claims makes the basic accounting equation true: Assets = Liabilities + Owner's Equity. Suppose a business purchases a new car which cost $9,500. It makes a down payment on the car of $1,500 and borrows the rest. This leaves the business owing $8,000 to the bank. If the business is an accounting entity and the car is its only asset, the accounting equation is:

Assets(A)	=	Liabilities(L)	+	Owner's Equity(OE)
$9,500	=	$8,000	+	$1,500
The car	=	Banks claim	+	Owner's claim

Although the mix of claims against the assets changes, the basic equation continues to hold true. In every entity, total assets are subject to some mixture of claims represented by liabilities and owner's equity (although either may sometimes be zero). Accordingly, the accounting system is built on this basic equation:

$$A = L + OE$$

Accounting Transactions LG 5

A transaction is an economic event that changes elements in the accounting equation. Businesses have hundreds of transactions each month that change elements of $A = L + OE$. To keep up-to-date with the changes, a business needs an accounting system to record each transaction.

The Recycle Consultants illustration in Chapter 1 shows how certain types of transactions change elements of $A = L + OE$. Note that before Transaction 1, the accounting equation had to be:

$0 = $0 + $0.

Immediately after Transaction 1, the equation became:

$90,000 = $0 + $90,000.

In studying the analysis of the ten transactions in Exhibit 1-5, you should note that individual elements increase or decrease with each transaction. For each transaction, we identify the elements of the equation that changed. Then we identify by how much they changed. After analyzing and recording each transaction, the basic equation ($A = L + OE$) is still valid. It must always be valid or there has been an error in recording. For example, after the December 9 transaction, the left side totals $98,000 and the right side totals $98,000. The Guided Study section will help you work through each transaction.

After we have analyzed all of the transactions using the accounting equation, we can use the information In Exhibit 1-5 to prepare the financial statements.

The Four Basic Financial Statements LG 6

A business prepares four basic financial statements--the income statement, the statement of owner's equity, the balance sheet, and the statement of cash flows. The chapter illustrates these statements using the information in Exhibit 1-5.

The *income statement* reports the revenues and expenses for a period of time. The excess of revenues over expenses is net income. If expenses exceed revenues there is a net loss. Exhibit 1-6 illustrates three of the statements for Recycle Consultants. Since revenues and expenses are changes in owner's equity, we find these items in the owner's equity column of Exhibit 1-5. We labeled each of the changes in owner's equity as investment, withdrawal, revenue, or expense as we recorded them. Now we pick out just the revenue and expense changes for the income statement.

The *statement of owner's equity* reports the changes in the owner's interest in assets for the period. It starts with the beginning capital balance. To that we add any additional owner investment and net income. We then subtract owner withdrawals. We also recorded these changes in the owner's equity column of Exhibit 1-5. We have already summarized the revenue and expense changes into the net income computation. Now we combine the net income with the investment and withdrawals to prepare the statement of owner's equity.

Most entities have more than one asset and usually have more than one type of creditor claim and ownership claim. The *balance sheet* is a financial statement that shows details of each of the three elements of the accounting equation. It is a snapshot of the financial position of an entity at a moment in time. Information of any type is more useful when we organize it into meaningful categories. The three basic elements of the accounting equation are each made up of many individual items. It is useful to group the individual items into similar classes on the balance sheet. One classification used for both assets and liabilities is *current*. An asset is a current asset if it is cash or is expected to be consumed or converted into cash within the year. A

14   Chapter 1

liability is a current liability if it will be liquidated (or paid off) with current assets within a year. This is usually the same as saying that a liability is current if it must be paid in one year.

Noncurrent assets have several classifications. The most common is property, plant, and equipment. A property, plant, and equipment asset is a long-term asset (not to be converted to cash in a year) used in operations of the entity. There are also long-term liabilities called long-term liabilities. Some of these are debts that are due to be paid over periods as long as twenty or thirty years.

Owner's equity in a single proprietorship (a business owned by one person) has only one classification. In Exhibit 1-6, the owner's equity is simply called "Debbie Starr, capital." Because of the basic accounting equation, we know that Debbie Starr has claims against $93,000 of the total assets. If $A = L + OE$, then $A - L = OE$. For this reason, we sometimes give another name to owner's equity--net assets. The owner's equity is the residual interest in the assets of the business. This means that if the business were forced to close, it would pay the creditors their cash first and any remaining cash would then go to the owners.

The last statement is the *statement of cash flows.*, Exhibit 1-7   This reports the cash inflows and outflows that occurred during the period. We categorize these cash flows into three categories--operating activities, investing activities, and financing activities. Operating activities are cash flows that relate to earning revenues and incurring expenses. Investing cash flows occur when we buy and sell long-term assets. Financing cash flows occur when the owner invests or withdraws money. Cash flows that occur when a business borrows money or pays it back are also financing activities. The information for this statement comes from the cash column of Exhibit 1-5.

GUIDED STUDY OF THIS CHAPTER

A. The Accounting Information System
Cover the questions on the following page with a piece of paper. Slide the paper down to reveal the first question. Use the text to find the answer to the question. Then slide the paper down to show the answer and the next question.

1. Babylonian textile mills kept production records and paid people based on work as early as ___600BC___ .

An Accounting Information System   15

A1. 600 BC

2. The three major authoritative accounting bodies in the United States are the _AICPA_, _FASB – Financial Accounting Standards Board_, and _SEC_.

A2. American Institute of Certified Public Accountants, Financial Accounting Standards Board, Securities and Exchange Commission

3. The independent nongovernmental body that develops and issues standards for financial accounting is the _FASB_.

A3. Financial Accounting Standards Board

4. We call the standards accountants follow _GAAP_.

A4. generally accepted accounting principles

5. The three major fields of accounting are (1) _Public accounting_, (2) _Private accounting_, and (3) _Government accounting_.

A5. public accounting, private accounting, government accounting

6. Public accountants offer their services to the public for a fee. Their three areas of service are _Auditing_, _Tax services_, and _Management advisory_.

A6. auditing, tax services, management advisory services

7. The independent review of the financial records of an organization is called _auditing_.

A7. auditing

8. Management advisory services range from the design of _computerized info systems_ to _finance planning_ and _cost studies_.

A8. computerized information systems, financial planning, cost studies.

9. Accountants that manage the accounting information system of a business are in _Private accounting_.

16 Chapter 1

A9. private accounting

A10. management accounting, cost accounting, internal auditing

A11. management accounting

B1. ethical issues

B2. fair and socially desirable

B3. experience, cultural background, and political beliefs

B4. the process which individuals use to evaluate their conduct in light of moral principles and values.

B5. above

B6. 56

10. The three major areas of private accounting are _Management Accounts_, _Cost acct._, and _Internal Auditing_.

11. The field that provides data and reports that enable the company managers to plan and control operations is _Management accts._.

B. Ethics

1. When competing issues come into conflict in a business _Ethical_ often arise.

2. Ethical conduct is _fair & socially desirable_.

3. A person's definition of ethics is affected by _Experience_, _Cultural_ _policies_, and _____.

4. Ethics is _the process that individuals use to evaluate their conduct in light of morals principles & values_.

5. Ethics often requires a level of behavior that is _above_ (at/above) the minimum level of the law.

6. A recent survey of U.S. companies indicated that _56_ % have corporate codes of conduct.

C. Building the Accounting Information System This next series of questions will help you understand basic accounting terms.

1. What is the name given to something of value owned by an accounting entity? _Asset_

An Accounting Information System   17

C1. An asset.

2. Which of the following are assets: cash, a delivery truck, a candy display case, serving trays in a cafeteria?
   cash, dT, cdc, + St

C2. All of them.

3. We value and record assets according to the Historical cost - cost principle

C3. cost principle

4. This requires that we record assets at the Historical cost.

C4. original price paid for them, called historical cost

5. The going-concern concept states that the company will continue to operate indefinitely unless there is evidence to the contrary.

C5. a company will continue to operate indefinitely unless there is evidence to the contrary

6. The stable dollar concept assumes that the dollar is sufficiently free from changes in purchasing power to be used as the basic unit of measure in accounting.

C6. sufficiently free from changes in purchasing power to be used as the basic unit of measure

7. What are the two types of claims against total assets of a business? liabilities + owners equities

C7. Creditor claims and owner claims.

8. What is the name for creditor claims? liabilities

C8. Liabilities.

9. What is the name for owner claims? Equity

C9. Owner's equity.

10. Owner's equity may change for one of four reasons. These are owners investments, Revenues, expenses, and owners withdrawals.

C10. investments, revenues, expenses, withdrawals

11. We call an inflow of assets that occurs when a business performs services or sells a product Revenue.

C11. revenues

12. Earning of revenue does not (does/does not) require a receipt of cash.

18   Chapter 1

C12. does not

13. Earning revenues causes an __↑__ *(increase/decrease)* in owner's equity.

C13. increase

14. When a business uses assets or incurs liabilities in generating revenues, it incurs an __expense__.

C14. expense

15. Expenses __↓__ *(increase/decrease)* owner's equity.

C15. decrease

16. When an owner removes assets from the business for personal use, it is called a __withdrawal__. This __↓__ *(increases/decreases)* owner's equity.

C16. withdrawal, decreases

17. Write out the basic accounting equation.
$A = L + OE$

C17. Assets = Liabilities + Owner's Equity.

18. What is the term for an economic event recorded by the accountant? __Transaction__ Give two or three examples of such events. __Investment__ __Selling of inventory__

C18. A transaction. Investment in a business, buying supplies, completing consulting services

19. If assets of Debbie Starr's delivery service were $10,000 and liabilities were $2,000, what would be the amount of owner's equity in that business? $ __8,000__

C19. 8,000.

20. Assume the same information as in C19; what is the amount of net assets of Starr's delivery service? $ __8000__

C20. 8,000.

21. Is *net assets* another term for owner's equity? __yes__

C21. Yes.

22. Suppose Starr paid the liabilities. Would this cause the basic accounting equation to be out of balance? __No__ Explain. __Because they would now be equity__

An Accounting Information System   19

C22. No. She would reduce cash by $2,000 and also reduce liabilities by $2,000.

23. In dollars, what would be the basic accounting equation for Starr's delivery service after she paid the liabilities?
_10,000 = 10,000_

C23. $8,000 = $0 + $8,000.

D. Recording Transactions
Study the recording of changes in the accounting equation by following the Recycle Consultants illustration.

1. In the December 1 transaction, items from two elements of the accounting equation changed. Cash increased from zero to $90,000. Also, owner's equity increased from zero to $ _90,000_ .

D1. 90,000.

2. In the December 5 transaction, what elements of the accounting equation changed? _~~Asset~~ cash land Building_

D2. Cash, land, and building.

3. Which items increased and by how much? _Building & land_

D3. Land by $20,000 and building by $50,000.

4. Classify the items that increased as assets, liabilities, or owner's equity. _assets_

D4. Both are assets.

5. What item(s) decreased and by how much? _cash - 70,000_

D5. Cash, by $70,000.

6. Classify the item that decreased as to asset, liability, or owner's equity. _asset_

D6. Cash is an asset.

7. After this exchange of cash for land and a building, do the total assets equal total equities? _yes_

D7. Yes.

8. Therefore, after recording the transaction total assets are equal to $ _70,000_ and total equities are equal to $ _90,000_ .

20 Chapter 1

D8. 90,000, 90,000

9. Analyze what has happened in the December 9 transaction. The asset entitled _Furniture_ has increased by $ _8,000_ . The liability entitled _A/P_ has increased by $ _8,000_ .

D9. Furniture, 8,000; Accounts Payable, 8,000

10. In the December 16 transaction, Recycle performed services and received an _asset_ .

D10. asset (cash)

11. Since Recycle received an asset by performing services, they have earned _Revenue_ .

D11. revenue

12. The dollar amount of revenue earned is $ _4,000_ . This is _equal_ to the value of assets received.

D12. 4,000; equal

13. We record the change in assets by _↑ Cash_ .

D13. increasing cash

14. We record the revenue by _↑ owners equity_ .

D14. increasing owner's equity

15. Why do we increase owner's equity? _Because owner has more claim to assets_

D15. Because the owner has more claim to assets after the revenue is earned.

16. In the December 23 transaction, Recycle again performed services. Was revenue earned? _Yes_ . Why? _Because services were performed_

D16. Yes; Because there was an inflow of assets (*accounts receivable*).

17. On December 26, there was a decrease in cash. Did Recycle buy an asset? _No_

D17. No.

18. What happened? _Incurred a expense_

D18. Recycle incurred an expense.

19. How much was the decrease in assets? $ _1,400_ How much was the expense $ _1,400_ .

D19. 1,400, 1,400

20. Thus we measure the amount of the expense by the __amount of assets used__.

D20. decrease in the assets

21. On December 27, Recycle received $1,500 cash from a client. Did it earn a revenue? __No__. Why? __Because it was recorded as a revenue when services were rendered__.

D21. No; It recorded the revenue on December 23 when it performed the service.

22. After recording the last transaction, does the accounting equation balance? __Yes__

D22. Yes.

23. What are total assets $ __94,000__.

D23. 93,600

24. What are total liabilities and owner's equity? $ __94,000__.

D24. 93,600

E. **Basic Financial Statements**
Using the results shown in Exhibit 1-5, we can prepare the four basic financial statements.

1. The four basic financial statements are the __Statement of Income__, __Statement of Owners Equity__, __Balance sheet__, and __Statement of Cash Flows__.

E1. income statement, statement of owner's equity, balance sheet, statement of cash flows

2. The income statement reports the details of the __Revenues__ and __Expenses__ for the period.

E2. revenues, expenses

3. The difference between revenues and expenses is __Net income / net loss__.

E3. net income *(if negative, it is a net loss)*

4. The heading on all financial statements includes __Name of Business__, __Name of Statement__, and __Date of Statement or period of time covered__.

22 Chapter 1

E4. name of the business, name of the statement, date of the statement or period of time covered

E5. 6,000, 2,000

E6. 4,000

E7. The statement of owner's equity

E8. capital balance at the beginning of the period

E9. additional investments, net income

E10. 0; It was the first period of operations.

E11. 90,000

E12. 1,000

E13. 93,000

E14. owner's equity

E15. we group the balance sheet items into items having a common basis

5. The total revenues for Recycle Consultants are $ __6,000__.
   The total expenses are $ __2,000__.

6. Thus the net income is $ __4,000__.

7. We also show this amount on which statement? __Statement of owner's equity__.

8. The first line of the statement of owner's equity is the __Balance from last statement__.

9. To this we add __Investments__
   and __net income__.

10. Starr's beginning capital balance was $ __0__. Why? __Because this is the 1st year.__

11. Starr made an investment in the business during December of $ __90,000__.

12. During December, Starr withdrew $ __1,000__ for personal use.

13. This makes the Starr's ending capital balance $ __93,000__.

14. This amount for ending capital is shown on the balance sheet in the __owner's equity__ section.

15. The balance sheet is classified. This means that __it is carried in groupings__.

16. The first classification of assets is __current assets__.

E16. current assets

17. Current assets include cash and other assets that a company expects to convert into cash in _one year_.

E17. one year

18. Recycle's total current assets on December 31, 1997, are $ _15,600_.

E18. 15,600

19. Recycle lists the following current assets: _cash & A/R_.

E19. cash and accounts receivable

20. Other examples of current assets are inventory and supplies.

E20. No answer required.

21. The second classification of assets is _Property, Plant & Equip_.

E21. property, plant, and equipment

22. Property, plant, and equipment includes assets _that continue into future & will cont. need to be used t con_

E22. used over a long period in the operation of the business

23. Recycle lists three property, plant, and equipment assets. They are _Land_, _Building_, and _Furniture_.

E23. land, building, furniture

24. The first category of liabilities is _Current liab_.

E24. current liabilities

25. Current liabilities include debts that _must be paid in current acct. period_

E25. must be paid in one year

26. Recycle has only one. It is _A/P_.

E26. accounts payable

27. Recycle has no other liabilities. The other classification would be _noncurrent liab_.

E27. long-term liabilities

28. These are liabilities that are not due in the _current acct period - next yr_

E28. next year

29. Recycle's total assets are $ _93,000_.

E29. 93,600

30. Recycle's total liabilities plus owner's equity is $ _93,100_.

24 Chapter 1

E30. 93,600

E31. No. An item may have been recorded in the wrong column or a transaction may have been completely left out.

E32. statement of cash flows

E33. cash flows from operating activities, cash flows from investing activities, cash flows from financing activities

E34. 5,500

E35. $500 of revenue was not collected as of December 31, 1997.

E36. The bill had not been paid.

E37. 15,100

E38. 15,100

E39. Yes.

31. Does this mean that Recycle's balance sheet is correct? __NO__ Why? _____

32. The last statement is the _statement of cash flows_.

33. The three classifications of cash flows are _Operating_, _Invest_, and _Financing_.

34. Because this statement reports changes in cash, we took the information to prepare this statement from the cash column of Exhibit 1-5. The cash received from customers was $ _5,500_ .

35. The income statement showed fees revenue of $6,000. Why isn't fees revenue and cash received from customers the same? _Because revenue are recognize at point of sale_

36. The statement of cash flows does not show payments for utilities. Why? _B_

37. The statement of cash flows shows the ending cash balance as $ _____ .

38. The December 31, 1997, balance sheet shows cash of $ _____ .

39. Will this relationship always be true? ___

F. Analyzing Information

1. In analyzing income statement information, we can look at the change in revenues. For L. A. Gear, total revenues _____ (increased/decreased) from 1987 through 1990 by $ _____

An Accounting Information System   25

F1.   increased, 749,000,000

2. The percentage change in total revenues from 1987 to 1990 was _____ %. We found this by dividing the change in revenue $ _____ by the revenue in _____ of $ _____.

F2.   1,060.9, 749,000,000, 1987, 70,600,000

3. The percent of total expenses to total revenues _____ (increased/decreased) from 1987 to 1989.

F3.   decreased

4. In 1987 the percent of total expenses to total revenues was _____ %. In 1989, the percent was _____ %.

F4.   93.8, 90.7

5. Then, in 1990 it _____ (increased/decreased) to _____ %.

F5.   increased, 96.2

6. Are total assets for L. A. Gear higher or lower for the four year period?
   _____

F6.   higher

7. The percentage change in total assets from 1987 to 1990 is _____ %.

F7.   889.1

8. We found this by dividing the change in total assets of $ _____ by the assets in 1987 of $ _____.

F8.   327,200,000, 36,800,000

9. By referring to the common-size percents, is the percent of total liabilities to total liabilities plus total owners' equity increasing or decreasing for the four year period?
   _____

F9.   increasing

10. In 1987, it was _____ %. And in 1990 it was _____ %.

F10. 39.9, 43.4

11. We can judge operating efficiency by dividing total _____ by average total _____.

F11. revenues, assets

12. This ratio is called _____
    _____.

26 Chapter 1

F12. total asset turnover

13. In 1990, total revenues for L. A. Gear were $_____ , and average total assets were $_____ .

F13. 819,600,000, 315,300,000

14. We find average total assets by adding _____ and _____ and dividing the total by _____ .

F14. beginning assets, ending assets, 2

15. For L. A. Gear in 1990 beginning assets were $_____ and ending total assets were $_____ .

F15. 266,600,000, 364,000,000

16. Total asset turnover _____ (increased/decreased) from 1989 to 1990.

F16. decreased

17. Is this favorable or unfavorable? _____

F17. unfavorable.

LEARNING GOALS ACHIEVEMENT TEST

1. (LG 1-3) Indicate whether each of the following statements is true or false:

   T a. Accounting has many purposes, but the primary purpose is to provide information that is useful to people in decision making.

   F b. The only people who would give careful study to financial reports of General Motors Corporation are its board of directors, officers, managers, and employees.

   T c. Even though you are not responsible for operations of the American Cancer Society, you could use its accounting reports to form an opinion of how much of its contribution receipts actually get through to persons intended to receive help under its charitable relief programs.

   T d. Federal and state governments have a legitimate reason to be interested in a business' financial reports.

   F e. Accounting began in the United States when the first income tax laws required individuals and corporations to report their incomes and pay income tax.

   T f. There is a natural relationship between the study of accounting and the study of management because all managers use accounting information in some way.

   T g. Many accountants work for federal, state, or local governments.

An Accounting Information System   27

__F__ h. As a student, it is unlikely that you are using actual accounting information today.
__F__ i. Businesses are organized as either single proprietorships or corporations.
__T__ j. The standards employed to make financial information meaningful for users are set today primarily by the Financial Accounting Standards Board.

2. (LG 4) Write out in words the basic accounting equation.

The Total Assets must be equal to total liability plus owners claims on assets

3. (LG 5) For each of the transactions listed below indicate how the accounting equation would be changed by placing a plus or minus in the appropriate columns.

		Asset	Liability	Owner's Equity
a.	L. Jones invested $5,000 cash in a new business.	+DR		+CR
b.	Purchased $200 in office supplies on account.	+DR	+CR	
c.	Earned $300 in revenue by performing services.	+DR		+DR (Rev)
d.	Bought $100 in office supplies paying cash.	+CR +DR		+DR
e.	Paid the account from (b) above.	CR —	−DR	
f.	Paid wages to employees.	CR —		—DR

4. (LG 7) Opposite each item listed below, indicate with a numeral whether it is:

1. A current asset.
2. A property, plant, and equipment asset.
3. A current liability.
4. A long-term liability.
5. An owner's equity item.

__5__ a. Eric Amash, capital.
__3__ b. Accounts payable.
__1__ c. Cash.
__1__ d. Accounts receivable.
__5__ e. Revenue.
__2__ f. Buildings.
__5__ g. Utilities Expense.
__4__ h. Mortgage payable (due in 20 years).
__3__ i. Notes payable (due in 60 days).
__3__ j. Wages payable.
__5__ k. Eric Amash, withdrawals.

ANSWERS TO LEARNING GOAL ACHIEVEMENT TEST

1.
   a. T f. T
   b. F g. T
   c. T h. F
   d. T i. F
   e. F j. T

2. Assets = Liabilities + Owner's Equity.

3.

	Asset	Liability	Owner's Equity
a.	+		+
b.	+	+	
c.	+		+
d.	+ −		
e.	−	−	
f.	−		−

4.
   a. 5 g. 5
   b. 3 h. 4
   c. 1 i. 3
   d. 1 j. 3
   e. 5 k. 5
   f. 2

Chapter 2

PROCESSING BUSINESS TRANSACTIONS

EXPLANATION OF MAJOR CONCEPTS

Accumulation of Data Using Accounts   LG 1

An accounting system has an account for each item that will appear on the financial statements. We record changes in the elements of the accounting equation in accounts. An **account** is a recording device that we use to sort accounting data into similar groups. As the dollar amounts of accounts (cash, accounts receivable, accounts payable, and so on) increase or decrease due to transactions, we record the changes in the account representing that subelement. For example, we record all the changes in cash in the Cash account. The balance in the Cash account on a specific date tells us how much cash we have as of that date.

Commonly Used Accounts and the Chart of Accounts   LG 2

We divide the accounts in an entity's accounting system into asset, liability, and owner's equity categories. We further subdivide assets into current assets and property, plant, and equipment. Common current assets are Cash, Accounts Receivable, and Prepaid Expenses. Commonly used property, plant, and equipment accounts are titled Land, Buildings, and Equipment. We divide liabilities into current and long-term. Current liabilities include Accounts Payable, Notes Payable, and Wages Payable. Long-term liabilities include Bonds Payable and Mortgages Payable. Owner's equity accounts include the Capital and Withdrawals account for the owner, revenues, and expenses.

The **chart of accounts** is a listing of all the accounts in the accounting system and the account numbers assigned to them. We arrange the accounts in order according to how they will appear on the financial statements. There should be an account in the system for each piece of information that appears in the accounting reports. The more detail desired in the reports produced by the accounting system, the more accounts that we include in the accounting system. When we assign account numbers, we should leave gaps so that we can add new accounts as the system grows.

We show the master chart of accounts used for all of the chapter illustrations, exercises, and problems, inside the front and back covers of the textbook. Review this to see the set up of a chart of accounts. Since the textbook uses a three-digit account number, we have used most account numbers because of the large number of

30 Chapter 2

accounts needed in the textbook.   Many businesses would use 10 to 15 digits in their system.

Debits and Credits   LG 3

Every transaction causes increases or decreases to two or more accounts in the accounting equation, *A = L + OE*. We use the words debit and credit to refer to these increases or decreases. In *any* account, a **debit** goes on the left side, and a **credit** goes on the right side. Using a T account to illustrate, then:

Any Account	
The debit side	The credit side

Since every transaction involves increases and decreases in elements of *A = L + OE*, we have a set of arbitrary rules to follow that show when an increase to an account is a debit and when it is a credit.   Actually, you need to memorize only one rule--an increase in an asset is a debit. You can derive all other rules from this basic rule and the position of the element in the equation.

The positive side of an account is its increase side. We determine the increase side of an account by its position in the accounting equation, *A = L + OE*. It is not normal for a subelement of the equation to have a negative balance. You might overdraw your bank account and have a temporary negative balance in cash, but can you imagine having a negative balance in a Furniture account? You could have a zero balance (no furniture) but never less than zero. Therefore, the following system falls into place:

ASSETS   =   LIABILITIES   +   OWNER'S EQUITY

Asset Accounts	=	Liability Accounts	+	Owner's Equity Accounts
Increase side		Increase side		Increase side

If an account is on the left side of the equation (as are Cash, Land, Furniture, and all other asset accounts), its increase side is the left or debit side of the account. If on the other hand, the account is on the right side of the equation (as are Accounts Payable, and Debbie Starr, Capital), its increase side is the right or credit side. Decreases in these accounts are just the opposite. If we increase an account by a debit, it is logical that we decrease it with a credit. If we increase the account by a credit, we decrease it by a debit. Keep this in mind as you decide whether to debit or credit specific accounts to record increases or decreases. Remember debit does not always mean increase. It is necessary to know what type of account you are dealing with to know whether debit means increase or decrease.

Processing Business Transactions

Changes in Owner's Equity

Owner's equity is the dollar amount of ownership rights in or claims against total assets. Owner's equity changes for four reasons: owner's investment, owner's withdrawals, revenues, and expenses. In Chapter 1 we studied how these transactions affected owner's equity. We now need to look at the debit/credit treatment.

If we record revenue and expense transactions directly in the owner's equity account, it would be difficult if not impossible to determine net income. It is possible, however, to accumulate changes in owner's equity related to income in separate *revenue* and *expense* accounts. At the end of an accounting period, we can use these accounts to prepare the income statement.

Revenue and Expense Accounts   To accumulate information about operating changes in owner's equity, we use revenue accounts and expense accounts. There are many types of revenues and expenses. We accumulate each in an account bearing a title that describes that particular revenue or expense.

A company earns **revenues** when it performs a service or delivers a product. The amount of the revenue earned is equal to the value of the asset received (typically cash or accounts receivable). A company incurs **expenses** when it consumes the economic benefits embodied in an asset. We measure the amount of the expense by the cost of the asset that was used up or that the company promised to give up in the future (accounts payable). You must bear in mind as you study this chapter that:

- Revenues cause an asset to increase and therefore cause owner's equity to increase.
- Expenses cause an asset to decrease or liability to increase and therefore cause owner's equity to decrease.

Because of the two foregoing statements, we would conclude that:

- Revenues increase owner's equity and have the same rules for debit and credit as an owner's equity account. You should credit a revenue to show an increase and debit a revenue to show a decrease.
- Expenses decrease owner's equity and have debit and credit rules that are the opposite of the rules for owner's equity. You should debit an expense to show an increase and credit an expense to show a decrease.

Withdrawals   The third type of account causing a change in owner's equity is the owner's withdrawals account. Just as an investment of assets increases owner's equity, a reduction of investment by withdrawing assets from the business causes a decrease in owner's equity. When an owner makes periodic withdrawals (usually of cash) to meet personal living expenses, we could debit the owner's capital account to show the reduction. In practice, however, we need to keep a separate record of periodic withdrawals. To do this, we use a new account with the title Withdrawals. We debit it because increases in withdrawals decrease the equity of the owner in the business.

32 Chapter 2

We have expanded the accounting equation to include three new account types. The equation now is:

Assets = Liabilities + Owner's Equity + Revenues - Expenses - Withdrawals

Owner's Equity as it appears in the equation includes the beginning amount plus any investments made by the owner during the period. We have recorded the changes in owner's equity during the period resulting from operating events and owner's withdrawals in revenue, expense, and withdrawals accounts.

This expanded equation can be restated as:

Assets + Expenses + Withdrawals = Liabilities + Owner's Equity + Revenues

You can use this expanded equation to review the rules for debit and credit. As we did earlier in this chapter of the Study Guide, accounts in classifications that are on the left side of the equation when positive have normal left-hand (or debit) balances. Accounts that are on the right side of the equation when positive have a normal right-hand (or credit) balance. Remember, it is not normal for any account to have a negative balance. Therefore, you should follow this pattern on how to increase an account:

Debit to increase:	Credit to increase:
Assets	Liabilities
Expenses	Owner's Equity
Withdrawals	Revenues

Decreases in accounts would be just the opposite.

Analyzing Transactions with Debits and Credits LG 4

As you analyze transactions, you should train yourself to go through a step-by-step process as follows:

1. Determine which items from the accounting equation, or accounts, the transaction changes.
2. Decide which category of the accounting equation that each account falls into--asset, liability, or owner's equity.
3. Decide how each account has changed, an increase or decrease.
4. Translate this information into a debit or credit.

Remember that in each transaction the total debits equals the total credits. This keeps the accounting equation in balance.

Processing Business Transactions 33

The Formal Ledger Account   LG 5

As we study the process of analyzing transactions, we often use a T account. However, an actual accounting system uses a more formal form for the account. Exhibit 2-4 shows one possible form. It has columns to enter the date, any extra information that might be necessary, the posting reference, the debit or credit transaction amount, and the debit or credit balance. It contains the same information as the T account but in a more formal format. The collection of all the accounts for an accounting entity is called the **general ledger**.

Journalizing and Posting   LG 6, 7

Time spent now learning the exact details of making journal entries and postings to the ledger accounts will save you hours of searching for errors in your homework. We call the process of entering information about a transaction into the accounting system **journalizing**. Exhibit 2-5 shows the journal entry for the December 1 transaction of the Recycle Consultants. The numbered explanations that accompany that journal entry tell you exactly how to record any journal entry. After journalizing the transactions, we must transfer the information contained in the journal to the general ledger. This process is called **posting**. Exhibit 2-6 illustrates exactly how to post that journal entry. After studying those two illustrations, go to the total illustration of Recycle Consultants transactions in Exhibits 2-7 and 2-8. This will help you understand and practice the debit/credit rules.

   The diagram on the next page shows the relationship of a journal to the general ledger (the entire group of accounts).

Trial Balance and Financial Statements   LG 8

After completing the posting, we should verify the equality of the debits and credits in the general ledger. We do this by preparing a trial balance. The **trial balance** is simply a listing of all the accounts in the general ledger along with their balances. If the sum of the debit balances and the credit balances is the same, we have some assurance of the accuracy of our work. It is not a guarantee of the accuracy, however. For example, we could have posted a debit amount as a debit to the wrong account. The trial balance would balance, but some of the account balances would be incorrect.

   We prepare the financial statements from the trial balance. We start with the income statement. Exhibit 2-10 shows how to use the trial balance to prepare the income statement. Exhibit 2-11 shows the preparation of the statement of owner's equity, and Exhibit 2-12 shows the preparation of the balance sheet.

GENERAL JOURNAL

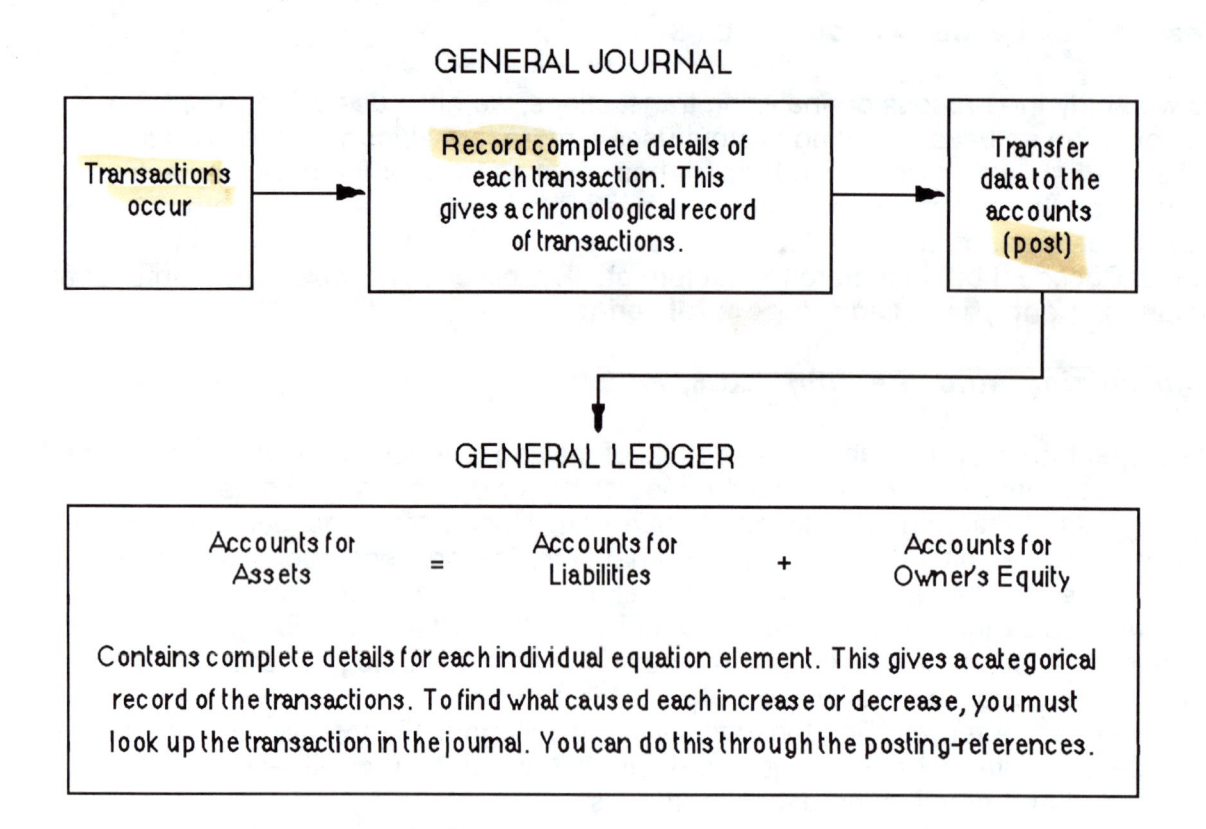

Transactions occur → Record complete details of each transaction. This gives a chronological record of transactions. → Transfer data to the accounts (post)

GENERAL LEDGER

| Accounts for Assets | = | Accounts for Liabilities | + | Accounts for Owner's Equity |

Contains complete details for each individual equation element. This gives a categorical record of the transactions. To find what caused each increase or decrease, you must look up the transaction in the journal. You can do this through the posting-references.

Overview of the Accounting System: The Accounting Cycle

Thus far we have developed a simple accounting system. This begins with the existence of objective evidence of a transaction, usually in the form of a business document. From the document, we make a record of the effect of the transaction in the journal or book of original entry. Next, we transfer or post the data in the journal to the ledger. Periodically we test the accounting system with a trial balance, which checks on the equality of debits and credits in the ledger. After completing this, we prepare the financial statements.

Analyzing Information LG 9

We can analyze the income statement by computing the dollar and percentage change in revenues over a period of time. We compute the dollar change by subtracting the revenues in the earlier period from those in the later period. We compute the percentage change by dividing the dollar change between two points by the dollar amount in the earlier period.

In analyzing the balance sheet, we can compute the dollar and percentage change in total assets over a period of time. We compute the percentage change by dividing the dollar change by the dollar amount in the earlier period. On the balance sheet, we

Processing Business Transactions 35

can also compute the percentage that total liabilities are of total liabilities plus owner's equity. We can then compare this percentage over time.

Integrating the income statement and balance sheet analysis also provides useful information. We can divide total revenue by average total assets. This gives a ratio called *total asset turnover*. A higher number is usually more favorable.

GUIDED STUDY OF THIS CHAPTER

A. The Account.
Begin our study with the account.

1. An account is _____

A1. a recording device used for sorting accounting information into similar groupings. One account will exist for each item in the financial statements.

2. Current assets consist of cash and other assets expected to be converted into cash or consumed in the operation of the business _____.

A2. within one year

3. Examples of current assets are _____.

A3. cash, accounts receivable, and prepaid expenses

4. The major classification of long-term assets is _____.

A4. property, plant, and equipment

5. Examples of property, plant, and equipment are _____.

A5. land, buildings, and equipment

6. Liabilities are divided into _____.

A6. current and long-term

7. Examples of current liabilities are _____.

A7. accounts payable, notes payable, and wages payable

8. Examples of long-term liabilities are _____.

36 Chapter 2

A8. mortgages payable and bonds payable

A9. capital, withdrawals, revenues, expenses

A10. the amount given up to purchase an asset

A11. use the purchased item in producing a revenue

A12. complete listing of all of the account titles used by an entity and their account numbers.

A13. We should set up an account for each type of information desired.

A14. We should arrange the accounts in the order that they will appear in the financial statements.

A15. We group accounts according to the classifications that will appear on the financial statements. Then we assign numbers, leaving gaps to add new accounts.

9. Owner's equity includes _____, _____, _____, and _____.

10. Cost is _____.

11. Cost becomes an expense when we _____.

12. The chart of accounts is a _____.

13. Describe the criteria used to determine the necessary accounts. _____

14. Describe the account ordering scheme used in setting up the chart of accounts. _____

15. Describe the scheme for establishing account numbers. _____

16. In the chart of accounts for Recycle Consultants in Exhibit 2-2, property, plant, and equipment accounts use what number sequence? _____

Processing Business Transactions 37

A16. 150-189.

17. Why were no account numbers assigned between Building and Furniture?
_____
_____
_____

A17. We did this to allow for the insertion of new accounts as the company expands.

B. Debits and Credits

1. The left side of an account is known as the _____ side, and the right side is known as the _____ side.

B1. debit, credit.

2. Entering a number on the debit side of an account means that we are increasing it. _____. (*True/False*) Why? _____
_____

B2. False; It depends on what type of account it is.

3. We find the balance of an account by
_____
_____
_____
_____

B3. finding the difference between the sum of the debits and the sum of the credits.

4. Rules for the use of debits and credits are developed from the accounting equation. Since assets are on the left side of the accounting equation, we increase asset accounts with _____.

B4. debits

5. And since liabilities and owner's equities are on the right side of the accounting equation, we increase them with
_____.

B5. credits

6. We record decreases in any account with the _____.

B6. opposite entry

7. Therefore, we decrease an asset account with a _____ and decrease liability and owner's equity with _____.

38 Chapter 2

B7. credit, debits

8. If you remember that assets are increased with debits, you can work out all of the other changes from that.

B8. No answer required.

9. A revenue describes the source of an inflow of assets (or reduction of liabilities). It is the result of providing goods or services to someone outside the business. Revenues _____ (increase/decrease) owner's equity.

B9. increase

10. Therefore, each time a transaction generates revenue, we should _____ (debit/credit) a revenue account.

B10. credit

11. From the following transactions, choose those that are revenue transactions (show only the letter representing them).
    a. Borrowed $1,000 from the bank.
    b. Billed customers for services rendered to them.
    c. Provided services to customers and received cash.
    d. Collected an amount from customers previously billed.
    e. Received the cash from customers for services billed in b.
    f. An owner invested additional funds in her own business.
    _____

B11. b, c.

12. From the foregoing, we see that borrowing is not revenue. Why? _____
    _____
    _____
    _____

B12. Although borrowing is an inflow of assets, it increases liabilities instead of owner's equity.

13. Why is revenue recognized when we bill customers for services rendered but receive no cash? _____
    _____
    _____
    _____
    _____

Processing Business Transactions 39

B13. There is an inflow of assets (accounts receivable) and an increase in owner's equity from an operating event.

14. When we collect these bills later, we do not have a revenue transaction. Explain. _____
_____
_____
_____

B14. There is an inflow of assets (cash), but it is in exchange for another asset (accounts receivable). We performed no additional services nor delivered goods. There is no change in owner's equity.

15. An owner's investments represent an inflow of assets and an increase in owner's equity. Therefore, is an investment by an owner a revenue?
_____

B15. No.

16. Why not? _____
_____
_____
_____

B16. It is not the result of providing goods or services to someone outside the business.

17. In your own words, describe an expense.
_____
_____
_____
_____
_____
_____

B17. It is an outflow of assets (or increase in liabilities) from business transactions that decreases owner's equity. It results when a business consumes the economic benefits of an asset in the process of generating revenues.

18. Would the expired costs of consuming office supplies be an expense? _____ . Why? _____
_____
_____
_____
_____

B18. Yes; An asset would be consumed in the process of generating revenues.

19. Wages and salaries of employees are expenses. The business is consuming what expired cost? _____
_____
_____
_____

40 Chapter 2

B19. The business receives the employee's services and gives up cash.

B20. No; It is simply an exchange of an asset for a liability.

B21. a. Wages Expense.
b. Interest Expense.
c. Repairs Expense.

B22. Debit; Each is an increase in expense.

B23. a. Cash.
b. Cash.
c. Accounts Payable.

B24. debit

20. Is the payment of an account payable an expense? _____. Explain.
_____
_____
_____

21. For each of the following transactions, suggest an appropriate expense account title.
a. Paid wages to employees
_____
b. Paid interest on money borrowed from the bank. _____
_____
c. Received a bill from a carpenter for repairing an office desk. _____
_____

22. In each case in B21, would we debit or credit the expense account? _____ . Why? _____
_____

23. To complete the recording of each of these three transactions, show the account title that we would credit.
a. _____
b. _____
c. _____

24. Another action that changes owner's equity is the withdrawal of assets by an owner. To record an additional withdrawal, which reduces owner's equity, we _____ (debit/credit) the withdrawals account.

25. Why did a debit increase the withdrawals account?_____
_____
_____
_____

B25. A withdrawal of assets by the owner has the effect of decreasing owner's equity (done with debits). The more withdrawals the owner makes, the less owner's equity there is. Debits decrease owner's equity.

26. Review the rules for debit and credit by completing the following table:

Type of Account	Increase	Decrease
Asset	Debit	_____
Liability	_____	_____
Owner's capital	_____	_____
Revenue	_____	_____
Expense	_____	_____
Withdrawals	_____	_____

B26. Debit   Credit
      Credit   Debit
      Credit   Debit
      Credit   Debit
      Debit   Credit
      Debit   Credit

C. **Recording Changes in the Accounts**
Begin the study of recording changes in accounts by following the Recycle Consultants illustration.

1. In the December 1 transaction, cash and owner's equity changed. Cash increased from zero to $ _____ . Also, owner's equity increased from zero to $ _____ .

C1. 90,000; 90,000

2. In the December 5 transaction, what elements of the accounting equation changed? _____

C2. Cash, land, and building.

3. Classify the items that increased as assets, liabilities, or owner's equity.

C3. Land increased and is an asset. Building increased and is an asset.

4. Classify the items that decreased as assets, liabilities, or owner's equity.

C4. Cash decreased and is an asset.

5. Which items increased and by how much in the December 5 transaction?

42 Chapter 2

C5. Land by $20,000 and building by $50,000.

6. What item(s) decreased and by how much? _____

C6. Cash, by $70,000.

7. If you were applying the rules of debit and credit, would the increases in assets be debits or credits? _____ .

C7. Increases in assets are debits.

8. Would the decrease in cash be a debit or a credit? _____

C8. A credit *(cash is an asset and assets are decreased with credits)*.

9. In this exchange of cash for land and a building, do the total debits equal total credits? _____

C9. Yes.

10. Therefore, we have a complete transaction with total debits equal to $_____ and total credits equal to $ _____ .

C10. 70,000, 70,000

11. Analyze what has happened in the December 9 transaction. The asset entitled _____ has increased by $_____ . The liability entitled _____has increased by $ _____ .

C11. Furniture, 8,000; Accounts Payable, 8,000

12. Is the $8,000 increase in Furniture a debit or is it a credit? _____

C12. A debit.

13. Is the $8,000 increase in the liability a debit or is it a credit? _____

C13. A credit.

14. If total debits equal total credits, we have completed the analysis of this transaction. Is this the case here? _____

C14. Yes.

15. Take note of the pattern that we use. Increases in assets are always debits, so decreases in assets must be _____ .

C15. credits

16. Increases in liabilities are _____ and decreases in liabilities are _____ .

Processing Business Transactions 43

C16. credits, debits

17. In Transaction 4, Recycle performed consulting services and received an asset. So it earned a revenue. What asset increased? _____ . What revenue increased? _____ .

C17. Cash, Fees Revenue

18. We _____ (debited/credited) Cash because a(n) _____ (increase/decrease) in Cash occurred.

C18. debited, increase

19. We _____ (debited/credited) Fees Revenue because it represents a(n) _____ (increase/decrease) in owner's equity.

C19. credited, increase

20. To double check your analysis of a transaction, use transaction 5 on December 18. First, what accounts changed, what are their classifications, did they increase or decrease?
_____
_____
_____
_____

C20. Cash, an asset, decreased; and accounts payable, a liability, decreased.

21. Translate these changes into debits and credits. _____
_____
_____
_____

C21. A decrease in cash is a credit. A decrease in accounts payable is a debit.

D. **Journalizing and Posting**
While studying journalizing and posting refer to Exhibits 2-5 and 2-6.

1. When recording a transaction in journal form what is the first step? _____
_____
_____

D1. The first step is to enter the year on the first line of the date column. *Note that we do not repeat it for each transaction.*

2. What is the second step in journalizing?
_____
_____
_____

44 Chapter 2

D2. Enter the month of the first transaction. *Note that we do not repeat it until we enter a transaction for a new month.*

D3. Enter the date of the transaction.

D4. Write the debit account title at the left margin of the explanation column.

D5. List all of the debit accounts at this point in the journal entry.

D6. Enter the debit dollar amounts into the debit amount column. We do not use dollar signs.

D7. List the credit account titles with an indentation from the left margin.

D8. Enter the credit dollar amounts into the credit amount column.

D9. Write an explanation below the credit account titles. *A short phrase is all that is necessary.*

3. What is the third step? _____

4. What is the fourth step in journalizing transactions? _____

5. If we are debiting more than one account, how many do we list at this point? ____ _____

6. What is the next step to journalize? _____

7. What is the sixth step? _____

8. What is the seventh step? _____

9. What is the last step? _____

10. The journal entry in Exhibit 2-6 shows a $90,000 debit to Cash. Does this mean that Cash increased or decreased? _____

Processing Business Transactions   45

D10. Increased.

D11. Owner's equity.

D12. Increase.

D13. Posting.

D14. 101, 301

D15. Locate the ledger account for the debit entry.

D16. Write the year at the top of the date column. Then enter the date, the journal page, and debit amount. Then determine the effect of the transaction on the balance and place the appropriate value in the Balance column.

D17. Enter the ledger account number for the debit entry in the posting reference column of the journal.

11. It also shows a $90,000 credit to Debbie Starr, Capital. Into what classification does this account fall? _____

12. Is the $90,000 credit an increase or a decrease to this owner's equity account? _____

13. What is the name of the process by which we transfer items entered in the journal to a ledger account? _____

14. Recycle Consultants' general ledger is made up of a set of accounts. What number is given to Cash? _____ ; To Debbie Starr, Capital? _____ .

15. What is the first step in posting this transaction? _____

16. What is the second step in posting this transaction? _____

17. What is the third step? _____

18. This is one of the most important steps in the process. Why? _____

46 Chapter 2

D18. Its presence in the journal means that this item has been posted. To enter it now *(not earlier or later)* helps prevent double posting or failure to post an item.

D19. Locate the ledger account for the credit entry.

D20. Enter the date, journal page number, and amount of the credit in the account Debbie Starr, Capital. Determine the new balance and enter it in the credit balance column.

D21. enter the number 301 (for Debbie Starr, Capital) in the posting reference column of the journal.

D22. No. That it occurred on December 1, 1997, and was posted from page 1 of the journal.

D23. No; That it occurred on December 1, 1997, and was posted from page 1 of the journal.

D24. That Debbie Starr invested $90,000 to start a business to be called Recycle Consultants.

19. What is the fourth posting step? _____

20. What is the fifth step? _____

21. The final step is to _____

22. If you only look in the ledger at the Cash account, can you identify the source of the $90,000 increase? _____ What can you tell about it? _____

23. If you only look at the Debbie Starr, Capital account, can you determine what caused the $90,000 increase? _____. What do you know about it? _____

24. However, if you look at the entry on journal page 1, what additional facts can you discover? _____

25. The function of the journal is to capture all the data of each transaction. The function of the ledger accounts is to bring together in one place all the changes that affect each account of the accounting equation.

Processing Business Transactions   47

D25. No answer required.

D26. No. *(Every posting in a ledger must come from a journal.)*

D27. No; We usually wait and post several journal entries at one time.

D28. Yes.

D29. Nothing, except that more than two accounts must receive postings.

E1. debited, 90,000; credited 90,000

E2. debit; debit, 90,000 *(Note that we do not use dollar signs in the journals and ledgers.)*

26. Is it acceptable to record some items directly into the ledger accounts without journalizing them first? _____

27. Should we post to the ledger immediately after making each journal entry? ____ . Explain._____

28. A journal entry with more than one debit or with more than one credit is called a compound entry. In a compound journal entry, do total debits equal total credits? _____

29. What is different about posting a compound entry? _____

E. Recycle Consultants' Transactions

Exhibits 2-7 and 2-8 show the journalizing and posting of Recycle Consultants transactions.

1. The December 1 transaction was for the investment by Debbie Starr. It _____ *(debited/credited)* Cash for $ _____ and _____ Debbie Starr, Capital for $ _____ .

2. When we post this entry, we enter the $90,000 increase in cash into the _____ column of the Cash account. We determine a new balance by adding this amount to the previous balance. Since this is the first entry, the new balance is a _____ *(debit/credit)* of _____ .

3. After posting the information into the Cash account. We enter the account number for Cash, _____ , into the _____ column of the journal.

48 Chapter 2

E3. 101, posting reference

E4. credit; credit amount, 301

E5. credit

E6. No answer required.

F1. (a) debit; (b) credit; (c) credit; (d) credit; (e) debit; (e) debit. *(Note, the normal balance of the account is on the same side as an increase.)*

F2. 95,500

F3. 80,400

4. After posting the debit, we post the _____ to Debbie Starr, Capital. We do this by entering 90,000 into the _____ column of account number _____.

5. We also determine the new balance for the Debbie Starr, Capital account and enter the balance into the _____ balance column.

6. You should take the time at this point to study the remaining journal entries and their postings. Trace each debit and credit in the journal to the appropriate ledger account. Remember that we enter the account number into the posting reference column of the journal only *after* posting the entry in the ledger.

F. Trial Balance

1. Looking again at the accounting equation, $A = L + OE$, we expect normal account balances to be as follows:

If the account is	Balance should be
a. An asset	_____
b. A liability	_____
c. Owner's capital	_____
d. Revenue	_____
e. Expense	_____
f. Withdrawals	_____

2. Find Recycle Consultants' Cash account in the general ledger in Exhibit 2-8. The total of the debit entries is $ _____.

3. The total of credit entries is $ _____.

4. Recycle had Cash account increases of $95,500 and decreases of $80,400. Since the company started with no cash on December 1, 1997, the amount of cash on hand at the end of the month is $ _____.

Processing Business Transactions   49

F4.   15,100

5. The amount of cash now on hand, $15,100, is called the account _____ .

F5.   balance

6. Each account in Recycle's general ledger has a balance. Some are debits and some are credits. Do you expect the total of all debit balances to equal the total of all credit balances? _____

F6.   Yes.

7. Why? _____

F7. Total debits and credits in each journal entry posted to the ledger were equal. So total debits in the general ledger should equal total credits.

8. In Recycle's trial balance (Exhibit 2-9), how many accounts have debit balances? _____ . Credit balances? _____ . The total of each column is $ _____ .

F8. Eight; Three; 96,600

9. Since Recycle's total debit and credit balances both equal $96,600, does this completely prove that we have done the journalizing and posting correctly? ___ . Explain. _____

F9. No; Errors could have been made, and debits would still equal credits. Posting a debit amount as a debit to the wrong account would not cause the trial balance to be out of balance. However, it offers evidence strong enough that we will assume there is no error.

10. Does a trial balance have dollar signs? _____

F10.   Yes.

11. Without looking at your textbook, write the heading for Recycle's trial balance.

50 Chapter 2

F11.

RECYCLE CONSULTANTS
TRIAL BALANCE
DECEMBER 31, 1997

G1. income statement

G2. revenues

G3. Fees Revenue

G4. 6,000

G5. expenses

G6. two

G7. Advertising Expense, Utilities Expense

G8. 2,000

G9. 4,000

G10. statement of owner's equity

G11. balance at the beginning of the period

G12. 0

G. Preparing Financial Statements

We will now use Recycle Consultants' trial balance to prepare financial statements.

1. First we prepare the _____ _____.

2. Exhibit 2-10 shows the preparation of the income statement. The first classification in the income statement is _____.

3. Recycle has one revenue account titled _____.

4. Its balance is $ _____.

5. It appears first. Next we list the _____.

6. Looking at the trial balance, Recycle has _____ expense accounts.

7. They are _____ and _____.

8. We list these under expenses. The total of the expenses is $ _____.

9. Net income is $ _____.

10. Next we prepare the _____ _____.

11. The first line on the statement is the _____.

12. Since Recycle was formed during December, the beginning balance is $ _____.

13. In this case, the balance in Debbie Starr, Capital was equal to the _____ _____. After this it will be equal to the beginning balance plus any additional investments.

Processing Business Transactions   51

G13. initial investment

14. The other amount from the trial balance that we use in preparing the statement of owner's equity is the balance in _____.

G14. Debbie Starr, Withdrawals

15. The beginning balance plus _____ _____, and _____ minus _____ equal the ending balance.

G15. initial investment, net income, withdrawals

16. The balance on December 31, 1997, is $_____.

G16. 93,000

17. This amount carries over to the balance sheet and appears in the _____ _____ section.

G17. owner's equity

18. The rest of the items on the balance sheet come directly from the _____ _____.

G18. trial balance

19. The first classification is _____ _____.

G19. current assets

20. For Recycle, it includes _____ of $_____ and _____ of $_____.

G20. Cash, 15,100, Accounts receivable, 500

21. The next classification is _____ _____.

G21. property, plant, and equipment

22. For Recycle, it includes _____ of $_____ and Building of $_____ and _____ of $_____.

G22. Land, 20,000, 50,000, Furniture, 8,000

23. There is only one liability. It is _____ _____ with a balance of $_____.

G23. Accounts payable, 600

24. The total liabilities and owner's equity is $_____.

G24. 93,600

25. Is this equal to the total assets? _____

52 Chapter 2

G25. Yes.

H1. decreased

H2. 32.8

H3. change in total revenues, 1991

H4. decreasing

H5. 110.7, 105.3

H6. Decrease.

H7. (31.5)

H8. change, earlier period

H9. Increasing.

H10. Unfavorable. it indicates more risk that L.A. Gear may not meet debt payments when they become due.

H. Analyzing Information
We continue our analysis of L.A. Gear.

1. Total revenues over the four year period have (increased/decreased) _____ .

2. The percentage decrease in total revenues from 1991 to 1994 was _____ %.

3. We find the percentage change in total revenues from 1991 to 1994 by dividing _____ by the total revenues in _____ .

4. Is the percentage of total expenses to total revenues increasing or decreasing? _____

5. In 1991, the expenses were _____ % of total revenues, and in 1994 expenses were _____ % of total revenues.

6. Did total assets increase or decrease over the four year period? _____

7. What is the percentage change in total assets? _____ %

8. We compute percentage change in total assets by dividing the _____ in total assets by the total assets in the _____ .

9. Is the percentage of total liabilities to total liabilities plus owner's equity increasing or decreasing? _____

10. Is this a favorable or unfavorable trend? _____
Why? _____

11. To determine if L.A. Gear is using a lower amount of assets to generate a given amount of revenue, we calculate a ratio called _____ .

Processing Business Transactions   53

H11. total asset turnover

12. From 1992 to 1994, did L.A. Gear's total asset turnover increase or decrease?
_____

H12. Increased.

13. Is this a favorable or unfavorable trend?
_____

H13. Favorable.

Note: You have now completed two chapters of *Guided Study* in this Study Guide. Are you using them exactly as suggested in the introduction by forcing yourself to make a commitment to try to answer the questions before checking the answer? If not, you are depriving yourself of the full benefit of the guided study of the textbook.

LEARNING GOALS ACHIEVEMENT TEST

1. (LG 1-3) Fill in the blanks opposite each account title below.

Account Title	Would we record an increase as a debit or a credit?	Is an accounts normal balance a debit or a credit?
Accounts Payable	CR	DR
Buildings	DR	CR
Furniture	DR	CR
G. Welch, Capital	CR	DR
Service Revenue	CR	DR
Notes Payable	CR	DR
Wages Expense	DR	CR
Accounts Receivable	DR	CR
Notes Receivable	DR	CR
Repair Supplies Expense	DR	CR

2. (LG 1-4) Reliable Auto Service uses the following accounts:

Cash
Repair Supplies
S. Bean, Capital
Service Revenue

Accounts Receivable
Accounts Payable
S. Bean, Withdrawals
Wages Expense

The following transactions occurred in February 1997:

1997		
Feb.	1	Sid Bean invested $10,000 by making a transfer from his personal bank account to the business bank account to establish the Reliable Auto Service.
	5	Purchased repair supplies on credit for $500.
	8	Received cash of $800 for repairing a customer's car.
	9	Since there was more work than one person could perform, hired an assistant at $350 per week to begin work on Monday, February 12.
	16	Sent bills to customers for whom repair work had been done this week; total amount was $2,500.
	16	Recorded collections of $2,000 cash for repair work performed. This work had not been previously billed.
	16	Paid the assistant his weekly salary of $350.
	21	Paid for all supplies purchased on February 5; total was $500.
	23	Received checks in payment of some of the bills sent out to customers on February 16; the total collected was $900.
	23	Withdrew cash for personal use, $600.
	23	Paid the assistant his weekly salary, $350.

Required: Set up T accounts for each of the accounts listed. Analyze the transactions and post the transactions directly to the accounts. Determine the balance in each account.

Cash

2/(1) 10,000	350 2/16
2/(3) 800	500 2/21
2/16 2,000	600 2/23
2/23 900	350 2/3
11,900	

Repair Supplies

2/(2) 500	
500	

A/R

2/16 2,500	900 2/23
1,600	

Wage Expense

2/16 350	
2/3 350	
700	

S. Bean - Cap

	10,000 2/(1)
	10,000

Service Rev

	800 2/(3)
	2,500 2/16
	2,000 2/16
	5,300

A/P

2/21 500 ~~350~~	500 2/(2) ~~350~~
	0

S. Bean - Withdrawals

2/23 600	
600	

56 Chapter 2

3. (LG 5-7) Record the following transactions for Happy Delivery Company in the general journal provided, and post them to the general ledger accounts (assume that Cash had a balance of $23,000 before these transactions):

1997
Aug. 8 Purchased repair supplies to be used during the next four months for $800, promised to pay in 30 days.

11 Purchased a new van for $15,000 paying Cash.

GENERAL JOURNAL — Page 27

Date		Accounts and Explanations	PR	Debit	Credit
1997					
aug	8	Repair Supplies		800	
		A/P			800
	11	Van		15,000	
		Cash			15,000

GENERAL LEDGER

Cash — Acct. No. 101

Date	Explanation	PR	Debit	Credit	Balance Debit	Balance Credit
1997					23,000	
aug 8				15,000	8,000	

Repair Supplies — Acct. No. 137

Date	Explanation	PR	Debit	Credit	Balance Debit	Balance Credit
1997						
aug 8			800		800	

Vans — Acct. No. 173

Date	Explanation	PR	Debit	Credit	Balance Debit	Balance Credit
1997						
aug 8			15,000		15,000	

58 Chapter 2

Accounts Payable   Acct. No. 201

Date	Explanation	PR	Debit	Credit	Balance Debit	Balance Credit

4. (LG 8) Following in alphabetical order are the account balances from the Valley Roller Rink on January 31, 1997. Beth made no additional investments during the month. All balances are normal.

Account Title	Balance
Accounts Payable	$ 5
Accounts Receivable	8
Cash	15
B. Sue, Capital	41
B. Sue, Withdrawals	2
Fees Revenue	35
Prepaid Rent	16
Rent Expense	4
Salaries Expense	12
Wages Expense	6
Equipment	18

Required:

a. Prepare a trial balance as of January 31, 1997.
b. Prepare an income statement for the month ended January 31, 1997.
c. Prepare a statement of owner's equity for the month ended January 31, 1997.
d. Prepare a balance sheet as of January 31, 1997.

a.

	DR	CR
AP	8	5
	8	
	15	

b.

4. (continued)
   c.

   d.

5. (LG 3, 4) Choose the word *increase* or *decrease* to fill in each blank space that follows:

   a. Revenues _____ owner's equity.
   b. A credit to a revenue account records a(n) _____ .
   c. A debit to a revenue account records a(n) _____ .
   d. Expenses _____ owner's equity.
   e. A debit to an expense account records a(n) _____ .
   f. A credit to an expense account records a(n) _____ .
   g. Withdrawals _____ owner's equity.
   h. A debit to the withdrawals account records a(n) _____ .
   i. If revenues are greater than expenses, the owner's equity will _____ .
   j. If expenses of an accounting period are greater than revenues, the owner's equity will _____ .

ANSWERS TO LEARNING GOAL ACHIEVEMENT TEST

1.

Account Title	Would we record an increase as a debit or a credit?	Is an accounts normal balance a debit or a credit?
Accounts Payable	Credit	Credit
Buildings	Debit	Debit
Furniture	Debit	Debit
George Welch, Capital	Credit	Credit
Service Revenue	Credit	Credit
Notes Payable	Credit	Credit
Wages Expense	Debit	Debit
Accounts Receivable	Debit	Debit
Notes Receivable	Debit	Debit
Repair Supplies Expense	Debit	Debit

2.

Cash					Accounts Receivable			
2/1	10,000	2/16	350		2/16	2,500	2/23	900
2/8	800	2/21	500					
2/16	2,000	2/23	600		Bal	1,600		
2/23	900	2/23	350					
Bal	11,900							

Repair Supplies				Accounts Payable			
2/5	500			2/21	500	2/5	500
Bal	500					Bal	0

62   Chapter 2

S. Bean, Capital			S. Bean, Withdrawals	
	2/1	10,000	2/23	600
	Bal	10,000	Bal	600

Repair Service Revenue			Wages Expense	
	2/8	800	2/16	350
	2/16	2,500	2/23	350
	2/16	2,000	Bal	700
	Bal	5,300		

No entry would be made for February 9, since no element of the accounting equation changed.

3.

GENERAL JOURNAL   Page 27

Date	Accounts and Explanations	PR	Debit	Credit
1997 Aug. 8	Repair Supplies Accounts Payable To record purchase of supplies on account.	137 201	800	800
11	Automobiles Cash To record purchase of new van paying cash.	173 101	15,000	15,000

GENERAL LEDGER

Cash   Acct. No. 101

Date	Explanation	PR	Debit	Credit	Balance Debit	Balance Credit
1997 Aug. 11	Assumed balance	J27		15,000	23,000 8,000	

Repair Supplies — Acct. No. 137

Date	Explanation	PR	Debit	Credit	Balance Debit	Balance Credit
1997 Aug. 8		J27	800		800	

Vans — Acct. No. 173

Date	Explanation	PR	Debit	Credit	Balance Debit	Balance Credit
1997 Aug. 11		J27	15,000		15,000	

Accounts Payable — Acct. No. 201

Date	Explanation	PR	Debit	Credit	Balance Debit	Balance Credit
1997 Aug. 8		J27		800		800

4. a.

VALLEY ROLLER RINK
TRIAL BALANCE
JANUARY 31, 1997

Account Title	Debits	Credits
Cash	$15	
Accounts Receivable	8	
Prepaid Rent	16	
Equipment	18	
Accounts Payable		$ 5
B. Sue, Capital		41
B. Sue, Withdrawals	2	
Fees Revenue		35
Rent Expense	4	
Salaries Expense	12	
Wages Expense	6	
Totals	$81	$81

b.

VALLEY ROLLER RINK
Income Statement
For the Month Ended January 31, 1997

Fees revenue..		$35
Expenses:		
Rent expense..	$ 4	
Salaries expense..	12	
Supplies expense...	6	22
Net income...		$13

c.

VALLEY ROLLER RINK
Statement of Owner's Equity
For the Month Ended January 31, 1997

B. Sue, capital, January 1, 1997...............................	$41
Add: Net income..	13
Subtotal..	$54
Deduct: Withdrawals...	2
B. Sue, capital, January 31, 1997.............................	$52

d.

VALLEY ROLLER RINK
Balance Sheet
January 31, 1997

Assets

Current assets

Cash...	$15	
Accounts receivable...	8	
Prepaid rent...	16	
Total current assets..		$39

Property, plant, and equipment

Equipment..	18
Total assets...	$57

Liabilities

Current liabilities

Accounts payable..	$ 5

Owner's Equity

B. Sue, capital..	52
Total liabilities and owner's equity............................	$57

5. a. increase   f. decrease
    b. increase   g. decrease
    c. decrease   h. increase
    d. decrease   i. increase
    e. increase   j. decrease

Chapter 3

ADJUSTING ENTRIES

EXPLANATION OF MAJOR CONCEPTS

Matching and Accounting Period Assumption LG 1

The accounting period assumption states that we divide the lifetime of a business into shorter time periods of equal length. This allows periodic reporting of financial information to users. Without this assumption, we could only prepare meaningful reports when the business ceased operations.

Recording expenses only when we pay them and recording revenues only when we collect them is the *cash basis* of accounting. The cash basis may be acceptable in some very small businesses that do not have many expenses or revenues to accrue. Most organizations, including government agencies and not-for-profit groups, have many types of expenses and revenues that accrue. Therefore, the accrual basis of accounting is usually the only system that will provide useful information to managers. The *accrual basis* requires that we recognize revenues in the period in which we perform the services or deliver the product.

The *matching principle,* then, states that we will record expenses in the period that the benefits from the expenditures help generate revenues. Proper matching of revenues and expenses gives more useful income information. Exhibit 3-1, in the textbook, diagrams the relationship between the accounting period assumption and the matching principle.

Adjusting Entries LG 2-7

If we use the accrual basis, we must make special accounting entries at the end of each accounting period. We call these entries *adjusting entries*. Adjusting entries bring the revenues and expenses up-to-date on an accrual basis. Thus, an income statement will contain the proper amounts of revenues and expenses and will more accurately reflect net income. Also, adjusting entries will correctly state assets and liabilities on the balance sheet. There are several types of adjusting entries, but they all have one purpose: to adjust the accounts to their proper amount on an accrual basis. Therefore, the adjusting process will be much easier for you if you think through each adjustment, keeping in mind that you are bringing the accounts up-to-date. In each case, ask yourself the following questions:

- *Identify the accounts that require adjustment and determine their unadjusted balances.* What has happened to make the current account balances outdated? Have we incurred an expense or have we earned a revenue?
- What income statement account is involved, and what is the related balance sheet account?
- *Determine the correct (adjusted) balance in each account requiring adjustment.* What should the actual expense or revenue be?
- *Prepare the adjusting entry to bring the accounts into agreement with the correct balances.* What must be done to the accounts to give them up-to-date balances?

In making adjustments, the following hints may be helpful:

- Every adjustment must involve either an expense or a revenue account.
- The way we recorded an original transaction entry determines the form and amount of the adjustment. Not all adjustments debit expense or credit revenue accounts. Sometimes a credit to an expense or a debit to a revenue account is required. (The Study Guide will illustrate this point later.)
- Adjusting entries *never* involve the Cash account. If you find yourself debiting or crediting Cash in an adjusting entry, something is wrong. Stop and analyze the situation again.
- Every adjusting entry has two parts: determination of the accounts that we will debit and credit, and computation of the amount. Separate them in your mind. Then determine each before you make the entry.

Accruals and Deferrals LG 3-7

Throughout Chapter 3, we use the terms *accruals* and *deferrals*. The accrual concept is relatively easy to understand. It is simply an item that has grown or accumulated with the passage of time that we have not recorded on the books. Interest on your savings account at the bank is an example. It accrues daily, but the bank only records it once per month. It isn't necessary to record it more often, and it would be very expensive to do so.

The term *deferral* really means "to defer or delay recognition of an expense or revenue." Deferrals refer to items that we have already recorded on the books. After we have recorded them, their status begins to change. However, as in the case of accruals, it is just not feasible or practical to recognize the continuous change. An insurance policy is an asset the moment we purchase it. As time passes, we use up the insurance protection, and the asset slowly changes to an expense. We defer (or delay) the recognition of that change until it is time to prepare financial statements. To make our financial statements more accurate, we must adjust the accounts to update the deferred recognition of expense. Exhibit 3-3 diagrams this deferral concept. The adjustment, like that for accruals, may involve either a revenue or an expense.

A summary of the logic process involved in making accruals and deferrals appears in Exhibits 3-4 and 3-5 of the textbook. It would be a good idea to review the exhibits at this point in your study and refer to them as you study the chapter.

Materiality LG 8

The *materiality concept* states that if an amount is so small that it would not affect the decision of an information user, the accounting need not follow generally accepted accounting principles. In the case of accruals and deferrals, this means that small amounts need not be accurately split between assets and expenses or revenues and liabilities. For example, we do not need to count the number of unused paper clips at the end of the year and make an adjusting entry to record the proper asset and expense amounts. We can simply expense the entire cost of paper clips purchased during the year.

Analyzing Information LG 9

In Chapter 3, we added the calculation of the percent of total expenses to total revenues. We calculate this by dividing total expenses by total revenues for each year. The chapter also added return on assets as a measure of efficiency. To calculate return on assets we divide net income by average total assets.

GUIDED STUDY OF THIS CHAPTER

A. Measuring Business Income

1. The only time we know true income is _____

A1. when the company goes out of business.

2. After selling all of the assets and paying the debts, we can determine income by _____

A2. comparing the ending cash with the beginning cash and adding total withdrawals.

3. To permit periodic reporting to users, we divide the life of a company into _____ _____

A3. shorter periods of time.

4. This division of a business' life into equal time periods is called the _____

A4. accounting period assumption

5. Generally the basic accounting period is a _____ month period of time.

A5. twelve-

6. There are two methods of accounting: the _____ basis and the _____ basis.

70 Chapter 3

A6. cash, accrual

7. Under the cash basis of accounting, when do we recognize revenue? _____ _____

A7. When we receive the cash.

8. Under the cash basis of accounting, when do we recognize expenses? _____ _____

A8. When we pay the cash.

9. Although the cash basis is a simple method to apply, what major problem does it cause? _____ _____ _____

A9. The income statement would be misleading.

10. Under accrual accounting, when do we recognize revenues? _____ _____

A10. When we perform the service or sell the product.

11. Under accrual accounting, when do we recognize expenses? _____ _____

A11. When we receive the benefits of the costs in producing revenue.

12. Accrual accounting determines income by _____ _____

A12. matching revenues and expenses.

13. The matching principle states that income information is better when we _____ _____ _____

A13. assign expenses to the same accounting period that we assign the revenues generated.

14. Adjusting entries are journal entries that _____ _____ _____

A14. update the general ledger accounts to state revenues, expenses, assets, and liabilities more accurately.

15. How will adjusting entries correct the potential mismatching of revenue and expense? _____ _____ _____

A15. Adjusting entries record the revenue in the period they earn it and the expense in the period they incur it, regardless of when the cash changes hands.

16. Name the two basic types of adjusting entries. _____
_____
_____

A16. Deferrals and accruals.

17. In a deferral, there is a _____ _____ in the current period. However, we defer a portion of the _____ or _____ until a future accounting period.

A17. cash payment; revenue, expense

18. We make this type of adjustment in two cases. When we pay cash in advance, we usually record the cost as an _____. Then we must _____
_____
_____

A18. asset; allocate these costs as expenses to the periods that receive the benefits.

19. In the other case, we receive the cash in advance and record the amount as a _____ . Then, we must _____
_____
_____

A19. liability; allocate these amounts as revenues to the periods in which we earn the revenues.

20. How do the accrual adjustments get their name? _____
_____
_____
_____

A20. Revenues or expenses have accumulated but have not been recorded. The term *accrued* simply means "accumulated."

21. All adjustments involve a(n) _____ account and a(n) _____ _____ account.

72   Chapter 3

A21. balance sheet, income statement

A22. No.

B1. to identify the accounts requiring adjustment and determine their balances.

B2. to determine the correct (adjusted) balance in each account.

B3. to prepare the adjusting entry to bring the accounts into agreement with the balances in step 2.

B4. One (Trucking Revenue).

B5. Four; 3,900. (Did you make the mistake of including the withdrawals account?)

B6. 7,500.

B7. 3,600.

22. Would the Cash account ever be involved in an adjusting entry? _____

B. Adjusting Entries To study adjustments, move directly to a study of Metro Delivery.

1. We follow three steps in preparing adjusting entries. The first step is _____

2. The second step is _____

3. The third step is _____

4. In Exhibit 3-2, how many different revenue items have already been recognized in the accounts? _____

5. How many different expense items appear in this trial balance? _____ .
The total amount of expenses in this trial balance is $ _____

6. What is the total amount of revenue in the trial balance in Exhibit 3-2?
$ _____

7. According to this trial balance, net income for December (total revenue minus total expense) would be $_____ .

8. Debbie Starr could make some poor decisions if she assumed that amount to be the net income. Let's study the adjustments needed to change that amount to the correct net income under the accrual basis.

Adjusting Entries 73

B8. No answer required.

9. The first adjustment involves insurance. How much insurance expense is shown in the trial balance in Exhibit 3-2? $ _____

B9. None.

10. When Metro Delivery paid the insurance for one year on December 1, it debited an _____ account, Prepaid Insurance, for $600. Is all of the amount a true asset on December 31? _____ . Explain. _____

B10. asset; No; Part of the asset has expired.

11. How much Prepaid Insurance remains prepaid as of December 31? $ _____

B11. 550.

12. The adjustment must reduce the asset account by $ _____ .

B12. 50

13. The reduction to the asset equals the value of the December insurance that has been used or has expired. What account should we debit to show use of the December insurance? _____

Why? _____

B13. Insurance Expense. To record December's insurance expense.

14. This adds a new expense account to the trial balance. What account should we credit? _____
Why? _____

B14. Prepaid Insurance. To show the reduction in the asset value.

15. In the first adjustment, the passage of time caused the accumulation of insurance expense. This is not true of the next adjustment. What is the factor that determines the amount of office supplies expense? _____

74 Chapter 3

B15. The actual consumption of supplies.

B16. Count the quantity left on hand December 31 and determine their cost. Then subtract from the total of the unused supplies amount available.

B17. 300, 100; 200

B18. No; We must credit Office Supplies with an amount that will reduce the asset account to its new balance, $100.

B19. In each case, part of a previously recorded cost is being deferred to a future period. *Part of the cost will be recognized as an expense in a future period.*

B20. 1,000

B21. 12,000 = ($13,000 - $1,000)

16. Since Metro Delivery kept no records to show how much of the office supplies were used, how do we determine that amount? _____
_____
_____

17. The amount available was $_____ and the physical count on December 31 showed $ _____ left on hand. Therefore, Metro Delivery must have used supplies amounting to
$ _____ .

18. Since the amount on hand on December 31 was $100, would it be correct to credit the Office Supplies account with $100 to make the adjustment? _____ . Explain.
_____
_____
_____

19. Again, we add a new expense account, Office Supplies Expense. Why is the process for these adjustments called a deferral? _____
_____
_____
_____
_____

20. The next adjustment introduces a new concept, depreciation. Depreciation is the process of allocating the original cost of a long-term asset to periods in which it is used. When Metro disposes of the trucks (purchased for $13,000 each), how much does it expect to sell each for as used equipment? $ _____ .

21. Metro Delivery's net cost of using one truck for five years is $ _____ .

22. Since five years is the same as 60 months, we assign 1/60 of $12,000 to each month as expense. The December expense per truck should be $ _____ .

B22. 200 = $12,000 ÷ 60

23. Instead of reducing the value in the long-term asset account with each adjustment, we use a contra account. Since a contra asset account reduces the asset valuation, its balance would be a _____ (*debit/credit*).

B23. credit

24. Each time we allocate an amount to Depreciation Expense–Trucks on Metro's books, we add to the balance in the _____ _____ account.

B24. Accumulated Depreciation–Trucks

25. An asset and its related contra asset account work together to determine the book value of the asset. If the balance in Accumulated Depreciation–Trucks was $10,000 on Dec. 31, 1997, what would the book value be? $ _____

B25. 16,000 ($26,000 - $10,000).

26. After Metro has recorded the last credit to Accumulated Depreciation at the end of five years, the book value of the two trucks is $ _____.

B26. 2,000 (*Note: This is equal to the expected residual value.*)

27. The fourth adjustment also illustrates a deferral. The unadjusted trial balance shows Unearned Rent of $ _____.

B27. 600

28. We are allocating a revenue to December and the five following months. How much is the actual December revenue? $ _____.

B28. 100

29. How much is the Unearned Rent at the end of December? $ _____.

B29. 500

30. What adjusting entry should we make to allocate the amounts you indicated in questions 28 and 29?
Account Title   Dr.   Cr.
_____
_____

Adjusting Entries 75

76 Chapter 3

B30. Unearned Rent   100
          Rent Revenue   100

31. Tom's Floral Shop, to whom Metro rented the truck, paid six months' rent in advance on December 1. Tom would credit cash and debit _____ _____.

B31. Prepaid Rent

32. As of December 31, how much of the Prepaid Rent would have expired?
$_____.
What would Tom's Floral's adjusting entry on December 31 be?
Account Title   Dr.   Cr.
_____
_____

B32. 100;
          Rent Expense   100
               Prepaid Rent   100

33. Note the relationship between the two parties to this transaction. Metro's revenue has increased by $100, while Tom's expense has increased by $_____. Metro's liability has a balance of $_____ while Tom's _____ has a balance of $500.

B33. 100; 500, asset

34. Accruals are items of expense or revenue that have increased but are _____ _____. Note that unlike deferrals, the amount we must adjust does not appear in any ledger account before adjustment.

B34. not yet recorded

35. Accrued revenues are revenues that are _____ in the current period but will be collected in _____ _____.

B35. earned, the next period

36. The interest revenue adjustment is an accrued _____.

B36. revenue

37. Metro had a $_____ note receivable dated _____.

B37. 1,200, December 11, 1997

38. Metro had recorded $_____ of interest.

B38. 0

39. Metro had earned _____ days of interest. This would be $_____ of interest.

B39. 20;
10 ($1,200 x 0.15 x 20/360)

B40. interest receivable

B41. Interest Receivable,
Interest Revenue

B42. expense

B43. 400; 80

B44. 80, have not

B45. Wages Expense, Wages Payable

B46. a liability, Wages Payable

40. Thus, Metro has _____ and interest revenue of $10.

41. The accrual adjustment would debit _____ and credit _____.

42. The adjustment for wages is an accrued _____.

43. Weekly wages at Metro are $ _____.
So daily wages are $ _____.

44. Assuming 1997 ends on Monday, Metro has incurred $_____ in wages that _____ (*have/have not*) been recorded.

45. The adjusting entry debits _____ _____ and credits _____ _____.

46. In adjustments for accruals, there is a relationship that is helpful to understand:
a. Accrued expenses increase liabilities.
b. Accrued revenues increase assets.
Therefore, the debit to Wages Expense in the adjustment was accompanied by a credit to _____.

47. Take time to record here the effect of all the adjustments made by Metro Delivery, using the following format:

Adjustment	Increased Expense	Increased Revenue
(a) Prepaid Insurance	$_____	$_____
(b) Office Supplies	$_____	$_____
(c) Trucks	$_____	$_____
(d) Unearned Rent	$_____	$_____
(e) Interest Receivable	$_____	$_____
(f) Wages Payable	$_____	$_____

78   Chapter 3

B47.　　Inc. Exp.　Inc. Rev.
　　(a)　　50
　　(b)　　200
　　(c)　　400
　　(d)　　　　　　100
　　(e)　　　　　　 10
　　(f)　　 80

B48.　730, 110; 620

B49.　3,600, 2,980

B50.　No answer required.

C1.　Manpower, Inc.

C2.　35.1

C3.　change, the earlier year (1993)

C4.　4,296,400,000,
　　3,180,400,000,
　　1,116,000,000

C5.　(1.6)

C6.　total assets, earlier

48. Adjustments increased total expenses by $_____ and increased total revenues by $_____ . This is a net increase of expenses in excess of revenues of $_____ .

49. Therefore, the net income we computed as $_____ in question B7 actually will be $_____ .

50. The adjustment process is necessary to get a correct matching of expenses and revenues in a period.

C. Analyzing Information

1. Chapter 3 compares Manpower, Inc. and Pinkerton's Inc. Which company has the higher total revenues? _____

2. What is the percentage change in total revenues for Manpower, Inc.? _____ %

3. We calculated this by dividing the _____ in total revenues by the revenue in _____ .

4. For Manpower the change in total revenue is $_____
   minus $_____
   or $_____ .

5. The percentage change in total assets for Pinkerton's is _____ %.

6. We find this by dividing the change in _____
   by the assets in the _____ year.

7. The change in total assets for Pinkerton was $_____
   and the total assets in the 1993 was $_____ .

Adjusting Entries   79

C7. (4,600,000), 282,700,000

C8. 4.22

C9. total revenues, assets

C10. beginning, end, 2

C11. total revenue, net income

C12. Manpower, Inc.

C13. Because it was higher.

D1. Insurance Expense

D2. 0, 600

8. Total asset turnover for Manpower was _____ times.

9. We compute this by dividing _____ _____ by total average _____.

10. We compute average total assets by adding total assets at the _____ of the year to total assets at the _____ of the year and dividing by _____.

11. The difference between total asset turnover and return on assets is the numerator. In total asset turnover, the numerator is _____ and in return on assets it is _____ _____.

12. Which company had the better return on assets? _____

13. Why was it better? _____ _____

D. Alternative Accounting for Deferrals (Appendix 3A)

1. When Metro paid the $600 for a one-year insurance policy, it debited Prepaid Insurance, or it could have debited _____.

2. If Metro had debited the expense when it made the payment, the balance in Prepaid Insurance on December 31, 1997, before adjustment would have been $_____ and the balance in Insurance Expense would have been $_____.

3. The adjusted balance in Prepaid Insurance should be $_____, and the balance in Insurance Expense should be $_____.

80 Chapter 3

D3.   550, 50

4. Thus, in this case the adjusting entry would be a debit to _____ for $ _____ and a credit to _____ for $ _____ .

D4.   Prepaid Insurance, 550,
      Insurance Expense, 550

5. Note that when we debit the original payment to an expense account, the adjustment requires the same accounts, but the entry transfers the unused portion from the expense to the asset. When we debit the original payment to an asset account, we transfer the used portion to an expense account.

D5.   No answer required.

LEARNING GOALS ACHIEVEMENT TEST

1. (LG 1) In one week, Sampson Company, a solid waste hauler, had the following transactions:

   a. Purchased $5,000 of fuel for trucks using credit cards. All of the fuel was consumed by the end of the month. No payments were made on this fuel.
   b. Hauled twenty contract loads of freight, collecting $9,500 for nine of them and billing customers a total of $13,500 for the other eleven loads.
   c. Paid last month's credit card bills for fuel for a total of $6,000.
   d. Paid no wages, but drivers earned $8,000 that will be paid next month.

   Required: Assuming that there were no other transactions, compute net income on (1) the cash basis and (2) the accrual basis. Explain which basis more accurately reflects the true income and why.

2. (LG 2-7) Plate Airlines needs to prepare financial statements each month for management control purposes. Plate owns a fleet of aircraft that have been financed through the issuance of interest bearing debt. Employees are paid on the fifth and twentieth day of each month. Many passengers purchase and pay for tickets in advance.

Required: List four adjustments that should be made at the end of a typical month, classify them by type, and show their effect on net income. Use the form that follows:

	Description of the Adjustment	Accrual or Deferral?	Effect on Income Increase / Decrease
1.	Interest payable / Interest expense	Accrual	Decrease
2.	Wages payable / Wages expense	A	Decrease
3.	Depreciation expense / Accumulated depreciation	D	Decrease
4.	Prepaid Expense / A/P	D	Increase

3. (LG 2-7) Prepare the end-of-period adjusting entries for each of the following situations that exist in Ft. Dodge Company on December 31, 1997. At the end of each explanation, show in parentheses whether the entry is an accrual or a deferral.

   a. The company borrowed $10,000 on a note payable on December 1, 1997, at an annual interest rate of 15 percent.
   b. A one-year fire insurance policy was purchased on December 1 at a cost of $1,200 and debited to Prepaid Insurance.
   c. The company purchased a building for $76,000 on December 1, 1997. They estimated the useful life at 40 years and the residual value at $4,000. Record depreciation for the month of December.
   d. On December 1, 1997, the company rented a piece of land it owns to a parking lot operator. Rent for one year of $12,000 was received in advance. It credited the rental receipt to Unearned Rent.
   e. The unadjusted balance in the Supplies account on December 31, 1997, was $2,800. A physical count shows that $900 of supplies is still on hand on December 31, 1997.

GENERAL JOURNAL

Date	Accounts and Explanations	PR	Debit	Credit

ANSWERS TO LEARNING GOALS ACHIEVEMENT TEST

1.

	(1) Cash Basis	(2) Accrual Basis
Revenue		
Trucking revenue	$9,500	$23,000
Expenses		
Fuel expense	$6,000	$5,000
Wages expense	0	8,000
Total expenses	6,000	13,000
Net income	$3,500	$10,000

The accrual basis more accurately reflects income because it matches expenses of this month with revenues actually earned this month. Both revenues and expenses exist at the time of incurrence, not when they are collected or paid.

2.

Description of the Adjustment	Accrual or Deferral?	Effect on Income Increase	Decrease
Depreciation of aircraft	Deferral		X
Interest on long-term debt	Accrual		X
Earned but unpaid wages	Accrual		X
Prepaid tickets that have been used	Deferral	X	

3.

GENERAL JOURNAL

Date		Accounts and Explanations	PR	Debit	Credit
1997 Dec.	31	Interest Expense Interest Payable To record December interest on $10,000 15% note. (accrual)		125	125
	31	Insurance Expense Prepaid Insurance To record one month's expiration of $1,200 one-year insurance policy. (deferral)		100	100
	31	Depreciation Expense--Building Accumulated Depreciation--Building To record one month's depreciation on building with 40-year life. (deferral--depreciation)		150	150
	31	Unearned Rent Rent Revenue To record one month's earnings. (deferral)		1,000	1,000
	31	Supplies Expense Supplies To record supplies used. (deferral)		1,900	1,900

Chapter 4

COMPLETION OF THE ACCOUNTING CYCLE

EXPLANATION OF MAJOR CONCEPTS

Steps in the Accounting Cycle LG 1

The complete accounting cycle is diagrammed in Exhibit 4-1. The steps in the accounting cycle are as follows:

During the accounting period:
- Collect transaction data from business documents
- Analyze transactions and journalize
- Post to the ledgers

At the end of the accounting period:
- Prepare a trial balance
- Prepare work sheet (including adjustments)
- Prepare financial statements
- Journalize and post adjusting entries
- Journalize and post closing entries
- Prepare a postclosing trial balance

The Work Sheet LG 2, 3

Accountants use work sheets to simplify the adjusting and closing process and to organize the information for preparing financial statements. They also use work sheets for other purposes, so it is important that you understand them well now. As you prepare a work sheet, follow the five steps discussed in the text. These five steps are:

1. Enter the headings at the top of the work sheet. Enter the account numbers, titles, and general ledger account balances in the Trial Balance columns (*the first set of columns*). This step completes the trial balance process and a separate trial balance is unnecessary.
2. Work out the adjustments and enter them in the Adjustments columns (*the second set of columns*). We use an identification letter to identify the corresponding debits and credits for each adjusting entry.

3. Combine the amounts in the first set of columns with those in the second set to arrive at the adjusted trial balance. Enter these amounts in the Adjusted Trial Balance Columns (*the third set of columns*). Remember to keep debits and credits straight as you do this.
4. Extend *each* amount in the Adjusted Trial Balance columns to *one* other set of columns. If the amount appears on the income statement, extend it to the Income Statement columns (*the fourth set*). If the amount appears on the balance sheet, extended it to the Balance Sheet columns (*the fifth set*). Remember to preserve the debit/credit nature of the amounts.
5. Subtotal the Income Statement and Balance Sheet columns. The difference between the Income Statement columns is the net income if the credits exceed the debits. The difference is a net loss if the debits exceed the credits. Enter the difference in the Income Statement debit or credit columns to force the columns to balance. Then enter the same amount in the opposite Balance Sheet column. If it required a debit to balance the Income Statement columns, place the same amount in the Balance Sheet Credit column. If your work sheet is mechanically correct, the Balance Sheet Debit and Credit column totals will now be equal.

As you work through these five steps, the following suggestions should make your work more accurate:

- Take each of the steps one at a time. Don't try to use short-cut methods such as moving amounts across the work sheet before you reach step 4.
- Stop after steps 1, 2, and 3 and total the columns. Be sure that you have kept total debits equal to total credits.
- Never introduce a new amount--for example, an adjustment amount--into the work sheet only once. You must enter any new amount into the work sheet both as a debit and a credit.
- In step 4, every amount in the Adjusted Trial Balance column is moved into one, and only one, of the four "financial statement" columns. This means the following:
  - Move assets, liabilities, and owner's equity (including withdrawals) account amounts into one of the two Balance Sheet columns. The reason is that these amounts go on the balance sheet.
  - Move revenue and expense amounts into one of the two Income Statement columns. The reason is that these amounts go on the income statement.
- Use the work sheet to prepare the financial statements, journalize adjusting entries, and journalize closing entries. Every dollar amount that you need to perform these tasks is on your work sheet.

At this point take the time to study the preparation of the Metro Delivery work sheet in Exhibits 4-4 through 4-8. The Guided Study section will do more with this work sheet.

Completion of the Accounting Cycle   87

The Financial Statements LG 4

The statements in Chapter 4 are excellent models. If you find that you still must look back at a sample to prepare financial statements, take the time now to study the format of the statements in Chapter 4, Exhibits 4-9, 4-10, and 4-11. Make sure that you understand what each section of each financial statement contains. It is important to understand the concept of the statements and not just memorize the format. This will save you time as the course progresses.

There is a definite sequence for preparation of the financial statements. The following explains the sequence and briefly comments on each statement:

1. **Prepare the income statement**. This is just an expansion of the equation, Revenues - Expenses = Net Income. You should first list the individual revenues from the Income Statement Credit column of the work sheet. The total revenues on the income statement will be the subtotal of Income Statement Credit column on the work sheet. Next, you should list the individual expenses from the Income Statement Debit column. The total of expenses on the income statement will be the subtotal of the Income Statement Debit column of the work sheet. Subtracting total expenses from total revenues should give the net income amount that you already have on the work sheet.
2. **Prepare the statement of owner's equity**. Select from two sets of columns, as follows:
   a. Take the beginning owner's capital amount from the Balance Sheet Credit column. This will be the case if no additional investments have been made during the year. If the owner made additional investments, the beginning capital is the amount shown on the work sheet less the additional investments.
   b. Add to the beginning capital the net income amount from the income statement or from the work sheet and the additional owner's investments, if any. (You will get a subtotal here.)
   c. Subtract the withdrawals amount that you obtain from the Balance Sheet Debit column.
   d. The result is the ending amount of owner's capital.
3. **Prepare the balance sheet**. Take all the amounts except owner's withdrawals and owner's capital (you've already used them) from the Balance Sheet columns of the work sheet. Follow these simple steps:
   a. The debits are assets. The work sheet lists current assets first. Stop at the end of them and compute a subtotal.
   b. The work sheet lists property, plant, and equipment assets next. Be sure to deduct each contra asset account from the asset to which it applies. You will find the contra asset accounts in the credit column. (A common error is to add contra asset accounts to liabilities.) Then add the total of current assets and the total of property, plant, and equipment to determine total assets.
   c. The credits other than contra assets are liabilities and owner's equity items. List the current liabilities first and subtotal them. Then list long-term liabilities (with a subtotal if more than one). Then compute a total for the liabilities.
   d. The owner's capital amount in the Balance Sheet Credit column is the beginning amount. You have already used it in the statement of owner's

equity. For the current balance sheet, obtain the new owner's capital amount from the statement of owner's equity that you have just prepared.

Adjusting Entries LG 5

Using the work sheet, journalize all of the adjusting entries and the closing entries. First journalize the adjusting entries and second post them.

For the adjusting entries, go to the Adjustments columns. Starting with adjustment (a), journalize the debits and credits and provide an explanation. Then go to adjustments (b), (c), and so on, until you have made a journal entry for each adjustment. Post these entries to the ledger.

The Closing Process LG 6, 7

The procedure called closing transfers the balances in the temporary accounts (revenues, expenses, and withdrawals) into capital. It also reduces the balances in the temporary accounts to zero. This prepares them to accumulate the next period's changes in owner's equity. If you left balances in revenue, expense, and withdrawals accounts, during the next period their balances would show more than one period's activity.

Most firms go through the closing process only once each year. In this textbook--especially in the earlier chapters--some illustrations and problems assume that the closing process takes place at the end of each month. This allows you to study the process with less complex data.

Note, to close a revenue account, simply record a debit to the account for its balance. To close an expense, simply record a credit to the account for its balance. We record the opposite debit or credit in an account called Income Summary. After you have done this, all expense and revenue accounts have equal debits and credits (their balances are zero). The debits and credits that were accumulated in expense and revenue accounts during the period have been moved into a single account, Income Summary. If that account has a credit balance, the company's total revenues were greater than expenses, and it had an income for the period. A debit balance would mean that expenses closed into Income Summary were greater than credits. This indicates a loss for the period.

Close the Income Summary account into the owner's capital account. If there was an income, the owner's equity increase appears as an increase in capital. The owner's withdrawals account is a decrease in capital. The owner's withdrawals account is also closed into the capital account. Since the withdrawals are the opposite of investment, this entry records a reduction in owner's equity. Note that any additional investments made by the owner would have been recorded directly to the capital account.

We can take the information for these closing entries from the Income Statement columns on the work sheet. Debit the accounts in the Credit column for their individual balances. Credit the subtotal of the Work Sheet Credit to Income Summary. Then, credit each account in the Debit column for its individual balance. Debit the subtotal of the Work Sheet Debit column to Income Summary. This should make the balance in the Income Summary account equal to the amount entered as the balancing amount in the Income Statement columns. You need two final closing entries:

1. Close the Income Summary balance (it is equal to the net income) into the owner's capital account.
2. Close the owner's withdrawals into the owner's capital account.

In summarized form, the closing entries appear as follows:

Revenue Accounts (each listed separately)	XXX	
	XXX	
Income Summary		XXX
To close revenue accounts.		
Income Summary	XXX	
Expense Accounts (each listed separately)		XXX
		XXX
		XXX
To close expense accounts.		
Income Summary	XXX	
Owner's Capital		XXX
To transfer net income to the owner's capital account. (Note, this would be opposite for a loss.)		
Owner's Capital	XXX	
Owner's Withdrawals		XXX
To close the withdrawals account to the owner's capital.		

Post these closing entries to the general ledger. After posting, the net income and withdrawals have been transferred to the capital account. The owner's capital account balance is now equal to the amount which appears on the balance sheet. Also, the temporary owner's equity accounts (revenue, expense, and withdrawals) all have zero balances. The real accounts (asset, liability, and capital) are the only accounts with a balance after posting the closing entries. Take the time at this point to review the accounts in Exhibit 4-16 to see that these summary statements are true.

Postclosing Trial Balance LG 8

After journalizing and posting the closing entries, we prepare another trial balance. This proves the equality of debits and credits in the ledger before journalizing and posting of transactions in the new period. The procedure for the preparation of this trial balance is the same as any other. List the accounts and their balances from the general ledger. Add the debit column and the credit column to prove the equality.

Analyzing Information LG 9

In Chapter 4, we break down the return on assets ratio into two parts. The first, profit margin, measures the firm's ability to control expenses relative to revenues. We compute the profit margin by dividing net income by total revenues. It measures the percentage of each sales dollar that becomes profit. The second part of return on assets is total asset turnover. We compute total asset turnover by dividing total revenues by average total assets. It measures the firm's ability to generate revenues with its assets.

Return on assets is then the product of profit margin and total asset turnover. A company can generate a good return on assets by either having a high profit margin or a high total asset turnover.

Reversing Entries (Appendix 4A)   LG A1, A2

A reversing entry is an entry made at the beginning of an accounting period and it is the opposite of one of the adjusting entries made at the end of the prior period. It is made to ease the subsequent recording of transactions. For example, if a company has a weekly payroll of $500 ($100 per day), they *normally* record payroll by a debit to Wages Expense and a credit to Cash for $500. If, on December 31, 1997, it is necessary to accrue two days wages, they would debit Wages Expense and credit Wages Payable for $200. On the next payday, January 3, 1998, the $500 payment would be paying off $200 in accrued liability and $300 in 1998 wages expense. If we made no reversing entry, we would have to take the adjusting entry into consideration when recording the January 3 payroll. We can eliminate this trouble by reversing the December 31, 1997, adjusting entry on January 1, 1998.

If the adjusting entry had been reversed on January 1, 1998, the accrued liability account would have been zeroed out. The wages expense would have a credit (negative) $200 balance. Then we could make the normal payroll entry on January 3, 1998, similarly to every other payday entry. We would debit Wages Expense and credit Cash credited for $500. The $500 debit to Wages Expense combined with the $200 credit in the reversing entry would make the balance $300, the proper amount of expense for 1998. The entries, as they would affect the Wages Expense and Wages Payable accounts, are summarized in T accounts below.

Wages Expense				Wages Payable	
a		b			a
12/31/97 200		12/31/97 200			12/31/97 200
Bal 0					Bal 200
d		c		c	
1/3/98 500		1/1/98 200		1/1/98 200	
Bal 300				Bal 0	

a. Adjusting entry.
b. Closing entry.
c. Reversing entry.
d. Regular payroll entry.

Completion of the Accounting Cycle 91

GUIDED STUDY OF THIS CHAPTER

A. The Work Sheet

1. Go back to Exhibit 3-2 and compare the items and dollar amounts in Metro Delivery's trial balance with the items and amounts in the Trial Balance columns of the work sheet in Exhibit 4-4. Are they the same? _____

A1. Yes.

2. What are the sources of the titles and amounts in the trial balance in Exhibit 3-2?
_____
_____

A2. The general ledger accounts.

3. We take the trial balance account titles and amounts on the work sheet directly from the ledger. Is it necessary to prepare a separate trial balance before entering it on the work sheet? _____

A3. No. (It was done in Chapter 3 because you had not studied the work sheet.)

4. Compare the adjustments in Chapter 3 with adjustments (a) through (f) entered on the work sheet in Exhibit 4-5. Are they the same? _____

A4. Yes.

5. In practice, which comes first--adjustments on the work sheet or the adjusting entries in the journal? _____
_____

A5. Adjustments on the work sheet. (Chapter 3 introduced adjustments in journal form because we had not studied the work sheet.)

6. Note that we key each adjustment in Exhibit 4-5 with a letter. Adjustment (a) in the debit column opposite Insurance Expense is in the amount of $ _____ .

A6. 50

7. Since total debits equal total credits on the work sheet, there must be one or more credit(s) for adjustment (a). Where and in what amount(s)? _____
_____

92 Chapter 4

A7. Opposite Prepaid Insurance, $50.

8. Adjustment (b) shows a credit to the asset Office Supplies. Is this credit of $ _____ increasing the asset or reducing it? _____

A8. 200; Reducing it.

9. Where is the debit for adjustment (b)? _____ _____

A9. Opposite Office Supplies Expense.

10. Is this debit increasing or decreasing Office Supplies Expense? _____

A10. Increasing it.

11. Read the explanation of adjustment (b) in Chapter 3. How much was the asset Office Supplies before the adjusting entry? $ _____ Can this number be found anywhere on the work sheet? _____ Where? _____ _____

A11. 300; Yes; The Trial Balance columns for Office Supplies.

12. The end-of-month count (inventory) shows only $ _____ of supplies left on hand, so usage of office supplies in December must have been $ _____ .

A12. 100, 200

13. Therefore, the adjustment on the work sheet will show a reduction to the asset by a _____ (*debit/credit*) of $200 and an increase in the expense account by a _____ (*debit/credit*) of $200.

A13. credit, debit

14. In adjustment (b), we are deferring a short-term _____ (*cost/revenue*).

A14. cost

15. Adjustment (d) shows a $100 debit to Unearned Rent. What is the account classification for Unearned Rent? _____

A15. A liability.

16. Entering a debit to a liability account _____ (*increases/decreases*) it.

A16. decreases

17. What account do we credit for adjustment (d)? _____

A17. Rent Revenue.

18. The account Rent Revenue is a(n) _____ (*expense/revenue*) account. A credit of $100 _____ (*increases/decreases*) it.

A18. revenue, increases

19. So adjustment (d) is a deferral. We are allocating an amount of $600: $ _____ to the liability and $ _____ to a revenue.

A19. 500, 100

20. Are the debit and credit totals in the Adjustments columns equal? _____ What is their amount? $ _____

A20. Yes, 840.

21. Why should total debits always equal total credits in the Adjustments columns?

_____
_____
_____
_____

A21. Because each individual adjustment had equal debits and credits.

22. Moving to Exhibit 4-6, examine the Adjusted Trial Balance columns of the work sheet. Each entry in these columns is the net sum of the Trial Balance and the Adjustments. For example, the $6,500 debit in Cash is the sum of the Trial Balance debit of $ _____ plus $ _____.

A22. 6,500, zero

23. In adding the Trial Balance to Adjustments, we must pay attention to debits and credits. In Office Supplies, a trial balance debit of $ _____ added to a credit of $ _____ equals a debit of $ _____.

A23. 300, 200, 100

24. In Wages Expense, a trial balance _____ of $ _____ added to a _____ of $ _____ equals a _____ of $ _____.

94 Chapter 4

A24. debit, 1,600, debit, 80, debit, 1,680

25. We must also bring the new accounts added during the adjustment process across to the Adjusted Trial Balance columns. In Wages Payable, for example, the amount in the Trial Balance columns is $_____.

A25. zero

26. Zero added to $80 brings $_____ into the Adjusted Trial Balance Credit column.

A26. 80

27. In the same manner, $_____ of Interest Revenue is brought over to the Adjusted Trial Balance _____ (*debit/credit*) column.

A27. 10, credit

28. The debit and credit totals of the Adjusted Trial Balance columns should be equal. In the example, they are $_____.

A28. 41,590

29. Once we have a balanced Adjusted Trial Balance, we must move each amount in that column to one of the columns on the right. The general rule is to follow the financial statement that we use the amount in. Therefore, we would expect assets to go into the _____ columns.

A29. Balance Sheet

30. Referring to Exhibit 4-7, trace a few assets. For example, we move Cash, Accounts Receivable, and Trucks into the Balance Sheet columns as _____ (*debits/credits*).

A30. debits

31. Contra asset accounts and liability accounts also help make up the balance sheet. Note that we moved Accumulated Depreciation--Trucks, Accounts Payable, and Unearned Rent into the Balance Sheet columns as _____.

A31. credits

32. Revenues and expenses make up the income statement. It would seem appropriate that we move their amounts into the _____ _____ columns.

Completion of the Accounting Cycle 95

A32. Income Statement

33. We moved three revenues into Metro's Income Statement columns as _____ (*debits/credits*). These three are _____ _____, and _____.

A33. credits; Trucking Revenue, Rent Revenue, Interest Revenue

34. We bring expenses to the debit side of the Income Statement columns. Looking at Exhibit 4-8, Metro's total expenses transferred were $_____.

A34. 4,630

35. Also on the Totals line, total revenues were $_____.

A35. 7,610

36. The difference, $_____ is net income. Enter on the side with the smaller subtotal and label it "Net Income."

A36. 2,980

37. Enter the same difference in the Balance Sheet columns. Since we inserted it into the Income Statement Debit column, we must enter it in the Balance Sheet _____ column in order to keep debits and credits equal on the work sheet.

A37. Credit

38. It is logical to enter the net income as a credit in the Balance Sheet columns, because it is going to _____ (*increase/decrease*) Debbie Starr, Capital, which has a normal credit balance.

A38. increase

39. If expenses had been greater than revenues, we would have entered the difference in the Income Statement columns as a _____, to balance the columns.

A39. credit

40. If balancing the Income Statement columns requires a credit, there must be a net _____ instead of net income.

A40. loss

41. This would mean entering a _____ in the Balance Sheet columns because a loss _____ (*increases/reduces*) owner's equity.

96   Chapter 4

A41.   debit, reduces

B. **Financial Statements**
Study the preparation of financial statements. Here is where the usefulness of the work sheet really shows.

1. We already know that there is a net income and that its amount is $ _____ .

B1.   2,980

2. We take the revenues directly from the work sheet. We can simply list the three revenue accounts and their amounts:
$ _____ , $ _____
and $ _____ .

B2.   7,500, 100, 10

3. We don't need to add for their total. The work sheet shows a subtotal of $_____ .

B3.   7,610

4. We can also list the seven expense items from the debit column. Again, we don't need to add. The work sheet gives us their total as $ _____ .

B4.   4,630

5. We already know net income, but we can subtract total expenses from total revenues on the Income Statement to have an accuracy check. $ _____
minus $ _____
equals $ _____ .

B5.   7,610, 4,630, 2,980

6. We can also take the statement of owner's equity directly from the work sheet. In Exhibit 4-10, the $32,000 amount came from the _____ column. We add the net income of $ _____ , and subtract withdrawals of $ _____ from the _____ _____ column.

B6.   Balance Sheet Credit; 2,980, 500, Balance Sheet Debit

7. In the same manner, the balance sheet data comes from the work sheet. Assets come directly from the debit column. If an asset has a contra account, the contra balance is _____ (*added to/subtracted from*) the asset. Be careful to pick up any assets added at the bottom of the work sheet.

B7. subtracted from

B8. Wages Payable

B9. statement of owner's equity

B10. No.

B11. Because we deduct the contra accounts in the balance sheet and deduct the owner's withdrawal from the capital amount. On the worksheet, they were added to their respective columns.

C1. six

C2. December 31, 1997

C3. we have posted the adjusting entries to those accounts

8. Liabilities come from the Balance Sheet Credit column. You must be careful to look for current liabilities added at the bottom of the work sheet. For the Metro Delivery, this is _____.

9. The work sheet does not show the subtotals for current assets and current liabilities. You must compute them. Also the work sheet does not show the new value of the owner's capital account. We get that amount from the _____ _____ just completed.

10. Do the totals of the Balance Sheet columns on the work sheet equal total assets and total liabilities and owner's equity on the balance sheet? (Exhibit 4-11) _____

11. Why don't they? _____
_____
_____
_____

C. **Adjusting and Closing Entries**
We also journalize adjusting and closing entries directly from the work sheet.

1. There are six adjustments on the work sheet and _____ adjusting entries.

2. Each adjusting entry in Exhibit 4-12 is dated _____.

3. The fact that the Posting Reference column of Exhibit 4-12 shows account numbers indicates that _____
_____
_____.

4. Compare Exhibits 4-8 and 4-15. The debits for the first closing entry came directly from the_____
_____ column of the work sheet.

98   Chapter 4

C4. Income Statement Credit

5. In the closing entry, we debit amounts that are credits in the work sheet because _____ .

C5. an offsetting debit will make their balances zero

6. The debit to Income Summary in the second closing entry in Exhibit 4-15 is $_____ . That amount came from the work sheet as the subtotal of the Debit _____ .

C6. 4,630; Income Statement columns

7. We credit the expense accounts in closing entry 2 because their balances are now _____ and we wish to bring the balances to _____ .

C7. debits, zero

8. The third and fourth closing entries in Exhibit 4-15 also come from the work sheet. The Income Summary balance is equal to credits of $_____ minus debits of $_____ . This is the net income amount on the work sheet that is closed into Debbie Starr, Capital.

C8. 7,610, 4,630

9. Debbie Starr, Withdrawals, is also a temporary account. The last closing entry changes its balance to $_____ and _____ (*increases/reduces*) Debbie Starr, Capital.

C9. zero, reduces

10. In the general ledger, which accounts do not have zero balances after closing? _____

C10. The real or permanent (asset, liability, and owner's equity) accounts.

11. In Exhibit 4-16, can you find any revenue or expense account with a nonzero balance? _____ Does the Withdrawals account have a balance? _____

C11. No; No.

12. In this entire end-of-period process, the work sheet has been the key. It is an informal document but an important tool. In the Metro Delivery illustration, there were only six adjustments. Think of the usefulness of a sheet when there are dozens of adjustments and hundreds of accounts.

Completion of the Accounting Cycle   99

C12. No answer required.

D1. profit margin, total asset turnover

D2. net income, total revenues

D3. sales dollar

D4. expenses, revenues

D5. total revenues, average total assets

D6. revenues, assets

D7. 3.38, 1.75, 5.92

D8. Compaq Computer

D9. Apple Computer

D. Analyzing Information

1. To study changes in the rate of return on assets, we break it into two parts: the _____ and _____.

2. We compute profit margin by dividing _____ by _____.

3. It shows the percent of each _____ _____ that results in net income.

4. It measures the firm's ability to control the level of _____ relative to _____.

5. We compute total asset turnover by dividing _____ by _____.

6. It measures a firm's ability to generate _____ from a given level of _____.

7. For Apple Computer, 1994's profit margin was _____ % and their total asset turnover was _____ times giving them a return on assets of _____ %.

8. Which of the three computer companies had the highest return on assets? _____

9. Which had the lowest return on assets? _____.

10. Compaq Computer's total asset turnover was almost as low as Apple Computer. How did they earn such a high return on assets? _____

100 Chapter 4

D10. They had a high profit margin.

11. Gateway 2000's profit margin was almost as low as Apple Computer's. How did they earn a return on assets almost as high as Compaq Computer? _____
_____
_____
_____

D11. Gateway 2000 had a very high total asset turnover.

12. So a company can earn a high return on assets by having either a _____
_____
or a _____
_____ .

D12. high profit margin, high total asset turnover

E. Reversing Entries (Appendix 4A)

1. The reversing entry is made on what date?
_____
_____

E1. The first day of the next accounting period.

2. The reversing entry involves the same accounts as the adjusting entry, but the entry is the _____ .

E2. opposite (or reverse)

3. In the chapter illustration for the wages adjustment, the December 31 adjusting entry _____ (*increases/ decreases*) wages expense and _____ (*increases/decreases*) the liability.

E3. increases, increases

4. The reversing entry on January 1 reduces the liability to a balance of $ _____ and creates a balance in the expense account of $ _____ .

E4. zero, (80) *negative*

5. The regular payroll entry on January 4 _____ (*debits/credits*) the expense for $ _____ .
This produces a balance in the expense account of $ _____ .
The proper amount of wages expense for 1998 thus far would be $_____ .

E5. debits, 400; 320; 320
($80 per day for 4 days)

6. The payroll entry on January 4 would be the _____ as every other payroll entry during the year.

E6. same

LEARNING GOALS ACHIEVEMENT TEST

1. (LG 1) Chapter 4 gave nine steps in the accounting cycle. List them in proper sequence.
   1. _____
   2. _____
   3. _____
   4. _____
   5. _____
   6. _____
   7. _____
   8. _____
   9. _____

2. (LG 2-7) The following is account balance information as of December 31, 1997, for the Fernandez Company:

Cash	$ 5
Equipment	30
Supplies	22
Accounts Payable	2
Notes Payable	6
M. Fernandez, Capital	20
M. Fernandez, Withdrawals	1
Service Revenue	30

   Required:

   (1) Enter the trial balance on the work sheet and complete the work sheet using the following supplementary data:
   a. Depreciation for the year is $3.
   b. Accrued interest on notes payable is $1 on December 31.
   c. A count of supplies on hand December 31 shows $4 remaining.

102 Chapter 4

(2) Prepare an income statement, a statement of owner's equity, and a balance sheet.

(3) Prepare the adjusting and closing entries from the work sheet.

(4) Prepare a postclosing trial balance.

(1)

FERNANDEZ COMPANY
WORK SHEET
FOR THE YEAR ENDED DECEMBER 31, 1997

Accounts	Trial Balance Dr.	Cr.	Adjustments Dr.	Cr.	Adjusted Trial Balance Dr.	Cr.	Income Statement Dr.	Cr.	Balance Sheet Dr.	Cr.

(2)

Income Statement

Statement of Owner's Equity

Balance Sheet

(3)

GENERAL JOURNAL

Date	Accounts and Explanations	PR	Debit	Credit

GENERAL JOURNAL

Date	Accounts and Explanations	PR	Debit	Credit

(4)

Postclosing Trial Balance

3. (LG A1, A2) Statewide Company recorded the following adjustment on January 31, 1997.

GENERAL JOURNAL

Date		Accounts and Explanations	PR	Debit	Credit

1997 Dec.	31	Wages Expense
		    Wages Payable
		    To accrue wages.
				450	450

Payday for the week will be Friday, January 4, 1998, when employees will be paid a total of $1,850.

Chapter 4

Required:

(1) Record the payment of the payroll on January 4, 1998, assuming no reversing.

GENERAL JOURNAL

Date	Accounts and Explanations	PR	Debit	Credit

(2) Record the reversing entry on January 1, 1998, and the payroll on January 4, 1998, assuming the reversing.

GENERAL JOURNAL

Date	Accounts and Explanations	PR	Debit	Credit

ANSWERS TO LEARNING GOALS ACHIEVEMENT TEST

1.
1. Collecting transaction data on business documents.
2. Analyzing transactions and journalizing.
3. Posting to the ledgers.
4. Preparing the trial balance.
5. Preparing the work sheet.
6. Preparing financial statements.
7. Journalizing and posting adjusting entries.
8. Journalizing and posting closing entries.
9. Preparing the postclosing trial balance.

2.
(1)

FERNANDEZ COMPANY
WORK SHEET
FOR THE YEAR ENDED DECEMBER 31, 1997

Accounts	Trial Balance Dr.	Trial Balance Cr.	Adjustments Dr.	Adjustments Cr.	Adjusted Trial Balance Dr.	Adjusted Trial Balance Cr.	Income Statement Dr.	Income Statement Cr.	Balance Sheet Dr.	Balance Sheet Cr.
Cash	5				5				5	
Supplies	22			(c)18	4				4	
Equipment	30				30				30	
Accts. Pay		2				2				2
Notes Payable		6				6				6
M. F., Capital		20				20				20
M. F., Withdrwls	1				1				1	
Service Rev.		30				30		30		
Totals	58	58								
Deprec. Exp.			(a) 3		3		3			
Accum. Deprec.				(a) 3		3				3
Interest Exp.			(b) 1		1		1			
Int. Pay.				(b) 1		1				1
Supplies Exp.			(c)18		18		18			
Totals			22	22	62	62	22	30	40	32
Net Income							8			8
Totals							30	30	40	40

(2)

FERNANDEZ COMPANY
INCOME STATEMENT
FOR THE YEAR ENDED DECEMBER 31, 1997

Revenue		
Service revenue		$30
Expenses		
Supplies expense	$18	
Depreciation expense--equipment	3	
Interest expense	1	
Total expenses		22
Net income		$ 8

FERNANDEZ COMPANY
STATEMENT OF OWNER'S EQUITY
FOR THE YEAR ENDED DECEMBER 31, 1997

M. Fernandez, capital, January 1, 1997	$20
Add: Net income for 1997	8
Subtotal	$28
Deduct: Withdrawals	1
M. Fernandez, capital, December 31, 1997	$27

FERNANDEZ COMPANY
BALANCE SHEET
DECEMBER 31, 1997
Assets

Current assets		
Cash	$ 5	
Supplies	4	
Total current assets		$ 9
Property, plant, and equipment		
Equipment	$30	
Deduct: Accumulated depreciation--		
Equipment	3	27
Total assets		$36

Liabilities

Current Liabilities		
Accounts payable	$ 2	
Notes payable	6	
Interest payable	1	
Total liabilities		$ 9

Owner's equity

M. Fernandez, capital	27
Total liabilities and owner's equity	$36

(3)

GENERAL JOURNAL

Date		Accounts and Explanations	PR	Debit	Credit

1997 Dec.	31	**Adjusting Entries**
		Depreciation Expense--Equipment
		    Accumulated Depreciation--
		        Equipment
		    To record depreciation for 1997.
				3	3

	31	Interest Expense
		    Interest Payable
		    To accrue interest.
				1	1

	31	Supplies Expense
		    Supplies
		    To adjust for used supplies.
				18	18

	31	**Closing Entries**
		Service Revenue
		    Income Summary
		    To close credit balance accounts.
				30	30

	31	Income Summary
		    Supplies Expense
		    Depreciation Expense--
		        Equipment
		    Interest Expense
		    To close debit balance accounts.
				22	18
					
					3
					1

	31	Income Summary
		    M. Fernandez, Capital
		    To close Income Summary.
				8	8

	31	M. Fernandez, Capital
		    M. Fernandez, Withdrawals
		    To close withdrawals.
				1	1

112   Chapter 4

(4)
FERNANDEZ COMPANY
POSTCLOSING TRIAL BALANCE
DECEMBER 31, 1997

Account Title	Debits	Credits
Cash	$ 5	
Supplies	4	
Equipment	30	
Accumulated Depreciation--Equipment		$ 3
Accounts Payable		2
Notes Payable		6
Interest Payable		1
M. Fernandez, Capital		27
Totals	$39	$39

3.

(1)
GENERAL JOURNAL

Date		Accounts and Explanations	PR	Debit	Credit

1998 Jan.	4	Wages Payable
		Wages Expense
		    Cash
		    To record payment of wages
		    without reversing entry.
				450
				1,400
					
					1,850

(2)
GENERAL JOURNAL

Date		Accounts and Explanations	PR	Debit	Credit

1998 Jan.	1	Wages Payable
		    Wages Expense
		    To reverse wage expense
		    accrual.
				450	
					450

	4	Wages Expense
		    Cash
		    To record wages expense
		    with reversing entry.
				1,850	
					1,850

Chapter 5

ACCOUNTING FOR A MERCHANDISING BUSINESS

EXPLANATION OF MAJOR CONCEPTS

Service versus a Merchandising Business LG 1

A service business earns revenue by performing a service for its clients. A merchandising business earns its revenue by delivering a product to its clients. The primary difference is in the need to determine the cost of goods sold of the merchandising business. Exhibit 5-1 highlights the differences between the income statement of a service business and a merchandising business. To record purchase and resale transactions, we need to add a new group of accounts, the merchandising accounts, to the general ledger.

Sales Accounts LG 2

It will be helpful to review the merchandising accounts and their use. The Sales account is a revenue account. We use it to record the revenues generated by the sale of goods. Like other revenue accounts, we credit it to record increases. Accordingly, it has a normal credit balance. Some businesses offer a trade discount as a method of reducing the list price of merchandise. The list price minus the trade discount equals the invoice price. We record the sale at the invoice price.

A trade discount may be a series of discounts from the list price. For example, we would calculate the invoice price of merchandise with a list price of $1,000 and a trade discount of 10%, and 20% as follows:

List price...	$1,000
Deduct: 10% of $1,000..	100
Remainder...	$ 900
Deduct: 20% of $900...	180
Invoice price...	$ 720

If a buyer returns goods or we grant a price concession to a buyer after delivery of the goods, we use a contra sales account rather than directly reduce the Sales account. Two common contra sales accounts are Sales Returns and Allowances and Sales Discounts. We use Sales Returns and Allowances to record the cost of merchandise returned or price reductions due to damages. We use Sales Discounts to record reductions allowed for early payment. For example, a 2/10 n/30 cash discount means that we will allow the customer to reduce the amount they owe by 2% if they pay within 10 days of the invoice date. Since they reduce sales, these accounts have normal debit balances. We increase them with debits.

In most states, retail stores must collect sales tax. The store is acting as a collecting agent for the state. So when the store collects the money it is not a revenue. It is a liability to the state. We credit the portion of the amount collected from the customer for sales tax to the account Sales Taxes Payable. When we forward this money to the state, we debit the liability account.

Cost of Goods Sold LG 3, 4

Merchandising firms may use either the periodic or the perpetual inventory system to keep records of the goods on hand. The perpetual system records changes in the inventory account each time we buy or sell merchandise. It records cost of goods sold as we sell the merchandise. The inventory account balance is perpetually correct. We study the periodic system in Chapter 5. It records the amount of purchases each period and calculates cost of goods sold at the end of the period. Several new accounts are necessary in the periodic system.

We use the Purchases account to record the invoice price of merchandise purchased. While it is not an expense account in the sense that Salaries and Wages Expense is, it has the same effect on owner's equity. When we purchase merchandise, we debit it to record increases. Its normal balance is a debit. If a business is responsible for the cost of shipping the merchandise to its store, this is an additional cost. We debit it to a separate account called Transportation In. F.O.B. terms determine whether the buyer or seller is responsible for freight. When it is F.O.B. shipping point the buyer has transportation in costs. When it is F.O.B. destination, the seller has transportation out expenses.

Contra purchases accounts exist to record transactions which decrease the cost of total purchases. We use separate accounts to provide management information about these events. We use Purchases Returns and Allowances to record the cost of merchandise returns or price concessions granted to keep the merchandise. We increase it with a credit, and it has a normal balance of credit. We use Purchases Discounts to record reductions in the amount owed due to paying within a discount period. We also increase Purchases Discounts with credits, and it has a normal credit balance.

The table on the next page summarizes accounting with the merchandise accounts:

Accounting for a Merchandising Business 115

Merchandise Accounts

Account	Increase	Decrease	Normal Balance
Revenue accounts:			
Cr Sales...	Cr	Dr	Cr
Contra revenues:			
Dr Sales Returns and Allowances................	Dr	Cr	Dr
Dr Sales Discounts...	Dr	Cr	Dr
Cost of goods sold accounts:			
Dr Purchases..	Dr	Cr	Dr
Dr Transportation In.......................................	Dr	Cr	Dr
Contra purchases:			
Cr Purchases Returns and Allowances.......	Cr	Dr	Cr
Cr Purchases Discounts................................	Cr	Dr	Cr
Current asset account:			
Dr Merchandise Inventory.............................	Dr	Cr	Dr

You can find a further review of the uses of these accounts in Exhibit 5-3 of the textbook. As you study the accounts in this chapter, be sure to note that we do not make entries to other than the normal side except to close the account. If, for example, you find yourself crediting Sales Discounts and you are not closing the account, you are doing something wrong.

Financial Statements LG 5, 6

We use the merchandise accounts in the income statement to determine cost of goods sold and to show the gross margin that a firm earns on sales. You must learn how to set up this section of the income statement. Start amounts in the right-hand column, moving to the left to develop subtotals. A summary of the multiple-step income statement for a merchandising firm is shown on the next page. Notice the details of the computation of net sales revenue, cost of goods sold, gross margin, net operating margin, and net income.

We divide the operating expenses into expenses associated with the selling activities of the business and the nonselling or general and administrative activities. Note that the income statement in Exhibit 5-4 shows only the primary revenue source, sales, at the top. We show secondary revenue sources, such as interest revenue and rent revenue, as "other revenues" in a special section at the bottom of the statement. In like manner, we show only the operating expenses in the expense section. We show nonoperating expenses, such as interest expense, as "other expenses" at the bottom of the statement.

FIRM NAME
PARTIAL INCOME STATEMENT *(multiple step)*
FOR THE (PERIOD) ENDED (DATE)

Gross sales revenue			$ X
Deduct: Sales returns and allowances...............		$ X	
Sales discounts....................................		X	X
Net sales revenue..			$ X
Cost of goods sold:			
Merchandise inventory, beginning.....................		$ X	
Purchases..	$ X		
Transportation in...	X		
Gross delivered cost of purchases		$ X	
Deduct: Purchases returns and allowances ...	$ X		
Purchases discounts...........................	X	X	
Net cost of purchases		X	
Cost of goods available for sale		$ X	
Deduct: Merchandise inventory, ending		X	
Cost of goods sold...			X
Gross margin on sales..			$ X
Deduct: Operating expenses:			
Selling expenses:			
list individually..	$ X		
....	X	$ X	
General and administrative expenses:			
list individually..	$ X		
....	X	X	
Total operating expenses...........................			X
Net operating margin			$ X
Other revenues and expenses................................			X
Net income...			$ X

   The balance sheet for a merchandising business is very similar to that of a service business studied in the first four chapters. Since Merchandise Inventory is a new current asset account, it will appear in the balance sheet. Note in the balance sheet, Exhibit 5-10, that we include Merchandise Inventory in the current assets section below Accounts Receivable.

Work Sheet Treatment of Merchandise Inventory   LG 7, A1

   The method of handling Merchandise Inventory on the work sheet is diagrammed in Exhibits 5-6 and 5A-1. The text illustrates two approaches--changing the Merchandise Inventory balance as a part of the closing entries (*the closing approach*) and as a part of the adjusting entries (*the adjusting approach*). You should learn and follow the approach required by your instructor. Do not try to learn both. It will be confusing.

Accounting for a Merchandising Business 117

In the closing entry approach, Exhibit 5-6, note that the amount that appears in the Trial Balance Debit column is the beginning inventory balance. On the work sheet we carry this amount across to the Income Statement Debit column. We do not enter any adjustments for this account, even though the ending amount is usually given to you in problems with the adjustment data. We enter the ending (new) inventory amount in the Income Statement Credit column and also the Balance Sheet Debit column. By entering this new amount in both a Debit and a Credit column, we preserve the equality of debits and credits on the work sheet. We also include all of the data that we will need to prepare the formal income statement from the Income Statement columns.

In the adjusting entry approach (Appendix 5A), we transfer the beginning inventory amount to the Income Summary account in an adjusting entry. This entry credits Merchandise Inventory and debits Income Summary. We establish the ending inventory amount in another adjusting entry by debiting Merchandise Inventory and crediting Income Summary. We carry both the debit and credit amounts on the Income Summary line across to the Income Statement columns. We need both when preparing the formal income statement.

Net Price Method   LG 8

Under the net price method of recording purchases, we initially record accounts payable and purchases at the amount that we will owe if we pay the account within the discount period. If we use the entire credit period, we debit the additional amount that we must pay to an account entitled "Purchases Discounts Lost." This account measures the additional cost of failing to pay the account within the available discount period.

Do not confuse cash discounts with trade discounts. Trade discounts are simply devices to determine the invoice price or cost. We do not show trade discounts in the accounting records. We record items at the invoice price determined after deduction of the trade discount.

Analyzing Information   LG 9

In Chapter 5, we learn to examine gross margin. Gross margin is net sales minus cost of goods sold. The gross margin percent is gross margin divided by net sales. We also calculate operating expenses as a percent of net sales. The key is that net sales is always the 100% number or the denominator. In our analysis, we then compare these percentages over a period of time.

GUIDED STUDY OF THIS CHAPTER

A. Merchandising Accounts
Let's first gain a thorough understanding of the new accounts in Chapter 5.

118   Chapter 5

A1.   increase

A2.   credit, credit

A3.   No.

A4.   Accounts Receivable.

A5.   Cash

A6.   trade discount

A7.   364.50

A8.   decreases

A9.   Sales Returns and Allowances

1. Sales is a revenue account. Each time we record a sale we ↑CR _____ (decrease/increase) revenue.

2. Since an increase in a revenue is a CR _____ (debit/credit), we should journalize a CR _____ (debit/credit) to the Sales account when we sell goods.

3. Should we wait until the customer pays for sales before recording a revenue? NO

4. When we journalize a sale that we make on account (for credit), what account do we debit? A/R

5. It is, of course, normal that we make some sales for cash. In that case, we debit the Cash _____ account while crediting Sales.

6. We record sales at the invoice price. In many cases, the invoice price is the list price less a TRADE DISCOUNT _____ .

7. If a product has a list price of $500 and a trade discount of 10%, 10%, 10%, the invoice price is $ 364.50 _____ .

8. In any business, customers may return merchandise because it is the wrong size or for many other reasons. Accepting such returns and giving the customer credit for them Decreases _____ (increases/decreases) total revenue from sales.

9. A decrease in a revenue is a debit, but if we debit Sales for such returns, there is no easy way for a manager to know how frequently these events occur. Therefore, we debit a contra account called ____ Sales Returns + allowances _____ .

10. When we debit Sales Returns and Allowances, the account we usually credit is A/R _____ .

Accounting for a Merchandising Business   119

A10. Accounts Receivable

11. Businesses offer cash discounts on sales to encourage customers to pay early. Discounts on sales _decrease_ (*increase/decrease*) revenue.

A11. decrease

12. Accordingly, we would debit another contra account when customers take advantage of cash discounts that we offer. We call it _Sales Discounts_.

A12. Sales Discounts

13. How would you determine net sales revenue for any accounting period? _Gross Sales − Discounts & Sales returns + allowance accts_

A13. Subtract both sales returns and allowances and sales discounts from sales.

14. Many states levy a sales tax on the customer but require the retail store _to collect_.

A14. to collect the tax

15. When the store collects the tax from the customer, it credits _Sales tax payable acct_ for the tax collected.

A15. Sales Taxes Payable

16. We credit a liability because the company must _pay_ the tax to the state.

A16. remit or pay

17. Purchases is a merchandising account that we debit with only the cost of _Merchandise for sale − Inv_.

A17. goods acquired for resale

18. Does each purchase of merchandise for stock increase the physical inventory of goods for resale? _yes_

A18. Yes.

19. And, doesn't each sale decrease the actual inventory of goods? _yes_

A19. Yes.

20. Why don't we make continuing debits and credits to the Merchandising Inventory account for the above transactions? _We do on the perpetual method._

120 Chapter 5

A20. In Chapter 5, we are using a periodic inventory system where we determine changes to Merchandise Inventory by physical count at the end of each period.

21. How do we maintain a record of the cost of new goods purchased for resale during a period? _Debit the true purchase acct_

A21. By debiting Purchases each time we buy goods. The Purchases account then accumulates gross purchases.

22. How do we keep a record of cost of merchandise that we sell in daily operations? _Debit sales_ ~~(crossed out)~~

A22. We don't. Under the periodic inventory system, we compute it at the end of each period.

23. A cost of buying merchandise is transportation. We use the _F.O.B._ terms to determine whether the buyer or seller is responsible for the cost of the transportation.

A23. F.O.B.

24. F.O.B. shipping point means that the title to the goods passes at the _Point of sale_ and the _Buyer_ bears the transportation cost.

A24. shipping point, buyer

25. F.O.B. destination means that the title to the goods passes at the _Destination_ and the _Seller_ bears the transportation cost.

A25. destination, seller

26. As in the case of sales, it is helpful to management to separate the gross cost of purchases. We show the amount of returns or allowances for defective merchandise in a contra purchases account called _Purchase Returns + Allowances_.

A26. Purchases Returns and Allowances

27. Since the Purchases account has a normal _Debit_ (debit/credit) balance, any account contra to purchases should have a normal _Credit_ (debit/credit) balance.

A27. debit, credit

28. We use the _Purchase Discounts_ account to record the cash discount allowed for early payments on merchandise.

Accounting for a Merchandising Business   121

A28. Purchases Discounts

29. We increase the Purchases Discounts account with a ~~Debit~~ CR (*debit/credit*).

A29. credit

30. Net purchases means purchases minus Purchases Returns & Allowances and Purchase Discounts.

A30. purchases discounts, purchases returns and allowances

31. Show, in summary, a computation to determine the cost of goods sold in a period. [Beginning Inv + Purchases + Transportation IN) − (contra accts)] − Ending Inv

A31. Beginning inventory + purchases (net) = total available − ending inventory = cost of goods sold.

32. The difference between net sales and cost of goods sold is called GROSS Margin on Sales.

A32. gross margin on sales

33. Go to Exhibit 5-4 in the textbook. The net sales revenue of $ 120,000 resulted from deductions of $3,000 and $ 2000 from gross sales revenue of $ 125,000.

A33. 120,000, 2,000, 125,000

34. TeleVideo's Sales account had a CR (*debit/credit*) balance of $ 125,000 on December 31, 1997.

A34. credit, 125,000

35. Sales Discounts had a DR (*debit/credit*) balance of $2,000 on the same date, and Sales Returns and Allowances had a DR (*debit/credit*) balance of $3,000.

A35. debit, debit

36. The beginning inventory for 1997 was $ 15000. It was a DR (*debit/credit*) balance in the Merchandise Inventory account.

A36. 15,000; debit

37. The Purchases account had a DR (*debit/credit*) balance of $ 65,000 on December 31, 1997. Also, Transportation In had a 5,000 (*debit/credit*) balance of $ DR - 70,000.

A37. debit, 65,000; debit, 5,000

A38. Yes.

A39. Yes.

A40. Purchases returns and allowances and purchases discounts.

A41. 79,000.

A42. 11,000.

A43. By physical count.

A44. 68,000

A45. 52,000

B1. 15,000

38. Therefore, Transportation In appears to be an addition to the cost of goods sold and not an operating expense. Is this correct? _yes_

39. Is Transportation In a part of net purchases? _yes_

40. What other items do we consider to be a part of net purchases? _contra accts: purchases returns & allowance_

41. What was the total cost of goods available for sale in the year 1997? $ _79,000_

42. How much of this remained unsold on December 31, 1997? $ _11,000_

43. This is the ending inventory. How did TeleVideo determine it? _By physical count_

44. Deducting ending inventory from cost of goods available for sale indicates that TeleVideo sold goods costing $ _68,000_ in 1997.

45. Subtracting this amount from net sales shows a gross margin on sales of $ _52,000_ .

B. Merchandise Inventory Account

1. TeleVideo Distributors had a merchandise inventory of $ _15,000_ on January 1, 1997.

2. This is the balance in the Merchandise Inventory account on December 31, 1996. They determined it by _physical count_ .

Accounting for a Merchandising Business 123

B2. physical count

B3. Purchases

B4. We extend it to the Income Statement Debit column of the work sheet.

B5. Income Statement Debit

B6. an increase

B7. 11,000; Income Statement

B8. a decrease

B9. on hand or unsold

B10. current asset

3. Since cost of goods sold was $68,000, it is obvious that additional merchandise was purchased. It was not debited to the Merchandise Inventory account, but to the ____purchase____ account.

4. Exhibit 5-6 shows the closing entry approach to handling inventories on the work sheet. What do we do with the beginning balance? _extend it to the Adjm Balance and the Income Statmt DR_

5. To what column do we extend the Purchases amount? _Income Statmt Stmt_

6. So, these two amounts, along with others, are reflecting ↑_____ (an *increase*/a decrease) in cost of goods sold.

7. Referring to Exhibit 5-6, what is the amount of the ending inventory? $__11,000__. We insert this amount on the work sheet as a debit in the Balance Sheet column and a credit in the _Income statemnt_ column.

8. The credit in the Income Statement columns will reflect _Decrease_ (an increase /a *decrease*) in cost of goods sold.

9. It makes sense that ending inventory should be a decrease in cost of goods sold because this is the portion of cost of goods available for sale that remains _available_

10. In the balance sheet, we would classify it as an _asset (current)_.

11. In Exhibit 5-10, the amount of inventory shown in the current assets is $__11,000__.

124 Chapter 5

B11. 11,000

12. This is, of course, the new December 31, 19 __97__ , amount determined by physical count.

B12. 97

13. (*Appendix 5A*) Under the adjusting approach to handling inventory changes, we make an adjusting entry _____ (*debiting/ crediting*) Merchandise Inventory for the beginning balance and debiting _____ _____ .

B13. crediting, Income Summary

14. We make a second adjusting entry _____ (*debiting/ crediting*) Income Summary and _____ Merchandise Inventory for the ending balance.

B14. crediting, debiting

15. We carry the adjusted balance on the Merchandise Inventory line to the _____ columns.

B15. Balance Sheet

16. We carry both amounts on the Income Summary line to _____ _____ .

B16. Income Statement columns

C. Net Price Method As discussed in the "Sales Revenue Accounts" section of the chapter, the TeleVideo Distributors granted sales discounts to customers in 1997 amounting to $2,000. In this review, we will use the concepts from the net price method discussion with a new set of data.

1. Referring to Exhibit 5-2, TeleVideo made a credit sale of $200 to J&Z Movie Rentals on December 6, 1997. The cash discount terms were 2/10, n/30. This means that J&Z may deduct __2%__ percent from the invoice price if they pay within __10__ days.

C1. 2, 10

2. On December 9, 1997, J&Z Movie Rentals returned $ __50__ of defective goods, leaving them owing a balance of $ _____ __150__ _____ to TeleVideo.

Accounting for a Merchandising Business   125

C2. 50, 150

3. J&Z Movie Rental paid the balance due on December 16, 1997. This __is__ (*is/is not*) within the discount period of ten days.

C3. is

4. J&Z may deduct 2% or $ __147__ from the balance due.

C4. 3 ($150 x 0.02)

5. J&Z actually paid only $ __147__ ; however, it debits Accounts Payable with the full $ __150__ remaining due.

C5. 147, 150

6. J&Z credits the discount taken, $3, to the __Purchase Discounts__ account.

C6. Purchases Discounts

7. The foregoing is an illustration of the gross price method. Under this procedure we know the total amount of discounts taken. Do we also know the amount of discounts not taken? __No__

C7. No.

8. Using the net price method, would J&Z know the amount of discounts not taken or lost? __yes__ .

C8. Yes

9. If J&Z used the net price method for recording purchases, it would record the purchase on December 6 by debiting __Purchases__ for $ __196__ and crediting __A/P__ for $. __196__ .

C9. Purchases, 196, Accounts Payable, 196

10. For the return on December 9, J&Z would debit _____ for $ _____ and credit _____ for $ _____ .

C10. Accounts Payable, 49, Purchases Returns and Allowances, 49

11. J&Z would record the payment entry on December 16 with a debit to _____ for $ _____ and a credit to _____ for $ _____ .

126 Chapter 5

C11. Accounts Payable, 147, Cash, 147

C12. No.

C13. Accounts Payable, 147, Purchases Discounts Lost, 3, Cash, 150

C14. income

C15. would not

C16. would

D1. They increased from $7,169.3 million to $8,745.6 million.

D2. 22.0%.

D3. We divide the change in net sales by the net sales in 1992.

D4. decreasing

D5. increasing

12. Would there be any indication of the discount taken by J&Z in this case? _____

13. If J&Z Movie Rentals did not pay until December 24 (and lost the discount), the payment would debit _____ _____ for $_____, debit _____ for $ _____, and credit _____ for $_____.

14. Purchases Discounts Lost is an expense account and would show as an expense in the _____ statement.

15. Thus, management _____ (would/would not) know amounts of cash discounts taken.

16. But the amount of lost discounts _____ (would/would not) be known.

D. **Analyzing Information**

1. Using Toys "R" Us income statements for 1992, 93, and 94, what happened to net sales? _____

2. What was the percentage change in net sales? _____

3. How did we calculate this percentage change? _____

4. Is the percentage of cost of goods sold increasing or decreasing? _____

5. With sales increasing and the percentage of cost of goods sold decreasing, gross margin should be _____.

6. Is this favorable or unfavorable? _____

Accounting for a Merchandising Business 127

D6. favorable

D7. 94.3 ($531.8 - $437.5)

D8. increasing

D9. unfavorable

D10. remained constant

7. The change in net income was $_____.

8. Is the percentage operating expenses increasing or decreasing?_____

9. Is this favorable or unfavorable? _____

10. Although net sales increased, net income as a percentage of net sales _____.

LEARNING GOALS ACHIEVEMENT TEST

1. (LG 1-4, 8) Indicate whether each of the following is true or false based on a periodic inventory system:

   __T__ a. We do not record recurring purchases and sales of merchandise during a year as continuous increases or decreases to the Merchandise Inventory account.
   __F__ b. We can determine the net cost of goods purchased during an accounting period by examining the entries to the Purchases account.
   __T__ c. Purchases Discounts is an account that reflects reductions in amounts paid for purchases.
   __T__ d. Sales Discounts is an account that reflects reductions in amounts collected from sales.
   __F__ e. We increase both the Purchases Discounts and Sales Discounts accounts by debits.
   __F__ f. The beginning inventory of 1997 is the same as the ending inventory of 1996.
   __T__ g. We must add the balance of Transportation In to the Purchases balance to determine the gross delivered cost of purchases.
   __F__ h. We determine the ending inventory valuation by a computation using data from the other merchandising accounts. physical count.
   __F__ i. The term 2/10, n/30 means that a buyer may take a 2 percent discount if they pay the bill in thirty days.
   __T__ j. A purchase of $3,000 of merchandise with terms of 2/10, n/30 recorded using the net price method would be debited to Purchases at $2,940.
   __F__ k. The income statement for both the service business and the merchandising business will have a cost of goods sold section.
   __T__ l. We categorize operating expenses into selling and general and administrative expense categories.

128 Chapter 5

2. (LG 4) Compute the missing figures in each of the following independent cases:

	Case A	Case B	Case C
Beginning inventory	$200	$ 100	$?
Purchases	800	1,000	500
Transportation in	50	50	10
Purchases discounts	20	30	5
Purchases returns and allowances	?	60	15
Cost of goods available for sale	990	?	540
Ending inventory	?	80	?
Cost of goods sold	840	?	510

3. (LG 7, A1) The following is a partial work sheet for the Wappacoma Company:

WAPPACOMA COMPANY
WORK SHEET
FOR THE YEAR ENDED DECEMBER 31, 1997

Accounts	Trial Balance Dr.	Trial Balance Cr.	Adjustments Dr.	Adjustments Cr.	Adjusted Trial Balance Dr.	Adjusted Trial Balance Cr.	Income Statement Dr.	Income Statement Cr.	Balance Sheet Dr.	Balance Sheet Cr.
Merch. Inven.	400		450		400		400	450	450	

The beginning inventory is $400; the ending inventory is $450.

Required: Using the approach specified by your instructor enter the inventory amounts in all locations in which they would normally appear when the work sheet is completed.

4. (LG 4, 5, 7, A1) Following are some of the December 31, 1997, account balances from Your Computer Retailer Company:

Account Title	Debits	Credits
Merchandise Inventory	$ 1,200	
P. Card, Capital		$12,270
P. Card, Withdrawals	8,000	
Sales		90,000
Sales Discounts	300	
Sales Returns and Allowances	800	
Purchases	50,000	
Purchases Discounts		1,000
Purchases Returns and Allowances		400
Transportation In	900	
Selling Expenses	4,000	

The ending inventory is $1,800.

Required:

(1) If your instructor requires the adjusting approach, record any necessary adjusting entries. IF NOT, skip this step.
(2) Record the closing entries.
(3) Compute the cost of goods sold.

130 Chapter 5

(1 & 2)

GENERAL JOURNAL

Date		Accounts and Explanations	PR	Debit	Credit
1997		CLOSING ENTRIES			
DEC	31	Merchandise Inventory		1,800	
		Sales		90,000	
		Purchase Disc		1,000	
		Purchase Returns + Allowances		400	
		Income Summary			93,600 93,200
	31	Income Summary		57,800	
		Purchases			50,000
		Transportation In			900
		Sales Disc			300
		Sales Returns + Allowances			800
		Selling Expenses			4,000
		Merchandise Inventory			1,800
	31	Income Summary		3,600 34,800	
		P. Card, Cap			3,600 34,800
	31	P. Card Cap		8,000	
		P. Card Withdraws			8,000

GENERAL JOURNAL

Date	Accounts and Explanations	PR	Debit	Credit

132 Chapter 5

(3)

5. (LG 2, 8) C. Cunningham Company sold merchandise to C. Rapids. The list price was $10,000 subject to a trade discount of 20, 10, and 5%. The invoice is further subject to a cash discount of 2/10, n/30.

Required:

(1) Compute the amount Rapids should pay if the invoice is paid thirty days after the purchase date.

$6840

(2) Compute the amount Rapids should pay if the invoice is paid nine days after the purchase date.

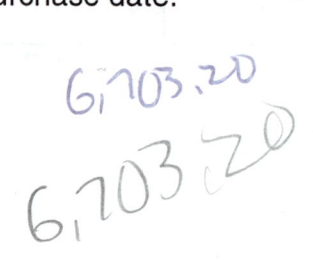

$6,703.20

(3) Explain how we should record the trade discount in the accounting records. _Should not show TRADE DISC., only to show the net amount_

(4) Explain how the cash discount would be shown in the accounting records:
   a. If lost and the net price method is used.

A/P	6,840	
Disc Lost	136.80	
Cash		6,703.20

   b. If taken and the gross price method is used.

A/P	6840	
Purchase Disc		136.80
Cash		6703.20

ANSWERS TO LEARNING GOALS ACHIEVEMENT TEST

1.
   a. T
   b. F (must also consider transportation in, discounts, and returns and allowances)
   c. T
   d. T
   e. F (Purchases Discounts is increased by a credit)
   f. T
   g. T
   h. F (it is determined by physical count)
   i. F (must pay in ten days to take discount)
   j. T
   k. F (the income statement for a service business does not have a cost of goods sold section)
   l. T

2.
	Case A	Case B	Case C
Beginning inventory			$50
Purchases returns and allowances	$ 40		
Total goods available for sale		$1,060	
Ending inventory	150		30
Cost of goods sold		980	

134 Chapter 5

3.
Closing approach:

WAPPACOMA COMPANY
WORK SHEET
FOR THE YEAR ENDED DECEMBER 31, 1997

Accounts	Trial Balance Dr.	Cr.	Adjustments Dr.	Cr.	Adjusted Trial Balance Dr.	Cr.	Income Statement Dr.	Cr.	Balance Sheet Dr.	Cr.
Merch. Inven.	400				400		400	450	450	

Adjusting approach:

WAPPACOMA COMPANY
WORK SHEET
FOR THE YEAR ENDED DECEMBER 31, 1997

Accounts	Trial Balance Dr.	Cr.	Adjustments Dr.	Cr.	Adjusted Trial Balance Dr.	Cr.	Income Statement Dr.	Cr.	Balance Sheet Dr.	Cr.
Merch. Inven.	400		450	400	450				450	
Inc. Summary			400	450	400	450	400	450		

4.
(1)
GENERAL JOURNAL

Date	Accounts and Explanations	PR	Debit	Credit
1997				
Dec. 31	Adjusting Entries (if required) Merchandise Inventory		1,800	
	Income Summary			1,800
	To establish ending inventory.			
31	Income Summary		1,200	
	Merchandise Inventory			1,200
	To remove beginning inventory.			

(2)

GENERAL JOURNAL

Date		Accounts and Explanations	PR	Debit	Credit
1997		Closing Entries			
Dec.	31	Sales		90,000	
		Purchases Discounts		1,000	
		Purchases Returns and Allowances		400	
		*Merchandise Inventory		1,800	
		Income Summary			93,200
		To close credit balance temporary accounts and enter ending inventory.			
	31	Income Summary		57,200	
		*Merchandise Inventory			1,200
		Sales Discounts			300
		Sales Returns and Allowances			800
		Purchases			50,000
		Transportation In			900
		Selling Expenses			4,000
		To close debit balance temporary accounts and remove beginning inventory.			
	31	Income Summary		36,000	
		P. Card, Capital			36,000
		To close Income Summary.			
	31	P. Card, Capital		8,000	
		P. Card, Withdrawals			8,000
		To close withdrawals account.			

* (If the adjusting approach had been used these accounts would not have been involved in the closing entries. The credit to Income Summary in the first closing entry would have been $91,400. And, the debit to Income Summary in the second closing entry would have been $56,000. The balance in Income Summary that would have been closed into P. Card, Capital would have been the same.)

(3) Computation of cost of goods sold:

Merchandise inventory, January 1, 1997		$1,200
Purchases	$50,000	
Transportation in	900	
Gross delivered cost of purchases	$50,900	
Deduct: Purchases discounts $1,000		
Purchases returns and allowances 400	1,400	
Net cost of purchases		49,500
Cost of merchandise available for sale		$50,700
Deduct: Merchandise inventory, December 31, 1997		1,800
Cost of goods sold		$48,900

5.   (1) $10,000 list price
           - 2,000 (20% of $10,000)
            $ 8,000
           -    800 10% of $8,000)
            $ 7,200
           -    360 (5% of $7,200)
            $ 6,840 invoice price

        OR $10,000 x 0.80 x 0.90 x 0.95 = $6,840

  (2) $6,840 - (0.02 x $6,840) = $6,703.20.
  (3)   We do not record it in the records. It serves to determine the invoice price. We record the invoice price or the net invoice price in the records.
  (4a)   We would debit it to Purchases Discounts Lost in the amount of $136.80.
  (4b)   We would credit it to Purchases Discounts in the amount of $136.80.

# Chapter 6

INTERNAL CONTROL AND CASH

EXPLANATION OF MAJOR CONCEPTS

Internal Control LG 1, 2

Internal control consists of the policies and procedures designed to provide reasonable assurance that errors or irregularities will be prevented or detected on a timely basis and that assets will be protected from improper use. The three elements of the internal control structure are (1) the control environment, (2) the accounting system, and (3) the control procedures.

The control environment consists of management's policies and actions that enable the business to meet its goals. It includes management's attitudes about the importance of internal control. The accounting system includes the methods and records used to identify, assemble, analyze, record, and report a firm's transactions. The control procedures include the methods to safeguard the assets and insure accuracy of the records. Exhibit 6-1 summarizes the elements of an internal control system.

Cash is easily subject to theft and requires extensive internal controls. Among the methods used to strengthen internal control over cash are:

- Separation of the duties and responsibilities of persons who handle cash transactions from those who record cash transactions.
- Use of mechanical devices (such as cash registers) to record cash transactions.
- Daily deposits of cash receipts intact (deposit the exact cash and checks received).
- Organization of the recording of cash so that, whenever possible, the work of one employee checks another employee.
- Periodical check of the operation of internal controls on a surprise basis by someone outside the cash area.
- Establishment of controls over the use of computers.
- Payments, except for minor amounts, made by check.
- Payment of minor amounts from a petty cash fund.

Petty Cash Fund LG 3

The preferred system for a petty cash fund is the imprest fund. Literally, imprest means advanced in trust. We advance a fixed sum to a designated petty cash fund custodian. At this point, the fund would have cash equal to the imprest amount. The custodian makes cash payments out of this fund for minor items. For each payment the custodian obtains a receipt on a petty cash voucher. We do not make journal entries to record these payments at the time the cashier makes the expenditure. We make the journal entires for these expenditures when we replenish the fund. We accomplish control over the cash in the petty cash fund by the fact that the total of the cash and petty cash vouchers should be equal to the imprest amount at all times.

Periodically, the we should replenish the petty cash fund. We should replenish the fund (1) when cash in the fund is low or (2) at the end of the accounting period in order to properly record all expenses. At that time, we "buy" the receipted petty cash vouchers from the custodian. That is, the custodian turns them over to the accounting department in exchange for sufficient cash to bring the cash in the fund back up to the imprest balance. We then debit the expenses represented by the petty cash vouchers and credit cash. If the amount represented by the vouchers is different from the amount of cash necessary to bring the fund up to the proper imprest balance, we use an account entitled Cash Over and Short to balance the entry. The fund is again wholly cash. As the cycle starts over, we make cash payments from the fund. The fixed sum becomes a mixture of cash and receipted vouchers until we make the next replenishment. We must remember one caution about an imprest fund. We must replenish the fund at an accounting period end in order to properly record all of the expenses.

Bank Reconciliation LG 4, 5

Good control requires that we deposit daily receipts of cash in the bank intact. Depositing daily cash receipts intact means that we pay no bills out of the cash received from sales or collections. The total of all daily sales and collections is deposited in the bank at the end of each business day. We should make all payments (except petty cash) by check. If we do this, the banks records should be a duplicate of the company's Cash account. Thus the balance in the Cash account should be equal to the bank balance. It rarely is because of:

- Timing differences. For example, we credit (reduce) Cash at the moment we write a check. The bank doesn't reduce our account until the check reaches the bank for payment.
- Actions by the bank not known to us. For example, the bank may deduct a monthly service charge. We do not know this amount until we receive the monthly bank statement.
- Errors. Our accounting department (or the bank) may make an error in recording a deposit or a check.

The bank reconciliation is a statement that explains the specific differences between our Cash account and the bank's recorded balance shown on the monthly statement. The preferred form of bank reconciliation begins with the balance in Cash and the bank statement balance (for the same date) and adjusts each to the same amount. Refer to Exhibit 6-5 for an outline of the format of a bank reconciliation. After listing all reconciling items, the bank reconciliation will show identical amounts for the adjusted book balance and adjusted bank balance. This is strong evidence that there are no errors in the Cash account. We must journalize every item on the "Per Books" side. The items on the "Per Bank" side do not require journal entries. Some, such as deposits in transit or outstanding checks, will clear automatically in a future period. We would refer others to the bank for correction.

The key to preparing a bank reconciliation is recognizing when to add to or subtract from the balance per book or the balance per bank. For each item that could cause the two balances to be different, you should ask yourself the following questions:

- Which balance (bank or books) is not reflecting the "true" cash balance because the item is not recorded or is incorrectly recorded? (For example, outstanding checks have not yet been reflected in the bank statement. Therefore, it is the bank balance that we should adjust.)
- Having decided which balance (bank or books) needs adjusting, ask: Is that balance as now stated too high or too low? (To use outstanding checks as an example again, the bank balance is now too high. When the checks actually arrive for payment at the bank, they will reduce our account. To adjust the bank balance, deduct them.)

In order to engage in this type of thinking, it is absolutely necessary that you understand the mechanics of bank transactions. Ask questions about any item you do not understand.

The Voucher System LG 6, 7

The voucher system gives better control over payments. Before writing any check, a person with proper authority must approve a form known as a voucher. Persons who prepare vouchers check such things as accuracy of prices and arithmetic on the vendor's bill or invoice. They also check the discount terms, compute the discount, and verify that we received the goods or services as authorized by the purchase order. Using account numbers from the chart of accounts, the person who prepares a voucher indicates the accounts debited. We always credit Vouchers Payable, a liability account, when recording a voucher.

The voucher register, Exhibit 6-8, is a special journal. Together with the check register, Exhibit 6-9, (another special journal), these journals replace the purchases journal and cash payments journal. We make postings to ledger accounts from these two journals either in total or individually, similar to postings from other special journals. You should review posting procedures for special journals (Appendix D) if you have any difficulty knowing when to post columns in total and when to post individual entries. Because every entry in the voucher register includes a credit to Vouchers Payable, there is a special column provided to post only the total. We post entries made in the Other Accounts section individually, as was the case with the cash payments journal. Note that the check register, Exhibit 6-9, has only special columns. All monthly postings from it are postings of totals only. Every entry in the check register must include a debit to Vouchers Payable and a credit to Cash. The Vouchers

140 Chapter 6

Payable account does not have a subsidiary ledger as does Accounts Payable. The unpaid vouchers themselves serve as a subsidiary record.

Analyzing Information LG 8

In analyzing financial statements, we should be aware of any restrictions that might exist on the cash balance. For example, must the company maintain a compensating balance to support free bank services or borrowing under a line of credit.

GUIDED STUDY OF THIS CHAPTER

A. Internal Control

1. The three elements of the internal control structure are the *The control environment*, *The acct. system*, and *control procedures*.

A1. control environment, accounting system, control procedures.

2. Referring to Exhibit 6-1, the control environment includes _____.

A2. management's philosophy and operating style, the organization structure, the audit committee, methods of assigning authority and responsibility, methods for controlling performance, and management's policies and practices

3. Internal control in the accounting system includes _____.

A3. identifying and recording all valid transactions, proper classification of transactions, proper measurement of dollar amounts, assignment of transactions to the proper accounting period, and proper presentation of financial statements

4. The control procedures include _____.

A4. proper authorization of transactions and activities, segregation of duties, documents and records that ensure proper recording, adequate control of assets and use of assets and records, and review of internal control

A5. deposited intact daily in a bank

A6. minor items paid from a petty cash fund

A7. naturally subject to theft or misuse

A8. inflow, outflow

A9. 6,246,900,000
6,423,000,000

A10. poor

A11. poor

5. For good internal control over cash, all cash receipts should be _Deposited Intact Daily to the bank_.

6. We should make all payments by check unless they are _a small or petty cash_.

7. Internal control over cash is important because cash is _the most liquid asset_ _theft_.

8. It is not the cash balance at any one time that is critical. It is the _inflow_ and _outflow_ of cash that we must control.

9. Exhibit 6-2 shows that Walt Disney had $ _6,246.9_ of cash inflows during 1994 and $ _6,423.0_ of cash outflows.

10. Having the same person receive cash and make entries into the cash receipts journal would be _poor_ (good/poor) internal control.

11. Having two or more persons making cash sales from the same cash register drawer is _poor_ (good/poor) internal control.

12. Should total cash receipts for any day be equal to the deposit to the bank account for that day? _yes_

142   Chapter 6

A12. Yes.

13. Would it be easier to pay some local bills by taking cash out of the cash register and leaving a copy of the bill to show what the payment was for? __yes__ .
What would be the danger in doing this? __lack of internal control__

A13. Yes; It creates opportunities (and temptations) to steal cash.

14. The safer way to handle small payments in cash is to use a __petty cash__ _____ assigned to a single custodian.

A14. petty cash fund

B. Petty Cash

1. Exhibit 6-3 illustrates a petty cash voucher. What is the purpose of this voucher? __To record & have a receipt__

B1. To describe and give evidence of a payment.

2. Who has received the payment and signed the receipt for it? __custodian__

B2. Jim Brady.

3. What was the payment for? __Postage expense__

B3. Postage Expense (special mailings)

4. We will debit this payment to Postage Expense. When? __when we replenish the petty cash fund__

B4. When we replenish the fund.

5. In what journal would we record the replenishment of the petty cash fund? __Petty cash acct__

B5. (Cash payments journal.)

6. If a petty cash fund is $100 and there are receipted vouchers totaling $62 in the safe in which the fund is kept, there should also be $ __38__ in cash in the fund.

B6. 38

7. Exactly what do we mean by replenishment of the petty cash fund? __exchange vouchers for cash__

Internal Control and Cash 143

B7. The custodian exchanges the receipted vouchers for a check.

8. What does the custodian do with the check? _Cashes it at the bank + puts cash back into the ???_

B8. Cashes it at the bank and puts the cash in the petty cash fund.

9. In the textbook example, what was the total amount of the petty cash vouchers turned in for replenishment? $ _____ .

B9. 451

10. What was the total amount of cash in the fund before making the replenishment? $ _____ .

B10. 47

11. We _____ (*debit/credit*) the expenses represented by the petty cash vouchers in the journal entry.

B11. debit

12. Was the proper cash amount in the petty cash fund? _____ . What was the difference? $ _____ . We record this amount to the account? _____ .

B12. No; 2; Cash Over and Short

13. In the textbook journal entry to replenish High Company's petty cash fund, we recorded a debit of $2 to Cash Over and Short. What type of account is this?

B13. It is an expense if it has a debit balance, a revenue if it has a credit balance.

14. Is it normal for persons handling cash to be over or short? _____ . Explain. _____

B14. Yes; The amounts should be small relative to total cash handled.

15. In case of an unreasonable cash overage or shortage, what action should a manager take? _____

B15. Investigate to determine and correct the cause.

C. Bank Reconciliation

144   Chapter 6

		1. How often do banks provide statements to their depositors? _____
C1.	Monthly.	2. Exhibit 6-4 shows the September 30, 1997, bank statement for Clearwater Company. The bank credited how many deposits to this account in September? _____
C2.	Nine, including credit memo. *(Ten if you include interest.)*	3. Is Clearwater practicing good internal control by depositing receipts intact daily? _____
C3.	No.	4. Clearwater Company had a balance of $_____in its bank account on September 30, 1997.
C4.	204.24	5. In Exhibit 6-4, the last transaction date is _____ .
C5.	September 30, 1997	6. Exhibit 6-6 reconciles the September bank statement (Exhibit 6-4) with Clearwater's Cash account. On September 30, Clearwater's Cash ledger account showed a debit balance of $_____ .
C6.	68.33	7. According to the textbook, the checks that were outstanding on August 31 were check numbers _____ through _____ .
C7.	637, 644	8. Clearwater had credited these checks to its Cash account but the checks _____ _____ The Bank of Connecticut for payment by August 31.
C8.	had not reached	9. Check number 637 appears on the September bank statement (Exhibit 6-4) as being paid on September 3. Check number 644 cleared through the bank on _____ .
C9.	September 4	10. Check number 639 was paid by the bank on _____ .
C10.	It has not been paid yet.	11. Therefore, check number 639 is one of the _____ checks on September 30, 1997.

Internal Control and Cash   145

C11. outstanding

12. On August 31, 1997, there was one deposit in transit in the amount of $_____ .

C12. 82.20

13. Clearwater deposited this $82.20 and debited Cash on August 30. The bank showed it as a deposit on _____ .

C13. September 2
(See Exhibit 6-4)

14. Clearwater's cash receipts journal indicates eight bank deposits made in September. The September bank statement shows how many of these eight as deposits? _____

C14. Seven.

15. The dollar amount of deposits recorded on Clearwater's books but not on the bank's books (in transit) on September 30 is $_____ .

C15. 421.50

16. To adjust the bank balance of $204.24 to the correct amount, it is necessary to _____ (*add/deduct*) the deposit in transit.

C16. add

17. When the outstanding checks reach the bank for payment, they will _____ (*reduce/increase*) Clearwater's balance.

C17. reduce

18. So, they should be _____ (*added to/deducted from*) the bank statement balance.

C18. deducted from

19. With these adjustments to the balance per bank, the adjusted bank balance on September 30, 1997 is $_____ .

C19. 540.47

20. Since Clearwater's Cash account has a balance of $_____, we must also adjust it.

C20. 68.33

21. The collection of our customer's note requires adjustment.

C21. No answer required.

22. Clearwater Company had given the bank a customer's note in the amount of $_____ for collection by the bank.

146 Chapter 6

C22. 500.00

23. To add $500.00 to Clearwater's account for this note, the bank recorded a _____ (*debit/credit*) memo, since Clearwater's account is a liability to the bank.

C23. credit

24. For performing the service, the bank charged Clearwater $_____ .

C24. 3.00

25. Thus, the bank has deposited the net amount of $_____ to Clearwater's account on _____ and issued a _____ memo.

C25. 497.00, September 16, credit

26. In effect, this transaction is the same as if the customer had paid the $500.00 in cash to Clearwater and then Clearwater immediately deposited it in the bank (except for the $3.00 collection fee).

C26. No answer required.

27. The bank statement showed that Clearwater had earned $_____ in interest. Since the company did not know of this amount before it received the statement, it must _____ (*add/subtract*) it to the book balance.

C27. 0.84; add

28. Clearwater made an accounting error with check number 640. The check was actually written in the amount of $_____ but was entered in the cash payments journal as $_____ . Thus, it will have to _____ (*add/subtract*) $_____ on the book side of the reconciliation.

C28. 200.16, 201.06; 0.90, added

29. We need two other adjustments. One was for the bank service charge of $_____ that was _____ (*added/subtracted*).

C29. 5.40, subtracted

30. The other adjustment was for _____ _____ . It subtracted $_____ from the book side. It must subtract it because _____ _____ _____

C30. a customer's NSF check; 21.20; the bank deducted the amount from our account when the check was dishonored by the maker's bank.

C31. 540.47

C32. Yes.

C33. journal

C34. Yes.

C35. Each one involves a debit or credit to Cash.

C36. general

C37. None. *(It may be necessary to report them to the bank.)*

31. After adding and subtracting the adjustments to Clearwater's Cash account, the adjusted Cash balance should be $ _____.

32. Is this amount the same as the adjusted bank balance? _____

33. Although the bank reconciliation is in balance, Clearwater has made no change to its Cash account. To make the change requires a series of _____ entries.

34. Is it correct that every adjustment made in the "Per Books" section of the bank reconciliation requires a journal entry on Clearwater's books? _____

35. There is something that every one of these journal entries will have in common. What is it? _____

36. If Clearwater has not totaled and posted the cash receipts and payments journals for the month, it should make the entries there. However, if it has already posted the cash journals, it could make the entries in the _____ journal.

37. Which of the items in the "Per Bank" section of the bank reconciliation require journal entries? _____

D. The Voucher System
A voucher is a specially designed form that serves as a check list to be gone over before we make a payment. It also shows which accounts to debit with specific amounts. A person in authority approves the voucher for payment after other persons have made various checks for accuracy and validity.

148   Chapter 6

		1. Exhibit 6-7 illustrates a typical voucher. The person approving this payment will do so by approving voucher number _____.
D1.	314	2. The due date on voucher 314 is 1/8/97. That is the date that they must write the check in order to _____ _____.
D2.	take advantage of the 2% cash discount	3. The Tennessee Aircraft Supply is using the gross procedure. Account Number 501 is the Purchases account debited with $ _____.
D3.	3,500.00	4. When it pays this approved voucher on 1/8/93, the actual amount of the check will be $ _____.
D4.	3,430.00	5. We will credit the difference of $70.00 to the _____ account in the check register.
D5.	Purchases Discounts	6. Exhibits 8-8 and 8-9 show the voucher register and check register. In the voucher register, we know the January 3 voucher to the Wheaton Company is for merchandise for resale because _____.
D6.	the debit is to the Purchases account	7. In the check register, we can see the journalizing of payment to the Wheaton Company on January 8. Since there is a Purchases Discounts column in the check register, we know that Tennessee Aircraft Supply uses the _____ (*gross/net*) method of recording purchases.
D7.	gross	8. In the voucher register, the credit to Vouchers Payable for the Wheaton Company purchase was in the amount of $ _____.

Internal Control and Cash   149

D8. 3,500

9. In the check register, we debited Vouchers Payable with $_____, but the amount of check number 709 is only $_____ . We credited the difference of $70 to the _____ account.

D9. 3,500, 3,430; Purchases Discounts

10. Is the debit ($3,500) posted individually to Vouchers Payable in the general ledger? _____

D10. No.

11. How does this entry get posted to the general ledger? _____

D11. It is part of the column total amount that they will post on January 31.

12. In the voucher register, the notation (206) beneath the Vouchers Payable column means that they have _____ (*debited/credited*) Vouchers Payable for $_____ .

D12. credited, 22,324

13. In the check register, the notation (206) beneath the Vouchers Payable column means that they have _____ (*debited/credited*) Vouchers Payable for $_____ .

D13. debited, 13,154

14. Are all items in the check register posted in total? _____

D14. Yes.

15. Are all items in the voucher register posted in total? _____

D15. No.

16. For example, in the purchase from Dover Company on January 3, they posted the $_____ entry individually to account number _____ .

D16. 800, Office Equipment, 171

17. The symbol (X) below the total of $11,826 in the Other Accounts column of the voucher register means that $11,826 _____ (*was/was not*) posted in total.

150   Chapter 6

D17. was not

D18. Voucher nos. 316, 333, and 334. (There may be others; the total page is not shown.)

D19. Attached to their respective invoice in the unpaid vouchers file.

D20. Yes.

D21. Vouchers Payable.

D22. no check is written except to pay an approved voucher. This improves internal control over cash

E1. compensating balance

E2. They consist of time deposits with a number of commercial banks with high credit ratings.

E3. No; To minimize credit risk.

18. Which vouchers in the voucher register (Exhibit 6-8) are unpaid on January 31, 1997? _____
_____
_____

19. Where would those unpaid vouchers be physically located? _____
_____

20. Should the total of vouchers in the unpaid vouchers file on January 31 be equal to the balance of a specific general ledger account? _____

21. Which account? _____
_____

22. The major advantage of the voucher system is that _____
_____
_____
_____ .

E. Analyzing Information

1. A bank balance that a business must maintain to support free bank services is called a _____
_____ .

2. What does Avon's cash equivalents consist of? _____
_____
_____
_____

3. Does Avon keep all of their cash in one bank? _____ Why or why not?
_____
_____
_____

4. How much does Avon have in lines of credit? _____

E4. $235,000,000.

E5. No.

E6. 0

5. Do they have any compensating balance requirements? _____

6. As of December 31, 1994, how much of their lines of credit has Avon used?
$ _____ .

LEARNING GOALS ACHIEVEMENT TEST

1. (LG 1-2) Answer the following true-false questions about internal control by placing a T or F in the space before the question.

    ___ a. Internal control consists of the policies and procedures used to provide reasonable assurance of accuracy and to safeguard assets.
    ___ b. A manager's attitude towards the full disclosure of financial information is a part of the internal control environment.
    ___ c. An effective accounting system is one that will disclose errors which are made in the journalizing and posting of transactions.
    ___ d. The use of prenumbered invoices is not a part of the internal control system but helps in filing.
    ___ e. A sound internal control system is not possible without the use of a voucher system.

2. (LG 3) Washington Company's management has decided that it needs a petty cash fund of $500.00. On June 1, 1997, a check for $500.00 was given to Maria Ortega, who was appointed the fund custodian. On June 30, 1997, the fund contained $330.00 in currency and coins and receipted vouchers for:

Postage expense paid............................	$ 60.50
Sales travel expense	110.30

    Required:

    (1) Prepare journal entries for the establishment and replenishment of the fund.
    (2) Assuming that June is a typical month, comment on the size of the fund.

152 Chapter 6

(1)   **GENERAL JOURNAL**

Date	Accounts and Explanations	PR	Debit	Credit

(2) _____

_____

_____

_____

_____

3. (LG 4, 5) Daniel Enterprise's Cash account has a balance of $582.00 on May 31, 1997. His bank statement on that date shows a balance of $834.50. Included in his statement are a group of deposits and check payments along with a $6.00 service charge. There is an item marked DM for $85.00 and John Gill's check in that amount. Daniel deposited the check last month. The bank returned the check stamped NSF. Daniel also cannot find a deposit of $218.50 that he made on May 31 recorded on the bank statement. He has listed outstanding checks for a total of $517.00, but his bank reconciliation is out of balance. In matching canceled checks with the check register, he finds that check no. 1685 in the actual amount of $216.00 was recorded as $261.00 in payment of insurance expense on May 8.

   Required:

   (1) Prepare a bank reconciliation.
   (2) Prepare general journal entries required.

(1)

(2)

GENERAL JOURNAL

Date	Accounts and Explanations	PR	Debit	Credit

4. (LG 7, 8) The following transactions are to be entered in a voucher register similar to Exhibit 6-8, a check register similar to Exhibit 6-9, or both. For each of them, fill in the blank spaces in the form on the following page. Use the gross price method. Transaction 1 is done as a sample.

Transaction Number — **Description**

1. Purchased merchandise on account for $5,000, terms 2/10, n/30. Prepared voucher no. 321 for payment.
2. Authorized voucher no. 322 to pay monthly rent of $350.
3. Prepared voucher no. 323 to authorize payment of a $10,000 note plus $1,200 interest.
4. Issued check no. 1830 to pay voucher no. 321 in time to take the cash discount.
5. Issued check no. 1831 to pay voucher no. 322.
6. Made arrangements to pay the interest and one-half the principal amount of the $10,000 note. A new note for $5,000 is issued for the balance. Voucher no. 323 is canceled; vouchers no. 324 and 325 are issued to replace it.
7. Paid voucher no. 324 by check.

SOLUTION FORM

Transaction Number	Entered in VR, CR, or Both	Columns in Which Entries Are Made and Amount of Each
1	VR	Voucher no. 321 Vouchers Payable, Credit, $5,000 Purchases, Debit, $5,000
————	————	
————	————	
————	————	
————	————	
————	————	

ANSWERS TO LEARNING GOALS ACHIEVEMENT TEST

1.   a. T   b. T   c. T   d. F   e. F

2. (1)

GENERAL JOURNAL

Date		Accounts and Explanations	PR	Debit	Credit

1997
Jun.
	1	Petty Cash
		    Cash
		    To establish petty cash fund.
				500.00	500.00

	30	Postage Expense
		Sales Travel Expense
		    Cash Over and Short
		    Cash
		    To replenish petty cash fund.
				60.50
				110.30
					.80
					170.00

(2)   Since $500.00 appears to be enough for about three months' petty cash needs, they should consider a reduction of the fund. About $200.00 should be enough. They can invest the remainder of the idle cash in a more productive asset. Also, too large a petty cash fund weakens internal control in that the custodian will need to seek replenishment (and thus be subject to review) less frequently.

3.

(1)

DANIEL ENTERPRISE
BANK RECONCILIATION
MAY 31, 1997

Balance per books, May 31		$ 582.00
Add: Error in check no. 1685		45.00
Subtotal		$ 627.00
Deduct: Bank service charge.................................	$ 6.00	
Customer's NSF check...........................	85.00	91.00
Adjusted balance per books, May 31.......................		$ 536.00
Balance per bank statement, May 31......................		$ 834.50
Add: Deposit of May 31 in transit.............................		218.50
Subtotal		$1,053.00
Deduct: Outstanding checks (per list)		517.00
Adjusted balance per bank, May 31.........................		$ 536.00

(2)

GENERAL JOURNAL

Date		Accounts and Explanations	PR	Debit	Credit

1997 May	31	Cash
		    Insurance Expense
		    To correct error in entering
		    check no. 1685 on May 8.
				45	45

	31	Service Charge Expense
		Accounts Receivable, J. Gill
		    Cash
		    To record service charge for
		    May and returned customer
		    check.
				6
				85
					91

4.

SOLUTION FORM

Transaction Number	Entered in VR, CR, or Both	Columns in Which Entries Are Made and Amount of Each
1	VR	Voucher no. 321 Vouchers Payable, Credit, $5,000 Purchases, Debit, $5,000
2	VR	Voucher no. 322 Vouchers Payable, Credit, $350 Other Accounts (Rent Expense), Debit, $350
3	VR	Voucher no. 323 Vouchers Payable, Credit, $11,200 Other Accounts Debit: Notes Payable, $10,000 Interest Expense, $1,200
4	Both	In CR, Vouchers Payable, Debit, $5,000 Purchases Discounts, Credit $100 Cash Credit, $4,900 In VR, enter date and check no. in Paid column
5	Both	In CR, Vouchers Payable, Debit, $350 Cash Credit, $350 In VR, enter date and check no. in Paid column
6	VR	Voucher no. 324, 325 Vouchers Payable Credit, $6,200 Other Accounts (Notes Payable), Credit, $5,000 Other Accounts (Vouchers Payable) Debit, $11,200 Paid column "Canceled by 324, 325"
7	Both	In CR, Cash, Vouchers Payable, Debit, $6,200 Credit, $6,200 In VR, enter date and check no. in Paid column

Chapter 7

ACCOUNTS RECEIVABLE AND BAD DEBTS EXPENSE

EXPLANATION OF MAJOR CONCEPTS

Sources and Classification of Receivables LG 1

A receivable represents a claim against other entities for assets or services. There are two sources of these claims: trade, sale of goods or services, and nontrade, sources other than trade. Trade receivables may be of three types: accounts receivable, notes receivable, or credit card receivables. There are a wide variety of sources of nontrade receivables, such as loans to officers, accrued interest on notes receivable, and claims for losses from an insurance company.

Bad Debts Expense LG 2

Bad debts expense is the result of making sales on credit and being unable to collect them later. We could record the bad debts expense at the time we determine an account to be uncollectible. However, we usually make these determinations in accounting periods after the one in which we made the sale. This will report revenue (sales) in one period and the related expense (bad debts expense) in another.

Estimating bad debts expense as an adjusting entry at the end of each accounting period allows us to assign the revenue and related expense to the same period. To record an estimate of bad debts expense, however, requires the use of a contra asset account to Accounts Receivable. If we credited Accounts Receivable with estimated bad debts expense, the general ledger account would not balance with its subsidiary ledger. We cannot credit a subsidiary account since we do not know at the time of the adjustment which individual customer will prove uncollectible. Therefore, we credit a *contra* or *valuation* account to allow us to show the net or collectible amount of accounts receivable on the balance sheet.

Allowance for Doubtful Accounts is the contra asset account credited when we record estimated bad debts expense. This account serves two purposes:

1. As a contra account, we deduct it from trade receivables on the balance sheet. Thus, it causes receivables to be stated at their net realizable (or collectible) value--a more realistic asset valuation.

160   Chapter 7

2. When we actually determine accounts to be uncollectible, we debit the allowance account for the account write-off. (We have already debited expense with an estimated amount. Often we made the expense debit in a prior period.)

Estimating the Expenses and Recording Transactions   LG 3, 4

We can use one of two approaches to estimate bad debts expense. Either is acceptable, but once we choose a method, we should use it consistently year after year.

- One method, called the *income statement approach*, bases the estimate on sales. A company simply determines from past experience the percent of each year's net sales that became uncollectible. Then, for the adjusting entry, we multiply the current year's net sales by the percent. We debit that amount to bad debts expense and credit it to the allowance. We ignore any existing balance in the allowance account in making the adjustment. Thus, when we use an income statement number, net sales, the amount being estimated is the desired balance in an income statement account, Bad Debts Expense.
- The other method called the *balance sheet approach* bases the estimate on accounts receivable. We make a study of the accounts receivable to estimate the amount of uncollectibles in them. We can do this study by dividing the individual receivables up into categories according to their age and multiplying each category by the appropriate percentage determined from past experience. Or, we can multiply the balance in Accounts Receivable by a percentage determined from past experience. The amount determined in this analysis is what the balance in Allowance for Doubtful Accounts should be. The expense, then, is the amount needed to adjust the allowance account to equal the estimated uncollectibles. Thus, when we use a balance sheet amount, Accounts Receivable, as a basis for the estimate, the amount we estimate is also a balance sheet amount, Allowance for Doubtful Accounts. Since the allowance account will have a balance in it before the adjustment, we must consider that balance in calculating the amount of the bad debts expense.

Here are five suggestions to help you avoid errors that students seem to make frequently:

1. The adjusting entry to record expense under the estimating method is always:

    Bad Debts Expense... XXX
        Allowance for Doubtful Accounts................ XXX

    Never involve the Cash account in an end-of-year adjustment, and never involve Accounts Receivable in this one.

2. Every write-off of an uncollectible account must credit Accounts Receivable.

3. Write-offs under the allowance method always debit Allowance for Doubtful Accounts. Write-offs under the direct write-off method always debit Bad Debts Expense.
4. Recoveries under the allowance method always credit Allowance for Doubtful Accounts.
5. In preparing an aging schedule, there must be a column for accounts not yet due. These are accounts less than thirty days old. It follows, then, that the age of an account in a past due column is thirty days plus the time in that column heading.

The Direct Write-Off Method LG 5

The direct write-off method is a simple approach. We make no attempt to estimate uncollectible accounts in advance. When we identify a specific account as being uncollectible, we debit the amount to Bad Debts Expense and credit Accounts Receivable. There is no adjusting entry made at the end of a year. We credit recoveries under the direct write-off method to a revenue, Bad Debts Recovered.

Comparison of Methods LG 6

Under the allowance method, the income statement shows an estimate of the bad debts expense in the same period as the sales which caused the expense to be incurred. The balance sheet will in turn show the net realizable (collectible) value of the accounts receivable. Under the direct write-off method the expense will not appear in the income statement until we write off the bad account. Thus, there is a mismatching of revenue and expense under this method. We show the accounts receivable at its gross amount which is greater than we expect to collect. Because of this, the direct write-off method is not generally recommended.

Credit Card Sales LG 7

Various types of institutions issue credit cards. The accounting for sales made to holders of these credit cards basically falls into two categories. The first is for sales on bank credit cards, such as VISA. Banks accept the charge slips from these sales as if they were cash. The bank simply deducts a percentage from the total sale as a service fee. The entry to record these sales then is a debit to Cash for the net amount, a debit to Credit Card Fees Expense for the service fee, and a credit to Sales for the total.

The second category is sales with nonbank type cards, such as the American Express card. In this case, we send the charge slips to the issuing institution for reimbursement. Again, the issuing institution charges a service fee and will reimburse only the amount of the sale less the service fee. The entry to record this type of sale is a debit to Accounts Receivable, Credit Cards for the net amount we will receive; a debit to Credit Card Fees Expense for the service charge; and a credit to Sales for the total amount of the sale.

162   Chapter 7

Internal Control LG 8

Internal control over receivables is primarily instituted through a separation of the duties of recording the sales transactions and recording the collections. Also, the customers can become a significant part of the control system through the use of monthly statements. This permits the outside party to check the accuracy of the accounting records.

Analyzing Information LG 9

In analyzing accounts receivable for real-life companies, we would be interested in whether accounts receivable were increasing or decreasing. We would also be interested in the change in bad debts expense over time. If sales were increasing and bad debts decreasing, that would be a favorable trend. Or if bad debts expense was too low that would be unfavorable. Also, we would look at the percent relationship between allowance for doubtful accounts and accounts receivable. If gross accounts receivable were increasing and allowance decreasing, that might indicate better anticipated collection, a favorable trend. Or, if the allowance were too low, that would be unfavorable.

GUIDED STUDY OF THIS CHAPTER

A. **Receivables** All types of receivables are assets. This chapter is concerned mainly with trade receivables that are current assets.

1. A trade receivable results from a _sale or service_.

A1. sale of goods or services to customers

2. The three major types of trade receivables are _A/R_, _notes receivable_, and _credit cards receivable_.

A2. accounts receivable, notes receivable, credit card receivables

3. _A/R_ receivable are not supported by formal written promises to pay at a specific date.

A3. Accounts

4. _Notes_ receivable are usually supported by formal written promises to pay at a specific date and often bear interest.

Accounts Receivable and Bad Debts Expense   163

A4. Notes

A5. Credit card, credit cards

A6. should not

B1. Allowance for Doubtful Accounts

B2. Bad Debts Expense

B3. a deduction from trade receivables (or from accounts receivable)

B4. income

B5. credit

5. **Credit Card** receivables result from the acceptance of **Credit Card** where banks do not accept the resulting invoices for deposit.

6. We **should not** (should/should not) combine loans to officers and employees in the same accounts as trade receivables.

B. Bad Debts Expense When we estimate bad debts expense under the allowance method, we record it only in an end-of-period adjusting entry.

1. The account credited in this adjusting entry is **A/D/A**.

2. The debit in the adjusting entry is to an expense account, **Bad Debt exp.**

3. Allowance for Doubtful Accounts is reported on the balance sheet as **a contra acct to A/R**.

4. The expense is reported in the **Income** statement, where it is a deduction from revenues of the same period as we report the revenues which cause the expense.

5. When we determine an individual's account to be uncollectible, we write it off. This requires a **CR** (debit/credit) to Accounts Receivable.

6. A debit reduces the contra account entitled **A/D/A**.

164 Chapter 7

B6. Allowance for Doubtful Accounts

7. Why isn't the write-off entry a debit to expense when we use the allowance method? _Because the expense is recorded during the acct period in which it occurred_

B7. Because we have already debited estimated total expense in a prior end-of-period adjusting entry.

8. One approach to estimating bad debts expense is the income statement approach. The amount of expense debited in the end-of-period adjusting entry is a percent of _net sales_.

B8. net sales (Sometimes net credit sales.)

9. How is the rate (percent) of net sales decided upon? _Past experience_

B9. We base it on an average of prior years' losses related to that period's net sales.

10. If there is a balance in the Allowance for Doubtful Accounts, what adjustment is made to the percent of net sales computed as bad debts expense? _None_

B10. None. *(The calculation has estimated the desired balance in the expense account. We do not consider the balance in the allowance account.)*

11. Another approach is the balance sheet approach. In this method, we estimate how much the Allowance for Doubtful Accounts ought to be at the end of each period by analyzing accounts receivable.

B11. No answer required.

12. Suppose we determine that the Allowance for Doubtful Accounts ought to have a balance of $4,000 on December 31, 1997. If the account has a credit balance of $500, we would need $ _3,500_ more to bring it up to $4,000.

B12. 3,500

13. But if it had a debit balance of $600, we would need a credit of $ _4,600_ to bring the account up to $4,000.

Accounts Receivable and Bad Debts Expense   165

B13. 4,600

14. So the debit to Bad Debts Expense under the balance sheet approach is the amount needed to bring the Allowance for Doubtful Accounts up to its _appropriate Cl level Balance_.

B14. desired balance

15. Does use of the balance sheet approach change the entries to write off uncollectible accounts? _NO_

B15. No. *(They are the same under either approach.)*

16. Referring to Exhibit 7-2, an amount will fall in the Not Yet Due column if it is less than _30 Days_.

B16. thirty days old (terms are 2/10 n/30)

17. Any amount in the 1-30 column is between _31 days_ and _60_ days old.

B17. thirty-one, sixty

18. E. Harris has amounts in more than one column. How can this happen? _Separate purchases at Different times_

B18. Harris has more than one unpaid invoice.

19. R. Travis has at least _2_ unpaid invoice(s).

B19. 2

20. Could there be additional columns on this work sheet? _yes_. Explain. _9t 90 · 120_

B20. Yes; Instead of Over 90 Days Past Due, there could be columns for 91-120 Days Past Due, etc.

21. Of the $47,000 in accounts Not Yet Due, the Simon Company expects _1_ % to become uncollectible.

B21. 1

22. We apply a different percentage against the accounts receivable from each column to determine the portion estimated to be uncollectible. For the "Not Yet Due" column, the percentage is 1%, giving an estimated amount uncollectible of $ _470_.

166 Chapter 7

B22. 470

B23. 4

B24. greater

B25. 2,600

B26. 2,500

B27. 2,900

B28. Bad Debts Expense

B29. the estimate of uncollectible accounts receivable, the balance in the allowance account

23. Of the $5,000 that is 1-30 Days Past Due, Simon expects that __4__ % will become uncollectible.

24. As the accounts become older, Simon has found that the estimated percent uncollectible becomes __greater__ (smaller/greater).

25. After estimating the dollar amount of uncollectible accounts in each segment, Simon Company believes that a total of $ __2,500__ of its accounts receivable are uncollectible on December 31, 1997.

26. If the Allowance for Doubtful Accounts already has a credit balance of $100, they need to add $ __100__ to bring the allowance up to $2,600.

27. But if the Allowance for Doubtful Accounts had a debit balance of $300, it would require a credit of $ __2900__ to bring the account up to $2,600.

28. The debit in the adjusting entry is always equal to the __Bad Debt exp__ account.

29. So in the balance sheet approach, the amount of bad debts expense depends upon two factors. One is __the estimate of uncollectable-A/R__ and the other is __Balance in the ADA__.

C. Write-Off and Recovery
When we determine a specific account is uncollectible, we write it off.

1. Under the allowance method, the write-off requires a debit to __ADA__.

Accounts Receivable and Bad Debts Expense 167

C1. Allowance for Doubtful Accounts

2. Accounts written off may later be wholly or partially recovered. If this happens, under the allowance method, there would be a credit to _ADA_ .

C2. Allowance for Doubtful Accounts

3. A second method of handling bad debts expense is to wait until they occur before recording them. In this case, there would be no end-of-period adjusting entry and no Allowance for Doubtful Accounts. We call this method the _Direct Write-off Method_ .

C3. direct write-off method

4. Under the direct write-off method, the account debited when we write-off an uncollectible account is _____ .

C4. Bad Debts Expense

5. A disadvantage of this method is that _____ .

C5. expense often falls into a period other than the one in which its related revenue was recognized (mismatching)

6. Under both the allowance method and the direct write-off method, we credit ~~ADA Bad Debt Exp~~ _A/R_ when we actually write-off an account.

C6. Accounts Receivable

7. Since we debited an expense on write-off under the direct write-off method, it is logical that we credit a revenue for recoveries under this method. The revenue account credited is _____ .

C7. Bad Debts Recovered

8. Exhibit 7-3 makes a complete comparison of the two methods and gives examples of transactions under each. It is worth careful study. Under the allowance method, bad debts expense for 1997 was $_____ . Under the direct write-off method, it was $_____ .

C8. 2,000; 800

9. Under both methods, the accounts written off amounted to $_____ .

168 Chapter 7

C9. 800

C10. 300

C11. The direct write-off method.

C12. No; There are probably other amounts in 1997 credit sales that will become uncollectible in later years.

C13. 79,200 = ($30,000 + $205,000 - $150,000 - $5,000 - $800 + $300 - $300)

C14.
    Cash . . . . . $XX,XXX
    Accts. rec. .   79,200

C15.
    Cash $XX,XXX
    Accts. rec $79,200
    Dct: Allow.
      for D.A.   2,500   76,700

10. Recoveries in 1997 under both methods were $_____.

11. Which method will report the recovery as a revenue? _____

12. Is the direct write-off method more accurate because the amount of expense recorded was equal to the uncollectible accounts written off? _____ . Explain.
_____
_____
_____
_____

13. In Exhibit 7-3 the balance in Accounts Receivable on January 1, 1997, was $30,000. What is the Accounts Receivable balance on December 31, 1997?
$_____.

14. Under the direct write-off method of recognizing bad debts expense, accounts receivable would appear on the December 31, 1997, balance sheet as:

Current assets:
  Cash $XX,XXX
  Accounts receivable   _____

15. Under the allowance method of recognizing bad debts expense, the balance sheet would appear (assume Allowance for Doubtful Accounts on December 31, 1997, to be a credit balance of $2,500):

Current assets:
  Cash $XX,XXX
    Accts. rec. $_____
                 _____
                 _____   _____   _____

16. Which method do you think gives the more realistic valuation of accounts receivable?
_____
Why? _____
_____

C16. The allowance method. Because it recognizes that they will not collect a portion of the $79,200.

D1. The institution that issued the credit card.

D2. It charges the seller a fee. (*Also, there is an interest charge on unpaid balances.*)

D3. 3,840.

D4. 4,000.

D5. Credit Card Fee Expense

D6. Accounts Receivable, *Credit Cards Company*

D7. same

D8. current asset

D. Credit Card Sales The introduction of internationally recognized credit cards allows a seller to sell on account without the risk of bad debt losses.

1. Who absorbs the bad debt expense when a bank credit card sale becomes uncollectible? _____

2. How does a credit card company compensate for its bad debt losses and still make a profit? _____

3. Assume that a company makes sales of $4,000 in a day to customers with bank credit cards. If the credit card companies charge 4%, how much is the amount of the debit to Cash? $_____

4. The credit to Sales is $ _____

5. Therefore, we make a debit of $160 to _____ .

6. If the same facts had existed, but the sales had been made to customers who used nonbank cards, the debit for $3,840 would have been to _____ .

7. The rest of the entry to record the sales would have been the _____ .

8. Accounts Receivable, credit cards is classified on the balance sheet as a _____ .

9. We should separate Accounts Receivable, credit cards from other trade receivables, however, because it is unlikely to have bad debt losses on credit card sales.

170 Chapter 7

D9. No answer required.

E1. increased

E2. decreased

E3. increased

E4. Increasing

E5. Increasing

E6. 11.9, 13.3

E7. They may believe it results from selling to customers with a higher credit risk.

E8. Increasing.

E9. It indicates that management believes a higher percentage of receivables are uncollectible.

E. Analyzing Information

1. Fingerhut's net sales _____ (*increased/decreased*) from 1993 to 1994.

2. Their net accounts receivable _____ (*increased/decreased*) from 1993 to 1994.

3. Their allowance for doubtful accounts _____ (*increased/decreased*) from 1993 to 1994.

4. Is their bad debts expense increasing or decreasing? _____.

5. Is the percent of bad debts expense to net sales increasing or decreasing? _____.

6. In 1993, this percent was _____ %, and in 1994 it was _____ %.

7. Why might management desire a higher percent? _____

8. For Fingerhut, is the percentage of allowance for doubtful accounts to gross accounts receivable increasing or decreasing? _____

9. What does this indicate? _____

Accounts Receivable and Bad Debts Expense 171

LEARNING GOALS ACHIEVEMENT TEST

1. (LG 2-5) The following applies to John's Appliance Company:

	1997	1998	1999
Net credit sales	$200,000	$260,000	$360,000
Uncollectible accounts written-off	600	3,200	4,200

When the business was formed in January 1997, John Johnson, the owner, estimated that bad debt losses would be 1% of net credit sales.

Required:

(1) Using the loss assumption, prepare general journal entries as of December 31 of each year to record (a) bad debts expense and (b) the write-offs for the year.

GENERAL JOURNAL

Date	Accounts and Explanations	PR	Debit	Credit
1997/12 31	Bad Debt Exp		2000	
	A/D/A			2000
	A/D/A		600	
	A/R			600
1998	Bad Debt Exp		2,600	
	A/D/A			2,600
	A/D/A		3,200	
	A/R			3,200
1999	Bad Debt Exp		3,600	
	A/D/A			3,600
	A/D/A		4,200	
	A/R			4,200

172 Chapter 7

GENERAL JOURNAL

Date	Accounts and Explanations	PR	Debit	Credit

(2) Do you consider John's estimate to be reasonably accurate? Explain.

NO all but the 1st year is estimates were Much too low

(3) Assume that 2000 sales are $400,000, accounts written off are $4,350, and analysis of accounts receivable on December 31, 2000, indicates that $5,200 is uncollectible. Change to the balance sheet approach and record the bad debts expense for 2000.

GENERAL JOURNAL

Date	Accounts and Explanations	PR	Debit	Credit

(4) In a competitor's business, a bad debt of $900 written off in 1996 was recovered in 1997. The account credited was Bad Debts Recovered. What approach or method was the competitor using? _____

_____

(5) If John's Appliance Company recovered an account in 1997 that has been written off in 1996, what account would be credited? _____

2. (LG 1) Wagner and Company had a balance of $74,500 in Accounts Receivable. Included as part of this balance are three customers who had overpaid their accounts by a total of $1,500. Also, included is a receivable from the owner of the business in the amount of $3,000, and a receivable from a credit card company in the amount of $5,000. How should the accounts receivable be disclosed on Wagner's balance sheet?

3. (LG 6) Bits and Bytes Shop has made the following credit sales on July 12, 1997:

To VISA and MasterCard customers .... $ 9,200
To American Express customers 16,000

The credit card companys' charge will be 5% of credit card sales. Record the credit sales for the day in a compound general journal entry.

GENERAL JOURNAL

Date	Accounts and Explanations	PR	Debit	Credit

ANSWERS TO LEARNING GOALS ACHIEVEMENT TEST

1.

GENERAL JOURNAL

Date		Accounts and Explanations	PR	Debit	Credit

1997 Dec.	31	Bad Debts Expense
		    Allowance for Doubtful
		        Accounts
		    To estimate expense for 1997.
				2,000	2,000

	31	Allowance for Doubtful Accounts
		    Accounts Receivable
		    To write off accounts for 1997.
				600	600

1998 Dec.	31	Bad Debts Expense
		    Allowance for Doubtful
		        Accounts
		    To estimate expense for 1998.
				2,600	2,600

	31	Allowance for Doubtful Accounts
		    Accounts Receivable
		    To write off accounts for 1998.
				3,200	3,200

1999 Dec.	31	Bad Debts Expense
		    Allowance for Doubtful
		        Accounts
		    To estimate expense for 1999.
				3,600	3,600

	31	Allowance for Doubtful Accounts
		    Accounts Receivable
		    To write off accounts for 1999.
				4,200	4,200

(2) No, his estimate is probably too low. The business will begin 2000 with only $200 in the allowance account. The balance at the beginning of a year should be adequate to cover prior year sales to be written off. He has probably understated expense of 1997, 1998, and 1999.

Accounts Receivable and Bad Debts Expense

(3)

GENERAL JOURNAL

Date		Accounts and Explanations	PR	Debit	Credit

2000 Dec.	31	Bad Debts Expense
		    Allowance for Doubtful
		        Accounts
		  To estimate expense for 2000.
		  ($4,350 + $5,200 - $200)
				9,350	9,350

(4) The direct write-off method.

(5) Allowance for Doubtful Accounts.

2. **Current assets**
    Cash .... $XX,XXX
    Accounts receivable, trade 68,000
    Accounts receivable, credit cards... 5,000
    Receivable from owner... 3,000

    Current liabilities
    Accounts payable... $XX,XXX
    Credit balances in customer accounts 1,500

3.

GENERAL JOURNAL

Date		Accounts and Explanations	PR	Debit	Credit

1997 Jul.	12	Cash
		Accounts Receivable, Credit Cards
		Credit Card Fees Expense
		    Sales
		  To record credit card sales.
				8,740
				15,200
				1,260
					25,200

Chapter 8

SHORT-TERM FINANCING

EXPLANATION OF MAJOR CONCEPTS

Promissory Notes LG 1

A promissory note is an unconditional promise to pay a specified sum of money to the order of a designated person or to the holder of the note at a fixed or determinable point in time in the future or on demand. They may be negotiable, meaning that the holder can transfer ownership. Notes have the following primary characteristics.

- Written and signed by the maker.
- Unconditional promise to a certain sum of money.
- May be payable to a specified person or to the holder.
- Must be payable on demand or at a specified future point in time.
- May or may not be interest bearing.

Maturity Dates LG 2

We may express the term of a note in years, months, or days. The maturity date is the date on which payment of the note is due. If we express the term of a note in years or months, the maturity date is the corresponding date in the maturity year or month. In other words, a 3-month note dated March 25, 1997, would be due on June 25, 1997. For a note with a term expressed in days, it is necessary to count forward the exact number of days, not counting the date the note was made but including the date the note is due. For example, if the note dated March 25, 1997, was a 90-day note, the maturity date would be June 23, 1997, computed as follows:

March 26 through 31 (31 - 25 = 6)	6 days
April	30 days
May	<u>31</u> days
Subtotal	67 days
June (90 - 67 = 23)	<u>23</u> days*
Total - term of note	<u>90</u> days

*Maturity date is June 23, 1997

178   Chapter 8

Since 67 days had run from when the note was made until the end of May, it required 23 additional days in June to complete the term. Also, note in the above computation that we counted the date the note was made, March 25, but that we did not count the date the note was due, June 23.

Interest Computations   LG 2

All interest in Chapter 8 is simple interest, and all rates are annual rates. The percent used is the fraction of 100 that is charged for the use of the specified amount of money per year. The principal times the rate--that is, *PR*--gives the amount of interest for one year. Because many interest-bearing notes are for periods greater than or less than one year, we must also multiply *PR* by time, *T*. This is the reason for the *T* in the formula *I* = *PRT*. You should note that computations in this chapter use a 360-day year. In the $1,000, 12%, 90-day note that Glen Chu gave Birgit Berry (see Exhibit 8-1), *T* is expressed as 90/360, which has the effect of reducing the 12% of $1,000 to one-fourth of a year.

The regular interest formula computation (*I* = *PRT*) is usually made by students with a calculator. To compute interest on the note in Exhibit 8-1, enter 1000 x 0.12 x 90 ÷ 360 in that sequence. The result on your calculator is:

```
1000 x .12   =      120.00
x 90         =   10,800.00
÷ 360        =       30.00
```

Since the principal ($1,000) is stated in dollars, the resulting interest (I) of 30 is also dollars ($30). This is not the maturity value (the total amount that Glen Chu must pay when the note is due). The maturity value is the principal plus the interest. In formula form, it is *MV* = *P* + *I*. On the Glen Chu note the maturity value would be $1,000 + $30 = $1,030.

It is essential that you learn to compute interest and maturity value. You can't concentrate on learning the accounting for notes if you can't do the arithmetic quickly and confidently.

Annual Effective Interest   LG 3

When a lender states interest rates for some period of time different than one year, for example one month, the true cost of borrowing is something different than the stated rate. For example, we may agree to purchase merchandise costing $1,000 by paying 24 equal monthly installments of $50 each. The annual effective interest rate is:

1. Calculate the average outstanding principal during the interest period.
   $1,000 ÷ 2 years = $500.
2. Calculate the annual interest cost.
   Total interest = ($50 x 24 months) - $1,000 = $200.
   Interest for one year = $200 ÷ 2 = $100.

3. Divide the Step 2 result by the Step 1 result.
   $100 ÷ $500 = 20% per year.

Notes Payable LG 4

To the maker of a note, the note is payable. We may use notes payable to pay for assets or to borrow money. We may give an interest-bearing note for the principal amount with a specified rate of interest to be paid to maturity. With such a note, we record the principal amount as a liability when the note is made. We record the interest expense when we pay the note at maturity. If the term of the note overlaps the end of an accounting period, we must make an adjusting entry to accrue interest.

When borrowing money, we may discount the note payable--that is, the lender may deduct the interest from the principal amount of the note when the money is borrowed. For a discounted note payable, the maturity value and the principal are the same. When we discount the note payable, we debit the amount of the discount to Discount on Notes Payable. (*Be careful in using this account. Students often confuse it with Notes Receivable Discounted, an account with totally different meaning.*) Discount on Notes Payable is a contra liability account. On the balance sheet, we deduct it from the total principal amount of the notes payable. If the entire term of the note falls within one accounting period, we transfer the discount to interest expense at maturity. If the note does not mature in the period it is made, we need an adjustment to recognize the amount of the discount that has become expense (expired) at the end of the accounting period. The remaining discount becomes an expense in the next year. If the entire term of the note falls within one accounting period, it is acceptable practice to debit the amount of the discount to interest expense. The reason is that all of the discount will become expense in the same period as the discounting occurred.

We should remember that whenever an interest-bearing note is outstanding at the end of an accounting period, we must make an adjusting entry to properly state the interest expense. We calculate the amount of the interest as discussed earlier. The form of the adjusting entry will vary, depending on whether it is for a note bearing interest on the principal or a discounted note.

Notes Receivable LG 5

To Birgit Berry, the note in Exhibit 8-1 is a note receivable. Basically the accounting entries for notes receivable are the opposite of those made by the maker of a note payable. Two concepts that seem to bother students most about notes receivable are:

1. The accounting for a dishonored note (one the maker fails to pay when due) held by a payee.

2. The accounting for notes receivable that are discounted at a bank.

Dishonored Note Receivable

As soon as a note reaches maturity, it loses its status as a negotiable instrument that the holder can pass on to another person (or bank) in exchange for something of value. If it is paid, its life cycle is over. If it is not paid, the debt still exists, but the life cycle of the note is over. A payee holding a dishonored note should recognize several things.

- The life cycle of the note receivable is over. We credit Notes Receivable for the principal amount because a valid note receivable no longer exists.
- The payee has earned interest. Even if not collected, the accrual basis of accounting requires the recognition of the amount of revenue earned. We credit the amount of interest that should have been collected to Interest Revenue.
- The debt is neither canceled nor uncollectible. The payee will take steps--including legal action, if necessary--to collect the total debt. Thus, we should debit the amount of both the principal and interest to Accounts Receivable. Also, by including the amount in accounts receivable, we will consider it in the bad debts estimate made at the end of the period.

Notes Receivable Discounted LG 6

When the holder of a note receivable (the payee) needs immediate cash, he or she may discount it at a bank. This means that the holder sells the note to the bank at a price determined by the bank discount rate and the number of days left in the term (or life) of the note. In recording discounted notes, remember these points:

- We apply the discount rate to the maturity value--not the principal--of the note. Thus, you must first compute maturity value before you can compute the amount of bank discount.
- The payee discounting a note receivable receives the proceeds. The proceeds are an amount equal to maturity value minus the discount. If the proceeds are greater than the principal, we have earned interest, and we should credit Interest Revenue in recording the discount transaction. If the proceeds are less than the principal (and it can be if the bank charges a high rate of discount), we have incurred an expense, and we should debit Interest Expense in recording the transaction.
- Notes receivable are discounted conditionally. That is, the discounter agrees to pay the bank the full maturity value if the maker dishonors the note at maturity. To recognize this possibility (called a contingent liability), we do not credit Notes Receivable when we discount a note. Instead, the credit is to a contra asset account called Notes Receivable Discounted. At maturity, either the maker or the discounter of the note pays the bank. In either event, both the contingent liability and the asset, notes receivable, no longer exist. We must make an accounting entry to eliminate both from the books.

For example, calculation of the proceeds from a $1,000, 14%, 90-day note receivable, discounted at the bank at 15% after holding the note 30 days would be as follows:

Principal	$1,000.00
Interest to maturity ($1,000 x 0.14 x 90/360)	+ 35.00
Maturity value	$1,035.00
Discount ($1,035 x 0.15 x 60/360)	- 25.88
Proceeds	$1,009.12

Entries at Discounting:

GENERAL JOURNAL

Date	Accounts and Explanations	PR	Debit	Credit
1997	Cash		1,009.12	
	Interest Revenue			9.12
	Notes Receivable Discounted			1,000.00

Entry at Maturity:

GENERAL JOURNAL

Date	Accounts and Explanations	PR	Debit	Credit
1997	Notes Receivable Discounted		1,000.00	
	Notes Receivable			1,000.00

Additional entry at maturing if note dishonored by maker:

GENERAL JOURNAL

Date	Accounts and Explanations	PR	Debit	Credit
1997	Accounts Receivable		1,035.00	
	Cash			1,035.00

Analyzing Information   LG 7

Under a revolving line of credit, a bank promises to advance cash on demand to a business up to a maximum amount. Usually the business must pay the balance down to zero for a certain number of days during the year. Businesses use these lines of credit to meet seasonal cash needs.

The financial statement user wants to determine the availability and adequacy of the credit sources. Issues that a user might raise include:

- What percentage of the line of credit is used?
- Is it likely that the bank will renew the line of credit?
- When does the line expire?

182 Chapter 8

- Are there any credit line requirements that are not being met?
- Is there sufficient credit to meet short-term financing needs?

GUIDED STUDY OF THIS CHAPTER

A. Recording Note Transactions

Let's begin with a careful examination of Exhibit 8-1 to get a complete understanding of the elements of a note.

1. Glen Chu, the _Maker_, will pay Birgit Berry the _Payee_.

A1. maker, payee

2. $1,000 is the _Principal/face value_.

A2. principal *or* face value of this note. (Note the spelling of this word; it is not "principle.")

3. The date of the note is _4-19-1997_, and the term of the note is _90_ days.

A3. April 19, 1997, 90

4. The maturity date of the note is _7-18-97_.

A4. July 18, 1997

5. On the books of Glen Chu, this is a note _Note Payable_.

A5. payable

6. On the books of Birgit Berry, it is a note _R. Receivable_.

A6. receivable

7. The $30 interest due at maturity is interest expense to Glen Chu, and interest _Revenue_ to Berry.

A7. revenue

8. A maker of a note must either receive an asset or cancel some other liability upon giving a note to a payee. In the Ace Company note payable (the first note payable example), the asset debited was _Office equipment_. The liability account credited was still _Notes Payable_.

Short-term Financing 183

A8. Office Equipment, Notes Payable

9. Interest is paid in addition to the principal at the maturity date. The Ace Company paid Triangle Company $120 interest on its 12% note for $4,000, causing the total payment of $ __4,120__ credited to __Cash__.

A9. 4,120, Cash

10. When Ace paid the note, it recorded a debit of $4,000 to __Notes Payable__. Ace debited the $120 interest to the expense account, __Interest Expense__.

A10. Notes Payable; Interest Expense

11. Note the method used to record notes given in exchange for merchandise. When Ace Company purchased merchandise from Boone Company in the next example, it first recorded the liability as __Accts Payable__.

A11. Accounts Payable, Boone Company

12. On the same date, it changed the liability to __Notes payable__.

A12. Notes Payable

13. Ace Company "washed" this purchase through Accounts Payable so that it would have __record of purchases it has had i Boone Company__

A13. a complete record in the subsidiary ledger of all transactions with Boone

14. Would Boone Company use the same procedure on their books? __yes__

A14. Yes.

15. Boone Company would record this sale as both a debit and a credit to __Accts Receivable__.

A15. Accounts Receivable

16. Ace Company could borrow money from the bank by giving the First National Bank a $10,000, 12% note, as shown in the March 1 transaction. A second way to borrow money is to __Discount__ Ace's own note as was done on May 1.

A16. discount

17. The amount of cash paid by the bank to a company (or person) discounting a note is called the __Proceeds__.

184   Chapter 8

A17. proceeds

18. We always compute discount on maturity value. The maturity value of Ace's note was $ __10,000__ because it was noninterest-bearing.

A18. 10,000

19. The amount withheld by the lender is called the discount. Although discount is always ultimately debited to Interest Expense, we may debit it directly to the expense account only if the note will __reach maturity in the same acct period__.

A19. reach maturity date in the same accounting period as the discounting occurred

20. When Ace Company discounted a 60-day note payable on May 1, it debited the amount of discount to __Discount on Notes payable (contra asset)__.

A20. Discount on Notes Payable

21. An entry is necessary on June 30, 1997, the maturity date, to recognize that the discount has become __an interest expense__.

A21. interest expense

22. The Adjusto Company illustration provides an example of apportioning the discount. When a $10,000, 45-day, 12% note was discounted at the Texas Bank on December 1, 1997, it debited Discount on Notes Payable for $__150__.

A22. 150

23. $150 will be the total amount of Adjusto's interest expense on this note. However, only __30__ of the 45 days are in the year 1997.

A23. 30

24. Accordingly, Adjusto should only debit $__100__ to Interest Expense in the December 31, 1997, adjusting entry.

A24. 100

25. This leaves $__50__ in the Discount on Notes Payable account. It is interest expense for the year __1998__. It must make another entry on January 15, 1998, to include that amount in 1998 expense.

A25. 50; 1998

B1. dishonors

B2. credit

B3. Accounts Receivable

B4. 50, Interest Revenue

B5. No. *(Efforts will be made to collect it.)*

B6. a revenue

B7. an expense

B. Notes Receivable Several situations can arise in recording note receivable transactions. One is the failure of the maker of the note to pay it when due.

1. By failing to pay a note at the maturity date, a maker defaults on the payment or _Dishonors_ the note.

2. A dishonored note receivable is no longer a negotiable instrument, so we must remove it from the Notes Receivable account by a _CR_ (*debit/credit*).

3. We debit the maturity value of the dishonored note receivable to _A/R_.

4. When Mark Biggs dishonored his $3,000 note to the Potter Company, Potter debited Accounts Receivable for the $3,000 principal plus $ _50_ interest or $3,050. It credited the interest portion of the receivable to _Interest Rev_.

5. Should it write-off this note as a bad debt? _No_

6. The need for adjusting entries to accrue interest at the end of an accounting period occurs with both notes receivable and payable which remain outstanding at year end. Accrued interest receivable gives rise to _Rev_ (a *revenue/an expense*).

7. Accrued interest payable gives rise to _Interest exp_.

8. We accrue the interest amount from the date of the note to _~~maturity~~ end of the acct. period_.

186 Chapter 8

B8. the end of the accounting period

9. The Emerson Company is shown as having one note receivable on December 31, 1997. A note from Linda Wilson is a 10%, 90-day note for $6,000 dated November 1, 1997. On this note, Emerson should accrue exactly __60__ days of interest and recognize this as income of 1997.

B9. sixty (Twenty-nine in November and thirty-one in December.)

10. Since it has not recorded this interest previously, we must debit __Interest expense__.

B10. Interest Receivable

11. We credit __Interest Rev__.
This adds $ __100__ to 1997 income.

B11. Interest Revenue; 100

12. The total interest it will earn on the note for the entire term would be $ __150__.

B12. 150

13. Since it has accrued $100 as earned in 1997, it will record the remaining $ __50__ as earned when it collects the note on __1-30-98__.

B13. 50, January 30, 1998

14. The total cash received on January 30, 1998, is $ __6,150__.

B14. 6,150

15. Of the total, $ ~~50~~ __100__ was the collection on 1997's interest, $ __50__ was 1998's interest, and $ __6000__ was the principal.

B15. 100, 50, 6,000

16. A third note receivable situation arises when we discount customers' notes receivable at the bank. Why might a company discount a customer's note? __Company needs cash__

B16. The company holding the note needs cash.

17. We compute discount on __maturity__ value.

B17. maturity

18. The maturity value of the note given by Edward Grande to the Fuller Company on April 1, 1997, is $6,000 + $ __120__ interest = $ __6,120__.

Short-term Financing 187

B18. 120, 6,120

B19. does not

B20. does

B21. discount, 6,001

B22. Interest Revenue

B23. Interest Expense

B24. contingent

B25. Notes Receivable Discounted

19. The discount period is the number of days that the bank will hold the note. April 11, the date of discount, __does not__ (does/does not) count as one of these days.

20. May 31, the due date, __Does__ (does/does not) count as one of the days of the period of discount.

21. The amount of discount is

$$\$6{,}120 \times \frac{14}{100} \times \frac{50}{360} = \$119.$$

The proceeds equal maturity value minus __Bank__, so Fuller Company receives $6,120 - $119 = $ __6001__ .

22. Fuller credits the amount they received in excess of face value to __Interest Rev.__ .

23. In some cases, the proceeds may be less than face value. In that case, we debit the difference to __Int. Exp__ .

24. When a business discounts a customer's note, it is usually with the requirement that the business must redeem the note if the customer fails to pay. This gives rise to a __Contingent__ liability.

25. To show this contingent liability, we do not remove the note receivable from the books when we discount it. Instead we credit a contra account, __Notes Receivable Discounted__ .

26. On the due date, Fuller must make an entry on their books. What does this entry accomplish? __It removes notes receivable + the contra acct.__

188 Chapter 8

B26. It removes the note receivable and the related contra account.

B27. 6,120

B28. the Fuller Company

B29. Accounts Receivable

B30. Because Fuller will now try to collect the total amount paid ($6,000 + $120 + $8 = $6,128) from Edward Grande.

C1. short-term revolving line of credit

C2. 50

C3. seasonal merchandise purchases

27. If Edward Grande fails to pay the note on May 31, the Fuller Company must buy it back from the bank at maturity value of $ 6120 .

28. In this case, the bank charged a protest fee of $8. This fee is paid to the bank by Fuller Company .

29. Fuller Company credits Cash with the full amount paid to the bank. It also debits that total to A/R _____ .

30. Students often ask why there is no Protest Fee Expense on Fuller Company's books when this dishonored note is paid by Fuller. What is the reason that we make no debit to an expense when Fuller pays the note? _____

C. Analyzing Information

1. When a bank promises to advance cash to a business up to a maximum, the business has a _____ .

2. Notes to the financial statements of The Bombay Company indicate that they have a revolving line of credit of $ _____ million.

3. The Bombay Company uses these primarily to fund _____ .

4. What restrictions does the credit agreement have? _____

C4. Dividend payments may not exceed 25% of net income, and they must meet certain financial ratios.

C5. Yes.

C6. 81.9

C7. December 31, 1994.

C8. No, Bombay does not currently pay dividends.

C9. We might want to know what financial ratios must be met.

5. Will the credit agreements be renewed? _____

6. What percent of The Bombay Company's revolving credit is used as of July 3, 1994 _____%.

7. When does the credit line expire? _____

8. Is the dividend restriction an issue? ___ Why? _____

9. What else might you want to know? _____

LEARNING GOALS ACHIEVEMENT TEST

1. (LG 1-6) Rebecca Levin gives to Juan Garcia a 90-day note promising to pay him $10,000 with interest at 14%. The note is dated March 4, 1997. Answer the following:

    a. The maker is _Rebecca Levin_.
    b. The payee is _Juan Garcia_.
    c. The term is _90 days_.
    d. The maturity date is _6-2-97_.
    e. The general formula to compute the interest is $I = P \times \% \times T$
    In this case, the specific computation of interest is:

    $350 = 10,000 \times 14\% \times 90/360$

    f. The maturity value is: 10,350

190   Chapter 8

g. If Garcia discounts the note at the Bank of Commerce at 16% on May 3, 1997, the discount period is _____.

$I = 10,350 \times .16 \times 40/360 \quad 30/360$

h. The amount of discount is computed as: ~~276~~ 138

i. The proceeds to Garcia is in the amount of $ ~~10,074~~ 10,212 .
j. Therefore, Garcia has $ ~~74~~ 212 of interest Rev
   (*revenue/expense*) in the discount transaction.
k. The journal entry for the discounting transaction on Juan Garcia's books is:

GENERAL JOURNAL

Date	Accounts and Explanations	PR	Debit	Credit
1997				
May 3	~~Notes~~ Cash		10,212 ~~10,074~~	
	Notes Disc Rec			10,000
	Int Rev			~~74~~ 212

l. The journal entry on Juan Garcia's books at maturity assuming Levin pays the bank:

GENERAL JOURNAL

Date	Accounts and Explanations	PR	Debit	Credit
1997				
June 2	Notes Receivable Disc		10,000	
	Notes Receivable			10,000

Short-term Financing 191

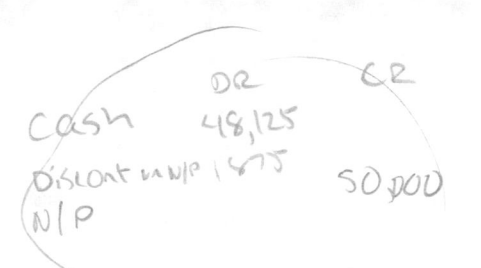

m. If Rebecca Levin fails to pay and the bank adds a protest fee of $20, the entry(ies) required on Garcia's books is/are:

GENERAL JOURNAL

Date		Accounts and Explanations	PR	Debit	Credit
1997					
June	2	A/R - Levin		10,370	
		Cash			10,370
	2	Notes Rec Disc		10,000	
		Notes Rec			10,000

2. (LG 4) If Samuel Jackson borrows $50,000 for his business by discounting his own 90-day note at 15% at the West Bank on November 28, 1997, the journal entry on his books will be:

GENERAL JOURNAL

Date	Accounts and Explanations	PR	Debit	Credit
NOV 28	Cash		48,125	
	Disc on Notes Payable		1,875	
	Notes Payable			50,000

192   Chapter 8

3. (LG4) Using the data from question 2, on December 31, 1997, Jackson's accountant must make an adjusting entry to apportion interest expense between 1997 and 1998. It is:

GENERAL JOURNAL

Date		Accounts and Explanations	PR	Debit	Credit
Dec	31	Interest exp		687.50	
		Disc on Notes Payable			687.50

ANSWERS TO LEARNING GOALS ACHIEVEMENT TEST

1. a. Rebecca Levin
   b. Juan Garcia
   c. 90 days
   d. June 2, 1997
   e. I = PRT. $10,000 x 0.14 x 90/360 = $350.
   f. $10,000 + $350 = $10,350 OR $10,000 (1.035) = $10,350.
   g. 30 days
   h. $10,350 x 0.16 x 30/360 = $138.
   i. $10,212 = ($10,350 - $138)
   j. $212, revenue
   k.

GENERAL JOURNAL

Date		Accounts and Explanations	PR	Debit	Credit
1997 May	3	Cash		10,212	
		Interest Revenue			212
		Notes Receivable Discounted			10,000
		Discounted Levin note at 16% at Bank of Commerce.			

Short-term Financing 193

l.

GENERAL JOURNAL

Date		Accounts and Explanations	PR	Debit	Credit
1997 Jun.	2	Notes Receivable Discounted Notes Receivable To record maturity of Levin note receivable.		10,000	10,000

m.

GENERAL JOURNAL

Date		Accounts and Explanations	PR	Debit	Credit
1997 Jun.	2	Accounts Receivable, R. Levin Cash Payment to Commerce Bank of dishonored Levin note plus protest fee.		10,370	10,370
	2	Notes Receivable Discounted Notes Receivable To record maturity of Levin note receivable.		10,000	10,000

2.

GENERAL JOURNAL

Date		Accounts and Explanations	PR	Debit	Credit
1997 Nov.	28	Cash Discount on Notes Payable Notes Payable Borrowing of $50,000 by dis- counting note payable at 15%.		48,125 1,875	50,000

3.

GENERAL JOURNAL

Date		Accounts and Explanations	PR	Debit	Credit
1997 Dec.	31	Interest Expense Discount on Notes Payable To record expiration of 33 days' discount.		687.50	687.50

Chapter 9

INVENTORIES AND COST OF GOODS SOLD

EXPLANATION OF MAJOR CONCEPTS

Costs Included in Inventory LG 1

Merchandise inventory includes all goods acquired for resale. We record inventories at cost. Cost includes all expenditures necessary to bring the merchandise to salable location and condition. Thus, it should include the invoice price of the merchandise minus any purchases discounts, plus transportation in and any other expenditures made to get the merchandise to the place of business such as insurance during the period of transit.

Two Inventory Systems LG 2

There are two basic issues involved in the accounting for inventories. They are:

1. *Item-by-item determination of quantities on hand* (physical count of inventory). Under the periodic method, we do this by physical count at the end of the accounting period. Under the perpetual method, we must make the item-by-item count to verify the inventory records. However, we may do it anytime during the period.
2. *Item-by-item determination of historical cost* (cost valuation of inventory). Since generally accepted accounting principles require historical cost for recording assets, it would seem to be a simple matter to record the cost of each item and use it to place a valuation on the inventory. Usually, this is not the case.

Under the periodic inventory system, we maintain no running record for items in the inventory. As described in Chapter 5, the physical count at the end of the accounting period establishes the quantity on hand. We can determine the quantity sold by the following computation:

Quantity on hand at beginning...	XX
Add: Quantity purchased during the period	XXX
Equals: Total quantity available for sale.................................	XXX
Deduct: Quantity on hand at end	XX
Equals quantity sold..	XXX

196   Chapter 9

In Chapter 5, we assumed that a specific cost could be associated with each unit on hand. In some cases for example, with new cars on an automobile dealer's lot, it is feasible. However, with most inventory items, the specific identification method is too costly or actually impossible to apply. Can you imagine using this method with a pile of oranges at a supermarket or with gasoline stored in an underground tank at the local service station? Accordingly, to place a cost valuation on inventory we must make some cost flow assumption. We will discuss these after discussing the perpetual system.

Under the perpetual inventory system, we maintain a continuous record of receipts and sales for units of each inventory item. Chapter 9 illustrates this record in the form of perpetual inventory cards or stock records. Many companies with thousands of different items in stock maintain this continuous record by computer, but the basic idea is the same. Maintenance of such a continuous record solves the problem of item-by-item determination of quantity on hand (although an annual count to verify the accuracy of stock records is still required). It does not, however, solve the second problem of placing a historical cost valuation on items on hand. When a customer selects a dozen oranges from the pile, which dozen did he or she take? Was it from those that were received on Wednesday at 48 cents per dozen or those received on Thursday at 51 cents per dozen? Or was it a combination of both? Even more impossible is the identification of the cost of gasoline a customer pumps from the storage tank. Last month the station may have had four or five deliveries, all at different cost prices. In the storage tank, they are mixed together. We know how many gallons the customer pumped, but from which cost batch? Again, as in the periodic inventory system, we must make some cost-flow assumptions.

Journal Entries

When we use the periodic inventory system, we can record the change in inventory balance with either closing entries or adjusting entries, as illustrated in Chapter 5. There is no ledger account for cost of goods sold. We determine it by computation and reduce income in the closing process. Under the perpetual inventory system, Cost of Goods Sold is a general ledger account that we debit with the cost of inventory items given up when making sales. We close this account balance into Income Summary at the end of the period to reduce net income. Carefully study the comparison of journal entries made under the two systems in Exhibit 9-1.

Cost-Flow Assumptions   LG 3, 4

We can make three alternative cost flows assumptions. You must understand that they are assumptions. They may or may not represent the actual flow of goods. The cost flow assumptions are:

- First-In, First-Out (FIFO). We assume that the cost of the earliest goods on hand is the cost of the inventory items sold first. Thus, we make up the ending inventory from the most recent purchases. *Note that the name of the cost flow assumption*

FIFO refers to the flow of costs out of inventory, not to the cost of goods that remain on hand in the inventory.
- Last-In, First-Out (LIFO). We assume that the cost of the latest goods on hand is the cost of the inventory items sold first. Thus, we make up the ending inventory from the earliest purchases, including the beginning inventory of the period.
- Weighted average. The idea of this assumption is that the cost of goods sold and the cost of inventory remaining on hand is an average of the cost of beginning inventory and purchases during the period. Under the periodic system, we apply a weighted average computation. Under the perpetual system, we use a moving average computation.

We use these cost-flow assumptions in both the periodic and perpetual inventory systems to determine (1) the valuation of ending inventory and (2) the cost of goods sold. The different assumptions usually yield different results. A manager must choose an assumption and apply it consistently from year to year. The assumption chosen does not relate to the physical flow of goods. It would be physically impossible for gasoline to flow through a storage tank in a FIFO or LIFO manner (gallons are mixed together). However, either FIFO or LIFO is an acceptable cost flow assumption for costing gasoline at a service station.

Financial Statement Impact   LG 5

During a period of changing prices, the alternative cost flow assumptions will produce different inventory values. Since we use the ending inventory in the preparation of both the income statement and balance sheet, the differences in value will affect both of the statements. On the income statement, cost of goods sold is affected. It in turn affects gross margin on sales and net income. The net income in turn affects the owner's equity on the balance sheet. Also, the inventory appears as a current asset on the balance sheet. Therefore, any differences in amount caused by the cost flow assumption will have effects on all of the statements.

Exhibit 9-5 summarizes the three cost flow assumptions and compares the financial statements that result. In a period of rising prices, FIFO will generally give the highest net income and highest total asset valuation. LIFO will generally give the lowest. In such a case, the lower net income shown under LIFO is more correct. This is because it provides a better matching of current revenues with current expenses.

Lower-of-Cost-or-Market (LCM)   LG 6

In order to present a conservative picture, inventory valuation may be reduced below cost if the market price should fall below the original cost. Chapter 9 presents three basic ways to compute LCM. These are applying LCM by item, major category, or total. Exhibit 9-7 shows the application of the three methods. Each of the three methods is an acceptable one. Application of LCM by individual item results in the most conservative (lowest) ending inventory valuation.

Estimating Inventories LG 7

There are many reasons that a business needs to estimate inventories. Perhaps we desire monthly financial statements. In many businesses, it is too expensive to make a physical count every month. Both the retail method and the gross margin method allow us to estimate the cost valuation of inventory at a specific date. They both require that we determine cost of goods as a percent of selling price, but in a slightly different way. The gross margin method uses previously experienced cost percentages; the retail method uses the current year cost percent. We will study the mechanics of the two methods in the Guided Study section.

Inventory Errors LG 8

Since the inventory amount affects both the income statement and balance sheet, an error in the determination of the inventory amount will have an effect on both statements. However, since we determine the inventory by physical count once each year, an error made in determining one year's inventory will correct itself in the next year. Exhibit 9-8 shows in a diagram the effect of making an error in one year's inventory computation. Review Exhibit 9-8 at this time.

Analyzing Information LG 9

We will want to use the notes to the financial statements to know the costing method being used. This will allow us to judge if cost of goods sold represents current value. It will also allow us to judge the inventory amount shown on the balance sheet.

GUIDED STUDY OF THIS CHAPTER

A. **Cost Assignment--Periodic System**
The questions in this section use the chapter example, designer sunglasses. We use the same transactions for each assumption. In all cases, the basic task is to allocate the $15,900 cost of 300 sunglasses available for sale between (1) the cost of 90 sunglasses remaining on hand and (2) the cost of 210 sunglasses sold. We will begin with weighted average.

1. The total number of sunglasses available for sale was __300__ and the total cost of goods available for sale was $__15,900__.

Inventories and Cost of Goods Sold   199

A1. 300, 15,900

2. So the weighted average cost per unit was $15,900 ÷ 300 = $ __53__ .

A2. 53

3. We assume the April 30 inventory cost to be __90__ sunglasses times $__53__ = $__4,770__ .

A3. 90, 53, 4,770

4. We compute cost of goods sold as $__15,900__ minus $__4,770__ = $__11,130__ .

A4. 15,900, 4,770, 11,130

5. Turn to FIFO. Under the periodic system, there is no record of units sold; we know only that 90 sunglasses are on hand on April 30. Since FIFO assumes that we transfer out the cost of the earliest goods first, the cost of the 90 units remaining in stock on April 30 must have been the __latest__ (earliest/*latest*) costs of units purchased.

A5. latest

FIFO
(LISH)

6. Therefore, the cost of the 90 units on hand on April 30 is from the purchase made on __4/16/97__ at $ __60__ each.

A6. April 16, 60

7. The April 30 inventory cost using the FIFO periodic assumption is 90 sunglasses at $__60__ = $__5,400__ .

A7. 60, 5,400

8. Cost of goods sold is equal to total cost of goods available for sale minus __ending inventory at FIFO__ .

A8. ending inventory

9. So, under FIFO periodic, cost of goods sold is $__15,900__ minus $__5,400__ = $__10,500__ .

A9. 15,900, 5,400, 10,500

10. We can verify cost of goods sold by adding the cost of the batches assumed to be sold. Under the FIFO assumption, we assume that sales included the entire beginning inventory ($2,400), the entire April 5 purchase ($4,500), and 60 sunglasses from the April 16 purchase ($3,600). This cost of $2,400 + $4,500 + $3,600 = $__10,500__ , which __is__ (*is*/is not) the same as already computed.

200   Chapter 9

FISH
—or—

A10. 10,500, is

11. The LIFO assumption says that the cost of the latest purchases are transferred out first. Therefore, the cost of the 90 sunglasses on hand on April 30 would be the ___earliest___ (earliest/latest) costs that we have experienced.

A11. earliest

12. The cost of the 90 earliest sunglasses purchased would be __60__ from the __4/1 purchase__ and __30__ from the __4/5 purchase__.

A12. 60, beginning inventory, 30, April 5 purchase

13. Thus, the LIFO periodic inventory is 60 sunglasses at $__40__ plus 30 sunglasses at $__50__ = $__3,900__.

A13. 40, 50, 3,900

14. Cost of goods sold is $15,900 minus $3,900 = $__12,000__.

A14. 12,000

15. Verify cost of goods sold by computing the cost of individual batches of sunglasses assumed to have been sold.

4/5/97 60 × 50 = 3,000
4/6/97 150 × 60 = 9,000
                    12,000

A15. 150 × $60 = $ 9,000
       60 × $50 =   3,000
       Total   = $12,000

16. Under each of the three methods, we allocated total cost of goods available ($15,900) between the April 30 inventory (90 sunglasses) and cost of sales in April (210 sunglasses). Each of the three cost flow assumptions give a different result.

A16. No answer required.

B. **Cost Assignment--Perpetual System**
Under the perpetual system, we keep a continuous record for each stock item, but we still must make cost-flow assumptions. They are moving average, FIFO, and LIFO. We will again use the transactions for the sunglasses. Start with moving average.

Inventories and Cost of Goods Sold 201

1. Under the moving average assumption, Exhibit 9-2, we do not need to keep batches separate. We add each new purchase to the previous quantity on hand and compute a _weighted average unit price_.

B1. new weighted average unit price

2. The receipt of 90 sunglasses on April 5 increases the total units on hand to _150_ and the total cost of units on hand to $ _6,900_ .

B2. 150, 6,900

3. Since a purchase occurred, we calculate a new average unit cost as $6,900 ÷ 150 = $ _46_ .

B3. 46.00

4. So, we will make the next sale at an assumed average cost of $ _46_ per pair of sunglasses.

B4. 46.00

5. Until we make another purchase at a different unit price, we will record future sales at the average cost of $ _46_ per pair of sunglasses.

B5. 46.00

6. A new purchase arrived on April 16 at a unit cost of $60. We now have on hand _200_ sunglasses with a total cost of $ _11,300_ .

B6. 200, 11,300

7. We must compute a new unit cost (this is why the method is called moving average). It is $ _11,300_ ÷ _200_ units = $ _56.50_ .

B7. 11,300, 200, 56.50

8. We record the next sale at the new average cost, leaving an April 30 inventory of _90_ sunglasses at $ _56.50_ = $ _5,085_ .

B8. 90, 56.50, 5,085

9. This inventory card has three basic sections: Purchased, _Sold_ , and _Balance_ .

202 Chapter 9

B9. Sold, Balance

10. The Sold section shows the _QTY sold, Unit cost, Total cost_

    The Balance section shows the _QTY, unit cost, & total cost_.

B10. cost of the units that were sold; cost of units remaining on hand

11. Turn to FIFO shown in Exhibit 9-3. Some parts have brackets around two or more lines. In the Balance section, the brackets mean that _some QTY come from different purchases_.

B11. all bracketed batches are on hand at that point in time

12. In the Sold section, the brackets mean that _cost of some units sold come from earlier purchase_.

B12. all bracketed batches were a part of one sale transaction

13. There is no bracket in the Balance section around the 60 sunglasses on hand on April 1. Why? _B/C all unit were purchase on 4/1 at the same price_

B13. Because the 60 units are at a single unit cost of $40.

14. The inventory after the April 5 receipt is now made up of two batches. One with a cost of $ __40__ per unit and one with a cost of $ __50__ per unit.

B14. 40, 50

15. On April 12, 100 sunglasses were sold. Why did we assume that the cost of these 100 sunglasses were made up of 60 at $40 and 40 at $50? _Because assuming the FIFO_

B15. FIFO assumes that we transfer the cost of the earliest units out first. This uses 60 sunglasses from April 1 inventory first and then requires 40 more from the April 5 purchase.

16. The balance on hand after the sale of April 12 is __50__ sunglasses at $ __50__ = $ __2500__.

Inventories and Cost of Goods Sold   203

B16. 50, 50, 2,500

17. The purchase of April 16 increases the balance by a second batch of __150__ sunglasses at $__60__. The balance is now $ __11,500__.

B17. 150, 60; 11,500

18. In the sale of 110 on April 28, we assume that we first transfer out the cost of the 50 earliest sunglasses. Thus, the sale also includes __60__ sunglasses from the April 16 purchase.

B18. 60

19. The final inventory is 90 sunglasses at $ __60__ = $ __5400__.

B19. 60, 5,400

20. To obtain cost of goods sold, we can add the Total Cost column of the Sold section for a total of $ __10,500__.

B20. 10,500

21. Consider Exhibit 9-4 which shows the same transactions recorded under the LIFO assumption. When we record the April 12 sale of 100 sunglasses, we show it as two batches of 90 and 10 units. Why? __LIFO assumes that transfer out of latest (100) (90) first & the from earlier purch (10)__

B21. LIFO assumes that we transfer the cost of the latest goods purchased out first. The April 5 purchase only has 90 units. Thus, we require 10 more units.

22. What units do we assume to be left on hand after the April 12 sale? __The 4/1/97 inventory at $40.00 each__

B22. 50 sunglasses from the April 1 inventory at $40.

23. The inventory valuation after the April 12 sale is 50 at $ __40__ = $ __2000__.

B23. 40, 2,000

24. A receipt on April 16 adds a second batch to inventory, so we must bracket the two to show that the total inventory valuation is now $ __11,000__.

B24. 11,000

25. We assume that the April 28 sale came from the cost of the latest goods on hand. We assume that the 110 sunglasses sold on April 28 came from the __4/16/97 PO of 150 @ $60 ea__.

204 Chapter 9

B25. April 16 receipt

B26. two; 40, 60, 4,400

C1. the same *(This will always be true for FIFO.)*

C2. different *(This is usually the case for LIFO.)*

C3. different *(This is usually true for the average methods.)*

C4. Rising

C5. highest

C6. lowest

26. This leaves on hand ~~to~~ two batches. One at a per unit cost of $ 40 and a second at a per unit cost of $ 60 with a total inventory cost of $ 4,400 .

C. Comparison of Methods

1. A comparison of FIFO periodic and FIFO perpetual shows that the April 30 inventory and cost of goods sold in April are _____SAME_____ (*the same/different*) amounts.

2. A comparison of LIFO periodic and LIFO perpetual shows that results were _____Different_____ (*the same/different*).

3. Weighted average (periodic) and moving average (perpetual) give _____Different_____ (*the same/different*) ending inventory and cost of goods sold.

4. Comparing the price of a sunglasses in the beginning inventory with the price per sunglasses for the purchases in April, would you say that prices are rising or falling? _____Rising_____ .

5. FIFO assumes that the costs of the earliest goods are transferred out first. Since we are in a period of rising prices, the April 30 inventory would be at the _____highest_____ (*lowest/highest*) prices.

6. On the other hand, LIFO assumes that we transfer the costs of the latest goods out first. Under LIFO, the April 30 inventory would be at the _____lowest_____ (*lowest/highest*) prices.

FISH 7. By assigning a lower price to ending inventory, LIFO automatically assigns a _____higher_____ (*lower/higher*) price to cost of goods sold for April.

Inventories and Cost of Goods Sold   205

C7. higher

C8. lower

C9. less

C10. Yes. The results would be exactly opposite.

D1. 5,200

D2. 1,000, 900, market

D3. 800, 1,200, cost

D4. No answer required.

D5. cost, 1,800, market, 3,700

8. And a higher cost of goods sold with LIFO means a ___lower___ (*lower/higher*) net income.

9. So, LIFO, with a lower income, should generally cause the owner of the firm to pay ___less___ (*less/more*) income tax than FIFO.

10. But remember that these transactions took place during a period of rising prices. Would it be accurate to expect the opposite results during falling prices? ___yes___

D. **Lower-of-Cost-or-Market (LCM)**

1. Exhibit 9-7 illustrates the three methods of application of lower-of-cost-or-market. The total inventory value under the item-by-item basis would be $ ___5,200___ .

2. We obtain this total by first comparing the cost and the market price of each item. For large beach towels, total cost is $ ___1,000___ and total market is $ ___900___ , so the lower is ___market___ .

3. For regular beach towels, total cost is $ ___800___ and total market is $ ___1,200___ , so the lower is ___800 cost___ .

4. We continue this process until we have found the lower-of-cost-or-market for each item. On a item-by-item basis, the LCM inventory valuation is the sum of these individual figures.

5. To use the class or category basis, we compare the total cost and total market for each category. For beach towels, LCM is ___cost___ at $ ___1,800___ , and for sunscreen, LCM is ___market___ at $ ___3,700___ .

6. So the LCM inventory valuation on a class or category basis is the sum of $ ___1,800___ and $ ___3,700___ = $ ___5,500___ .

206   Chapter 9

D6.   1,800, 3,700, 5,500

D7.   market, 5,800

D8.   lowest, highest
      (This will always be true.)

E1.   total cost of goods available

E2.   40

E3.   60 (100% - 40%)

E4.   120,000

E5.   beginning inventory, net purchases

E6.   30,000, 137,000, 167,000

7. On the total inventory basis, we simply price the total inventory at cost and at market. Of these two figures, the lower is ___Market___ at $ __5,800__ .

8. Note that the item-by-item basis provides the ___lowest___ (lowest/highest) valuation and the total inventory basis provides the ___highest___ (lowest/highest) valuation.

E. Estimating Inventories

1. The gross margin method of estimating inventories requires that you estimate cost of goods sold. If we know estimated cost of goods sold, we can subtract it from __Total cost of goods available for sale__ to find ending inventory at cost.

2. In the textbook example, Kleer Pool Company has experienced an average gross margin rate of __40__ %.

3. If the gross margin equals 40% of sales, cost of goods sold must be 100% minus 40% = __60%__ %.

4. Net sales of $200,000 times 60% means that cost of goods sold in 1997 was $ __120,000__ .

5. You must also find the total cost of goods available for sale. It is equal to __Beginning Inventory__ plus __Net purchase__ .

6. For Kleer Pool Company in 1997 this was $ __30,000__ plus __138,000__ = $ __167,000__ .

7. Ending inventory is equal to total goods available for sale minus __estimated cost of goods sold__ .

Inventories and Cost of Goods Sold   207

E7. estimated cost of goods sold

8. For Kleer Pool Company, this is
$ 167,000 minus
$ 120,000 = $ 47,000.

E8. 167,000, 120,000, 47,000

9. The accuracy of the gross margin estimate depends on the accuracy of the estimate of gross margin percent.

E9. No answer required.

10. To use the retail method, it is necessary to record all receipts both at cost price and at Retail.

E10. selling price or retail price

11. In the example, the beginning inventory at cost is $28,000, and the retail price of this inventory is $ 40,000.

E11. 40,000

12. Purchases at cost must be net purchases (including transportation in). They were $182,000, and their retail price was $ 260,000.

E12. 260,000

13. Total goods available for sale at cost were $ 210,000 and were recorded at a retail price of $ 300,000.

E13. 210,000, 300,000

14. The current cost as a percent of retail is $ 210,000 divided by $ 300,000 = 70%.

E14. 210,000, 300,000, 70

15. We recorded actual sales at retail price in the Sales account. In this company, the sales are $ 250,000.

E15. 250,000

16. Total goods available for sale at retail price ($300,000) minus sales of $250,000 leaves an ending inventory at retail of $ 50,000.

E16. 50,000

17. To convert this figure to estimated ending inventory at cost, we multiply it by the cost/retail % percent, which is 70%.

E17. cost-to-retail

18. Estimated inventory at cost = .70 times $ 50,000 = $ 35,000.

208   Chapter 9

E18. 50,000, 35,000

E19. No; A physical count is required at least once per year to check on other measures.

F1. overstate, understate

F2. understate, understate

F3. understate, overstate

F4. correct

G1. LIFO

G2. Yes. LIFO charges cost of goods sold with relatively current costs.

19. Does using the perpetual or estimating methods to find inventory values eliminate the need for physical count? _No_
Explain. _A physical count is required at least once a year to check on other measures_

F. Inventory Errors

1. An understatement of ending inventory in 1997 will _overstate_ cost of goods sold and _understate_ net income.

2. This error will also _____ inventory on the balance sheet and will _____ owners' equity on the balance sheet.

3. This same error will _____ cost of goods sold in 1998, and it will _____ net income in 1998.

4. On the 1998 balance sheet, owner's equity will be _____.

G. Analyzing Information
Use the Caterpillar information shown in Exhibit 9-6.

1. What inventory method is Caterpillar using? _____.

2. Does this provide a good matching of revenues and expenses on the income statement? _____
Why? _____

3. If Caterpillar uses LIFO does this give a representative amount on the balance sheet? _____
Is the inventory understated or overstated?
_____

G3. No. Understated.

G4. Yes.

G5. 3,870 million

G6. LIFO reserve

G7. cumulatively how much extra cost the company has charged to cost of goods sold since it began using LIFO.

G8. 814 million

4. Can we use the notes to the statements to determine how much? _____

5. Caterpillar's inventory at a current value would be $ _____ .

6. The excess of FIFO value over LIFO value is known as the _____ .

7. The LIFO reserve indicates _____ _____ _____ .

8. We can also use the LIFO reserve to estimate how much, income tax the company has saved. In Caterpillar's case, this is $ _____ .

LEARNING GOALS ACHIEVEMENT TEST

1. (LG 2) The following questions pertain to inventory systems. Each can be answered with the word "periodic" or "perpetual."

   a. We change the inventory balance in adjusting or closing entries under the __PERIODIC__ system.
   b. Cost of goods sold is a separate ledger account title under the __perpetual__ system.
   c. We add transportation in cost to the Inventory account under the __periodic perpetual__ system.
   d. We deduct the cost price of items sold from the Inventory account under the __perpetual__ system.
   e. We use the Purchases account only under the __periodic__ system.
   f. We credit purchases returns and allowances to the Inventory account under the __perpetual__ system.
   g. Under the __PERIODIC__ system, Purchases Returns and Allowances is an account that we close to Income Summary.
   h. The system that would be best for the Produce Department of a supermarket is the __perpetual periodic__ system.
   i. The system that would be best to record the inventory of a jewelry store is the __perpetual__ system.
   j. The higher degree of inventory control is found in the __perpetual__ system.

210 Chapter 9

2. (LG 2) Record the receipt of a purchase of $1,000 of merchandise and the return of $200 in defective merchandise, using (a) the periodic system and (b) the perpetual system. Date all transactions May 10, 1997.

GENERAL JOURNAL

	Date		Accounts and Explanations	PR	Debit	Credit
(A)	May	10	Purchases		1,000	
			A/P			1,000
		10	A/P		200	
			Purchase Returns + allowances			200
(B)	May	10	Merchandise Inventory		1,000	
			A/P			1,000
		10	A/P		200	
			Merchandise Inv			200

3. (LG 3-5) Assume the following activity for an inventory item in March 1997:

    Mar. 1   Beginning balance, 100 pounds at $0.50.
             4   Sold 60 pounds.
           12   Purchased 100 pounds at $0.60.
           14   Sold 75 pounds.
           20   Purchased 50 pounds at $0.70

Inventories and Cost of Goods Sold   211

Required:

(1) Compute ending inventory using a <u>periodic system</u> for (a) FIFO, (b) LIFO, and (c) weighted average.

(a) FIFO

(b) LIFO

(c) Weighted average

(2) Compute ending inventory using a perpetual system for (a) FIFO, (b) LIFO, and (c) moving average (round off moving average unit amounts to the nearest cent).

Chapter 9

(a) **FIFO**

Date	Purchased	Sold	Balance	
3/1			100 lb @ .50	50
3/4		60 × .50 = 30	40 × .50	20
3/12	100 lb at .60 = 60		40 × .50	
			100 × .60	80
3/14		40 × .50 20		
		35 at .6 = 21	65 × .60	39
3/20	50 lb × .7 35		65 × .60	
			50 × .70	74
	150		65	

(b) **LIFO**

Date	Purchased	Sold	Balance	
3/1			100 × .50	50
3/4		60 × .5 = 30	40 × .50	20
3/12	100 × .6 = 60		40 × .50	
			100 × .60	80
3/14		75 at .60 = 45	40 × .50	
			25 × .60	35
3/20	50 lb × .70 = 35		40 × .50	
			25 × .60	
			50 × .70	70

(c) Moving average

Date	Purchased	Sold	Balance	
3/1			100 × .50	50
3/4		60 × .50 = 30	40 × .50	20
3/12	100 × .60 = 60		140 × .57	80
3/14		75 × .57 = 43	65 × .57	37
3/20	50 × .70 = 35		(115 × .63	72)

(3) Which cost flow assumptions may give different results under periodic and under perpetual? Why?

LIFO

Moving average / weighted average

4. (LG 6) Lower-of-cost-or-market valuation can be computed on an item-by-item, class, or total inventory basis. The LCM inventory valuations produced by each basis are:

(a) Highest on the __Total INV__ basis.

(b) Lowest on the __item-by-item__ basis.

(c) In between on the __Class__ basis.

5. (LG 7) Uber Company had a June 1, 1997, inventory valued at a cost of $1,500 and a retail price of $2,000. Purchases were $5,500 at cost and $8,000 at retail. Sales were $8,500. Estimate the cost of the June 30 inventory using the retail method.

		Cost	Retail
6/1	Beginning INV	$1,500	$2,000
	Purchases	5,500	8,000
	CG for Sale	7,000	10,000
	Cost to Retail % = 70% (7000/10,000) × 100		
	Sales		8,500
6/30	Ending Inventories	$1,050	$1,500

6. (LG 7) Assume the same facts as in Problem 5 above except that Uber Company has had an average gross margin percent of 40% for the past three years. Estimate the ending inventory using the gross margin method.

Sales (Rev)		$8,500
CGS	× 60%	5,100
GM	× 40%	3,400
Beginning INV		1,500
+ Purchases		5,500
Cost of Goods available for Sale		7,000
(× CGS % of 5100)		(5,100)
END INV valuation		$1,900

7. (LG9) In assigning a cost valuation to the December 31, 1997, inventory, the Dexif Company overstated the value by $2,000. Complete the following table regarding the effects of the error.

	Error Amount	Overstated/ Understated
1997 cost of goods sold	2000	under
1997 gross margin on sales	2000	over
1997 net income		
Owner's equity, December 31, 1997		
Current assets, December 31, 1997		
1998 cost of goods sold		
1998 gross margin on sales		
1998 net income		
Owner's equity, December 31, 1998		
Current assets, December 31, 1998		

ANSWERS TO LEARNING GOALS ACHIEVEMENT TEST

1.
   a. periodic   f. perpetual
   b. perpetual   g. periodic
   c. perpetual   h. periodic
   d. perpetual   i. perpetual
   e. periodic   j. perpetual

2.

GENERAL JOURNAL

Date		Accounts and Explanations	PR	Debit	Credit

(a) 1997 May	10	Purchases
		    Accounts Payable
		    Receipt of merchandise.
				1,000	1,000

	10	Accounts Payable
		    Purchases Returns &
		      Allowances
		    Return of defective goods.
				200	200

GENERAL JOURNAL

Date	Accounts and Explanations	PR	Debit	Credit

(b) 1997 May 10	Merchandise Inventory
	    Accounts Payable
	    Receipt of merchandise.
			1,000	1,000

10	Accounts Payable
	    Merchandise Inventory
	    Return of defective goods.
			200	200

3. (1) (a) FIFO
    Ending inventory:
      50 pounds at $0.70 = $35.00
      65 pounds at $0.60 = 39.00
     115 Total $74.00

   (b) LIFO
    Ending inventory:
     100 pounds at $0.50 = $50.00
      15 pounds at $0.60 =   9.00
     115 Total $59.00

   (c) Weighted average

	Pounds	Cost
Beginning inventory	100	$ 50.00
Purchases (100 pounds at $0.60)	100	60.00
(50 pounds at $0.70)	50	35.00
Total available for sale	250	$145.00

Weighted average unit price = $145.00 ÷ 250 = $0.58
Ending inventory: 115 pounds at $0.58 = $66.70.

(2)
(a) FIFO

	Purchased	Sold	Balance	
3/1			100 @ $0.50 = $50	$50
3/4		60 @ $0.50 = $30	40 @ $0.50 = $20	$20
3/12	100 @ $0.60 = $60		40 @ $0.50 = $20	
			100 @ $0.60 = 60	$80
3/14		40 @ $0.50 = $20		
		35 @ $0.60 = 21	65 @ $0.60 = $39	$39
3/20	50 @ $0.70 = $35		65 @ $0.60 = $39	
			50 @ $0.70 = 35	$74

(b) LIFO

	Purchased	Sold	Balance	
3/1			100 @ $0.50 = $50	$50
3/4		60 @ $0.50 = $30	40 @ $0.50 = $20	$20
3/12	100 @ $0.60 = $60		40 @ $0.50 = $20	
			100 @ $0.60 = 60	$80
3/14		75 @ $0.60 = $45	40 @ $0.50 = $20	
			25 @ $0.60 = 15	$35
3/20	50 @ $0.70 = $35		40 @ $0.50 = $20	
			25 @ $0.60 = 15	
			50 @ $0.70 = 35	$70

(c) Moving average

	Purchased	Sold	Balance	
3/1			100 @ $0.50 =	$50
3/4		60 @ $0.50 = $30	40 @ $0.50 =	$20
3/12	100 @ $0.60 = $60		140 @ $0.57 =	$80
3/14		75 @ $0.57 = $43	65 @ $0.57 =	$37
3/20	50 @ $0.70 = $35		115 @ $0.63 =	$72

(3) The LIFO and moving average methods may give different results when applied to periodic and to perpetual. With LIFO it is due to the fact that under perpetual the costs assigned to goods sold are dependent upon what cost were in inventory when the sale took place. Under periodic the timing of the purchases and sales is ignored and the earliest goods are assumed to be in inventory. With moving average, the periodic method calculates the average cost based on all the units that were available during the period, whereas, the perpetual calculates an average each time goods are purchased based on the goods on hand at that moment.

4. (a) total
   (b) unit
   (c) class

5.

	Cost	Retail
Beginning inventory	$1,500	$ 2,000
Purchases	5,500	8,000
Total goods available for sale	$7,000	$10,000
Cost as a percent of retail	70%	
Sales		8,500
Ending inventory at retail		$ 1,500
Estimated inventory at cost ($1,500 x 0.70)	$1,050	

6. 100% - 40% = 60%   cost as a percent of sales.
Cost of goods sold = $8,500 x 0.60 = $5,100.
Ending inventory = $7,000 - $5,100 = $1,900.

7.

	Error Amount	Overstated/ Understated
1997 cost of goods sold	$2,000	Understated
1997 gross margin on sales	$2,000	Overstated
1997 net income	$2,000	Overstated
Owner's equity, December 31, 1997	$2,000	Overstated
Current assets, December 31, 1997	$2,000	Overstated
1998 cost of goods sold	$2,000	Overstated
1998 gross margin on sales	$2,000	Understated
1998 net income	$2,000	Understated
Owner's equity, December 31, 1998	$0	Correct
Current assets, December 31, 1998	$0	Correct

Chapter 10

LONG-TERM ASSETS

EXPLANATION OF MAJOR CONCEPTS

Tangible Plant Assets LG 1, 2

Long-term assets (assets whose use will extend beyond one year) fall into three groups: tangible plant assets, natural resources, and intangible assets. The term property, plant, and equipment includes all plant assets and natural resources with tangible existence (meaning they have substance and can be touched). A business acquires them for use in regular operations and will use them for more than one accounting period. Buildings, equipment, and delivery trucks are examples of tangible plant assets. Coal reserves and timber are examples of natural resources. Intangible assets are those which exist in concept but do not have substance in the sense that you can touch or feel them. They do, however, contribute to the operation of the business. Patents, copyrights, and franchises are examples of intangible assets. One thing common to all of these assets is a long useful life. All have estimated useful lives (EUL) extending over two or more accounting periods. Except for land, however, they have limited useful lives.

We record long-term assets in the accounting records at their cost. This includes the purchase price less any cash discount, plus all other expenditures made to prepare the asset for use. These other expenditures should be reasonable and necessary, benefit the whole useful life, and be made before the asset is put into use. We say that all costs debited to the asset account are *capitalized*.

The major accounting problem with regard to a long-term asset is to assign portions of its cost in some rational manner to the accounting periods benefited by the use of the asset. The process of allocating the cost of long-term assets to accounting periods is called depreciation, depletion, or amortization. While the three terms cover the same basic concept, their specific meanings are different:

- Depreciation refers to the process of allocation of cost of tangible plant assets to specific periods.
- Depletion refers to recording the consumption or extraction of natural resources.
- Amortization refers to recording the expiration of an intangible asset. However, amortization is sometimes used as a general term to describe all three concepts.

Depreciation Methods LG 3

There are several methods of computing depreciation. A company may choose any of them or may use a combination of methods. After choosing a method for a specific plant asset (or group of assets), we should use that method consistently year after year. We must make two estimates for each asset: estimated useful life and estimated residual value. Estimated useful life is the period of time over which the business plans to use the asset. Estimated residual value is the amount the business expects to recover from disposal at the end of the useful life. Following is a summary of the methods of depreciation explained in the textbook:

- The straight-line method assumes that we assign an equal share of depreciation expense to each accounting period. The formula is:

$$\frac{\text{Cost - Residual value}}{\text{EUL in years}} = \text{\$ Depreciation per year.}$$

  The straight-line percent (rate) is another tool to compute annual costs. Straight-line percent is:

$$\frac{100\%}{\text{EUL in years}} = \text{Annual straight-line percent.}$$

  (Cost - Residual value) x Annual straight-line percent = $ Depreciation per year.

- The production unit method assigns expense to each period on the basis of amount of production per period. The formula is:

$$\frac{\text{Cost - Residual value}}{\text{Estimated Life in Units}} = \text{Depreciation per unit.}$$

$$\text{Depreciation Expense per Unit} \times \text{Units Produced during Period} = \text{Depreciation Expense}$$

- Accelerated methods assign greater depreciation expense in earlier years of life. Two accelerated methods illustrated in Chapter 10 are:
  1. Declining balance method which we view as a fixed percentage of declining balance. The beginning point for this method is the straight line rate (explained earlier in this Study Guide section). Double declining-balance (or 200%-declining balance) uses twice the straight-line rate applied to the carrying value. Since carrying value equals cost minus accumulated depreciation, the carrying value gets smaller each year as accumulated depreciation increases. (Thus we give the name declining-balance to the method.) You must be careful when using the declining-balance method not to deduct residual value. We apply the rate chosen to the remaining carrying value. Also, you must be careful in the declining-balance method not to take so much depreciation that the carrying value drops below the residual value.

2. **Sum-of-the-years'-digits method** uses a fraction of the total digits in the years of EUL. The fraction applies each year's digit in reverse order as a percent of the total. You should learn and should use the arithmetic progression formula to compute the sum of the year's digits. It is:

$$\frac{n(n+1)}{2} = SYD,$$

where n = estimated useful life. For example, if EUL is 8 years, then

$$\frac{8(8+1)}{2} = 36.$$

Then, to find depreciation, use cost minus residual value. In the foregoing 8-year example, depreciation expense is:

```
First year    = 8/36 x (Cost - Residual value).
Second year   = 7/36 x (Cost - Residual value).
Third year    = 6/36 x (Cost - Residual value).
   . . .
   . . .
Eighth year   = 1/36 x (Cost - Residual value).
```

- **Modified Accelerated Cost Recovery System** is a method permitted for income tax reporting. Depreciable personal property falls into eight cost recovery classes for income tax purposes. Within each class, the law provides a percentage of cost that a taxpayer can deduct as depreciation each year in computing their federal income tax liability.

Capital and Revenue Expenditures   LG 4

Often it is necessary to make expenditures on a long-term asset after it is put into use. We must segregate these into capital and revenue expenditures. We classify an expenditure made to an asset during its life as a capital expenditure if it extends the useful life or increases the capacity of the asset. We debit capital expenditures to Accumulated Depreciation if they are an extraordinary repair that extends the life of the asset. Otherwise, we debit them to the asset account. If an expenditure does not qualify as a capital expenditure, it is a revenue expenditure. Then we debit it to an expense account such as Repairs Expense.

Revisions of Depreciation   LG 5

The depreciation may require revision as a result of either an extraordinary repair that extends the useful life or an error in estimating the life of an asset. In either case, we depreciate the remaining book value at the time of the revision over the new estimate of the remaining useful life.

Disposal and Trade-In LG 6

Most tangible plant or equipment items have some value at the end of their useful lives. Disposal by sale or scrapping often causes a gain or loss. If the amount recovered is greater than book value (cost minus accumulated depreciation), there is a gain. If the amount recovered is less than book value, there is a loss. We always record losses or gains from disposal by a means other than trade-in and report them in the income statement. A loss account has a normal debit balance; a gain account a credit.

At the end of the EUL, businesses often trade assets in on new assets. The accounting for gains and losses is more complex in a trade-in situation. We must distinguish between two types of trade-in cases:

- Trade-in on a similar asset. The word similar has a broad interpretation here. Any asset that serves the same productive function is similar. Thus, the trade-in of a bookkeeping machine used to produce monthly bills on a small computer to produce bills (in addition to other functions) is a trade on a similar asset.
- Trade-in on a dissimilar asset. This would be the trade-in of an asset on another asset that performs an entirely different function. A grinding machine traded in on a parcel of land for a parking lot is a trade for a dissimilar asset.

The rules for recording a gain or loss on trade-ins recognize the concept that a trade-in on a similar asset continues the earnings process of the old asset. A trade-in on a dissimilar item terminates the old earnings process. The rules are:

- Recognize all losses on trade-ins for similar or dissimilar assets.
- Recognize gains on trade-ins for dissimilar assets.
- Do not recognize gains on trade-ins for similar assets. When we do not recognize the gain, we record the new asset at a cost equal to the list price less the gain.

Other Asset Concepts LG 7

Depletion records the consumption of natural resources. Because we are recording the actual consumption, we usually use the production methods to record depletion cost. Note that depletion--unlike depreciation--is not an expense immediately upon recording. Along with other production costs, it becomes part of the inventory. Accordingly, it reduces income not as an expense but as part of cost of goods sold.

Amortization records the consumption of the economic benefits of intangible assets. We compute amortization by the straight line method. Intangible assets do not have residual value. We compute amortization on the full cost.

Analyzing Information LG 8

The financial statement user will want to assess whether the assumptions used in computing depreciation and amortization are reasonable. We might ask

Long-term Assets 223

- Are the methods, asset lives, and residual values reasonable?
- What is the impact of any changes during the period?
- If they capitalized some interest cost, what was total interest? We would use total interest cost in calculating times interest earned.

GUIDED STUDY OF THIS CHAPTER

A. Cost and Depreciation

1. Cost includes _The purchase price less any cash discount, plus all other reasonable and necessary expenditures to prepare the asset for operations_.

A1. the purchase price less any cash discount, plus all other reasonable and necessary expenditures to prepare the asset for operations

2. In the example of the computer in Chapter 10, the cost included _____

A2. the purchase price less discount plus transportation, cost of wiring, and construction of special desk

3. Since depreciation is the allocation of cost to more than one accounting period, we must know how many periods to use. The life of an asset cannot be accurately known in advance, so we must establish an _EUL_.

A3. estimated useful life (EUL)

4. Also, since we expect to recover something (at least scrap value) on disposal of an asset, we must estimate the _Residual Value_.

A4. residual value

5. One method of computing depreciation does not require use of estimated residual value in the computation. Which one is it? _Declining-Balance_

A5. Declining-balance method.

6. All methods require an estimate of _EUL_

224   Chapter 10

A6. useful life

7. The simplest method is the straight-line method. Compute the 1997 depreciation for a typewriter costing $795 at the beginning of 1997 with a residual value of $45 and an estimated useful life of 10 years. _72 (075)_____ .

A7. ($795 - $45) ÷ 10 = $75

8. The straight-line percent for this typewriter is 100% divided by EUL = _10_____ %.

A8. 10 (This can be computed as a decimal fraction by using 1 ÷ EUL.)

9. Compute the straight-line depreciation for 1997, using the straight-line percent. _(795-45) × 10% = 75_____ .

A9. 0.10 x ($795 - $45) = $75.

10. Using the double declining-balance method. The rate would be _20_____ %.

A10. 20 (2 x 0.10)

11. Using double declining-balance, 1997 depreciation would be 20% of $ _795_____ = $ _159_____ .

A11. 795, 159

12. The carrying value for 1998 depreciation would be $795 minus $159 = $ _636_____ . The 1998 depreciation would be _20_____ % of $ _636_____ = $ _127.20_____ .

A12. 636; 20, 636, 127.20

13. Notice that the depreciation for 1998 is less than that for 1997 because we are using a fixed percent of a _Declining Balance_____ .

A13. declining-balance

14. Note in the illustration of DDB in the textbook that total depreciation never reduces the book value of the asset below the estimated residual value. In the last year, depreciation was equal to the book value minus the residual value.

A14. No answer required.

15. Use this same typewriter example and compute depreciation by the sum-of-the-years'-digits (SYD) method. The sum of the years' digits is _55_____ .

Long-term Assets 225

A15. 55 [Computed as follows:
$$\frac{10(10+1)}{2} = 55$$]

16. ~~Assume that~~ it had been purchased on January 11, 1997. Do we compute a full month for January? __yes__

A16. Yes.

17. So the 1997 depreciation using SYD is __10/55__ x ($795 - $45) = $ __136.36__ .

A17. 10/55, 136.36

18. And for 1998, it is __9/55__ x ($795 - $45) = $ __122.73__ .

A18. 9/55, 122.73

19. At the end of ten years, we will have recorded 55/55 of ($795 - $45), leaving $ __45__ of undepreciated cost.

A19. 45

20. Suppose this typewriter were estimated to have 10,000 hours of useful life. By the units of production method, depreciation per hour would be $ __.08__ .

A20. 0.075 (or 7 1/2 cents) = ($795 - $45) ÷ 10,000

21. If it were used 1,800 hours in 1997, the depreciation charge would be $ __1800__ x __.08__ = $ __144__ .

A21. 0.075, 1,800, 135

22. Suppose instead we estimate that the typewriter can type a total of 30,000 pages in its EUL. The depreciation per page would be $ __0.025__ .

A22. 0.025 (or 2 1/2 cents)

23. If we used it to produce 4,600 invoices in 1997, the depreciation charge would be $ __4600__ x __.025__ = $ __115__ .

A23. 0.025, 4,600, 115

24. Exhibit 10-4 compares the asset book values. With which method does the book value decrease the fastest? __Double DB__

A24. Double declining-balance.

25. Which method decreases the slowest? __Straight line__

A25. Straight-line.

26. From this we can conclude that the method with the largest depreciation deductions in early years is __DDB__ .

226 Chapter 10

A26. double declining-balance

A27. 45

A28. Yes; All four methods end with the same book value. *It will always be equal to the estimated residual value.*

A29. whole month

A30. sum-of-the-years' digits

A31. take the remaining partial period

B1. capitalized

27. At the end of the useful life the book value of the typewriter in our Study Guide example under all methods is $ __45__ .

28. Will this always be the case? __yes__, Why? __As is capitalized__

29. If an asset is bought during the accounting period, we must take a fraction of a year's depreciation in the year of acquisition and the last year of life. We normally calculate depreciation to the nearest __whole month__ .

30. One method requires allocation of the depreciation for an asset's year to the affected accounting periods for every accounting period. It is __SDY__ .

31. In the straight-line and double declining-balance methods, it is only necessary to take a fractional period the first year and then follow the normal pattern for all full periods until the final period when we __take the remaining partial portion__ .

B. **Capital versus Revenue Expenditures**

1. A capital expenditure is an expenditure that increases the carrying value of a long-term asset. We say the expenditure is __capitalized__ rather than expensed.

2. In the purchase of a computer, expenditures could include (a) invoice cost less discount, (b) transportation in, (c) assembly, (d) installation, and (e) testing and trial runs. How many of these are capital expenditures? __All of them__

Long-term Assets 227

B2. All of them.

B3. revenue

B4. capital

B5. capital

B6. an asset

B7. Accumulated Depreciation

B8. Accumulated Depreciation-- Engines

B9. Trucks

B10. Repairs Expense

B11. book value, remaining life

3. A routine repair on this computer would be a _Revenue expense_ expenditure.

4. Additional memory to enable the computer to run larger programs would be a _Capital_ expenditure.

5. A major overhaul that extended the EUL of this computer would be a _Capital_ expenditure.

6. We debit revenue expenditures to expense, but we usually debit capital expenditures to _asset Accumulated Dep_ _an asset_.

7. In some cases, we may view capital expenditures that extend useful life as cancellation of some of the depreciation. We debit these expenditures to _accumulated Depreciation_.

8. For example, if an overhaul added 2,000 flight hours to an aircraft engine, we would debit _accumulated Depreciation 2000_.

9. If we better a delivery truck by having a hydraulic lift installed on it, we would debit the cost to _an asset - Truck_.

10. We would debit the replacement of a broken headlight on the delivery truck to _Repairs expense_.

11. After a capital expenditure, we must revise future depreciation. We allocate the remaining _Book value_ over the new estimate of the asset's _Remaining life_.

12. The textbook example of a $2,500 overhaul to a truck _DR_ accumulated depreciation and increased useful life by _2_ years.

228 Chapter 10

B12. decreased, two

B13. 10,500, 8,200

B14. four

B15. 2,050 ($8,200 ÷ 4)

C1. Depreciation Expense

C2. Accumulated Depreciation

C3. Income Summary

C4. income statement

C5. WE do not close it.
(Did you get caught on this one?)

C6. Office Equipment, balance sheet

13. The adjusted book value was $ 10,500 and the new depreciable cost was $ 8,200.

14. We depreciate the $8,200 over the remaining useful life of 4 years.

15. This gives a new annual depreciation of $ 2,050.

C. **Accounting Entries and Disposal**

1. The entry to record the annual depreciation would debit Depreciation expense.

2. It would credit Accumulated Depreciation.

3. At the end of 1997, we close the expense into Income Summary.

4. The expense amount appears in the Income statement.

5. We close the Accumulated Depreciation--Office Equipment account into Not close it.

6. It serves as a valuation (or contra) account to Asset account - office equipment and reduces the carrying value of property, plant, and equipment on the office equipment balance sheet.

7. The illustrations of asset disposal in the textbook began with a truck which cost $ 20000 that was acquired on January 1, 1997. The truck has an EUL of 5 years and a residual value of $ 2000.

C7. 20,000, January 1, 1997; five, zero

C8. December 31, 2000

C9. 3,000, 4 3/4

C10. 1,000; gain, 200

C11. Income Statement

C12. 200

C13. loss on disposal

C14. Income Statement

C15. credit, debit

8. If sold on October 1, 2001, the first task is to record depreciation for the year of disposal. The last annual depreciation entry already recorded was an adjusting entry on 12/31/00 .

9. Depreciation for 3/4 year is $ 3000 ; after recording that amount, 4 3/4 years of depreciation have accumulated.

10. The carrying value (or book value) on October 1, 2001, is $ 1000 . If we sold the truck for $1,200, there would be a 200 (gain/~~loss~~) of $ 200 .

11. We report the Gain on Disposal of Plant Assets account on the Gain on Disposal of Plant assets .

12. Example 2 shows the entry to record the sale of this truck at a gain of $ 200 .

13. Example 3 shows the entry to record the sale of the truck for $400. This produces a $600 Loss .

14. We report the Loss on Disposal of Plant Assets on the ~~Loss~~ Income Statement .

15. In all entries for disposal, we CR (debit/credit) the asset account for the full amount of cost, and DR (debit/credit) the Accumulated Depreciation for the amount of accumulated depreciation to date.

16. In each example of disposal of this truck, we credited the Trucks account for $ 20,000 and debited the Accumulated Depreciation account for $ 19000 .

230   Chapter 10

C16. 20,000, 19,000

17. Whenever we dispose of an asset by sale, scrap, trade-in, or any other means, we must remove both the __asset acct.__ and its __contra asset acct.__ from the books.

C17. asset cost, accumulated depreciation

18. The method of recording asset trade-ins depends upon whether we trade the asset for a dissimilar or a similar asset. Which situation could prohibit the recording of a gain? __Similar asset__.

C18. Trade-in on a similar asset.

19. The textbook uses the example of a computer traded in on a delivery truck. Is this trade for a similar or dissimilar asset? __Dissimilar trade__

C19. Dissimilar.

20. In Example 1, the trade-in allowance for the computer is $500. We assumed its fair market value is $ __500__ .

C20. 500

21. The book value of the old asset is $ __500__ . Since the fair market value and the book value are the same, there is no gain or loss.

C21. 500

22. The cash paid is equal to the selling price of the new asset $ __$12,000__ minus the trade-in allowance for the old asset $ __500__ , or $ __11,500__ .

C22. 12,000, 500, 11,500

23. In Example 2, the list price of the truck is still $12,000; the trade-in allowance is $ __300__ . Accordingly, there is a loss of $ __200__ .

C23. 300; 200

24. Example 3 holds the list price of the truck at $ __12,000__ . Therefore, the $ __800__ trade-in allowance for the computer brings a gain of $ __300__ .

C24. 12,000; 800, 300

25. We record the gain because the trade-in was for __a dissimilar asset__ .

C25. a dissimilar asset

C26. book value of the old computer, the cash paid

C27. unrecorded gain

C28. record

C29. does not recognize

C30. $11,700

C31. the book value of the old computer

C32. 500; 11,200, 11,700

26. Where the trade-in is for a similar asset, we must recognize a loss, but we do not recognize a gain. If we do not recognize the gain, we record the new asset at the value of the assets given up. This would be the **Book Value of the Old Computer** plus **the cash paid**.

27. This would be the same amount as the list price of the new asset minus the **unrecorded gain**.

28. If the trade-in for a similar asset results in a loss, we **record** (record/do not record) the trade-in in the same manner as a dissimilar trade-in.

29. If the trade-in results in a gain and the trading entity is making a cash payment, it **Does not Recognize** (recognizes/does not recognize) the gain.

30. In the example of the computer traded for a new computer at a gain, we record the new computer at $ ~~12,000~~ 11,700 .

31. Therefore, instead of recording the gain, they must record the new computer at a valuation equal to **the Book Value of Old Computer** plus cash paid.

32. The book value of the old computer is $ **500** . The cash paid is $ **11,200** , for a total valuation for the new asset of $ **11,700** instead of $12,000.

33. The nonrecognition of the $300 gain reduces net income of 1997 (the trade-in year) by $ **300** .

232   Chapter 10

C33. 300

C34. Yes; An asset costing $3,700 instead of $4,000 will be depreciated over the EUL. This means lower depreciation expense and higher net income ($300 over the EUL).

D1. natural resources (or wasting assets)

D2. production unit

D3. 180,000, 20,000

D4. 160,000

D5. 0.40

D6. 4,000

D7. inventory (or ore inventory)

34. Is this unreported income compensated for in future years? _yes_ . Explain. *An asset costing 3,700 instead of 4,000 will be depreciated over the EUL. This means lower depreciation expense & higher net income*

D. Depletion

1. The term depletion applies to _natural resources_ .

2. In the textbook illustration, the method used to compute depletion is similar to the _production unit_ method of computing depreciation.

3. We base the cost per ton on a mine that costs $ _180,000_ with the land expected to be resold for $ _20,000_ after removing the ore.

4. The net value of the ore, therefore, must be $ _160,000_ .

5. $160,000 ÷ 400,000 tons = $ _.40_ per ton.

6. The 10,000 tons of ore removed in this period represent a cost of $0.40 x 10,000 which equals $ _4000_ .

7. The depletion cost of $4,000 is not expense; instead it becomes a part of the cost of _inventory_ awaiting sale.

8. Since they sold only 8,000 tons (or 8/10) of the ore mined, _2000_ tons remain in inventory as an asset.

Long-term Assets 233

D8. 2,000

D9. wages of miners

D10. 1.40

D11. 11,200

D12. 2,800

D13. 800 *(This is a critical question. If you missed it, you need more study of depletion.)*

E1. intangible asset

E2. straight-line

E3. expense

E4. the asset account

E5. shorter

9. The inventory valuation includes not only depletion costs but other production costs such as __wages of miners__.

10. When we add $10,000 of other production costs to the depletion, the cost per ton becomes ($4,000 depletion + $10,000 production cost) ÷ 10,000 tons = $__1.40__.

11. 8,000 tons costing $1.40 were sold for a cost of goods sold of $__11,200__.

12. This leaves 2,000 tons in inventory at the end of the period with a cost valuation of $__2,800__.

13. Of this $2,800 inventory value, $__800__ is depletion cost.   2,000 × .40 = 800 depletion cost

E. **Amortization**

1. Amortization records the periodic cost expiration of an __intangible asset__.

2. We use the __straight-line__ method to compute amortization.

3. As is the case with depreciation, we debit the amortization charge to a(n) __expense__ account.

4. Unlike depreciation, we do not use a contra account. In the annual adjusting entry to recognize amortization, the credit is to __the asset acct__.

5. We may amortize intangible assets over their legal lives or estimated useful lives, whichever is __shorter__.

6. Goodwill is the ability of a firm to generate __above normal__ earnings.

234 Chapter 10

E6. above normal

E7. purchase of all or part of a business

E8. expenses

E9. we establish technological feasibility

F1. straight-line

F2. higher

F3. lower

F4. No.

F5. times interest earned

F6. No.

F7. Some of the interest paid might be capitalized.

7. We record it on the books only as the result of the _acquisition/sale_.

8. Business people sometimes argue that we should treat research and development costs as capital expenditures. *FASB Statement No. 2* requires that we treat most as _expenses_.

9. We must record computer software development costs as expenses until _we establish technological feasibility_.

F. **Analyzing Information**
We use the 1994 and 1995 financial information from Toys "R" Us, Inc.

1. What method of depreciation is Toys "R" Us using? _____.

2. If they were using an accelerated method, depreciation expense would be (*higher/lower*) _____.

3. And net income would be _____.

4. Did Toys "R" Us make any changes in depreciation methods? _____

5. We can measure a firm's ability to pay annual interest charges by calculating _____.

6. For a fair calculation of times interest earned, we must include all interest paid by the company. Does all interest always show on the income statement? _____

7. What else might have happened to interest payments? _____

8. Did Toys "R" US capitalize any interest during fiscal 1994? _____

F8. Yes

F9. 6,926,000

F10. 90,826,000

F11. income tax expense, interest expense, total interest cost

F12. 10.22

9. How much interest did they capitalize? $_____.

10. Their total interest cost during fiscal 1994 was $_____.

11. To calculate times interest earned, we add net income plus _____, plus _____ and divide by _____.

12. Times interest earned for Toys "R" Us was _____ times.

LEARNING GOALS ACHIEVEMENT TEST

1. (LG 1-3) Rupert Company purchased a computer on January 4, 1997, with an invoice price of $51,000 and a cash discount of 4/10 n/30. The company paid $1,040 for installation. It estimates that the useful life will be eight years and the residual value will be $2,000. Record the purchase of the computer and then depreciation for the year 1997 under each of the following methods.

    a. Straight-line method.
    b. Double declining-balance method.
    c. Sum-of-the-years'-digits method.
    d. Production unit method with an EUL of 32,000 hours with 3,500 hours of operation in 1997.

GENERAL JOURNAL

	Date		Accounts and Explanations	PR	Debit	Credit
	Jan	4	Computer		50,000	
			Cash			50,000
(a)	Dec	31	Computer Depreciation exp		6,000	
			Acc/Dep-Computer			6,000
(b)	Dec	31	Computer Depreciation exp		12,500	
			Acc/Dep-Computer			12,500
(c)	Dec	31	Computer Depreciation exp		10,667	
			Acc/Dep-Computer			10,667
(D)	Dec	31	Computer Depreciation exp		5,250	
			Acc/Dep-Computer			5,250

Long-term Assets 237

2. (LG 4, 5) Duterium Company had purchased a delivery truck on January 3, 1995, for $10,000. It estimated the useful life to be 10 years and the residual value $1,000.

   a. Assume that on January 5, 1997, Duterium spent $2,000 to increase the capacity of the cargo area. This expenditure is a ~~2,000~~ _Capital_ expenditure. It would debit it to _Acc Dep TRUCKS_ .

   b. Assume that on March 8, 1997, Duterium spent $1,500 on a major overhaul that extended the useful life of the truck by 2 years. This expenditure is a _Capital_ expenditure. It would debit it to _Accumulated Depreciation_ .

   c. Assume that on October 28, 1997, Duterium spent $800 to replace the worn out tires. This is a _Revenue_ expenditure. It would debit it to _Repair expense_ .

3. (LG 6) On January 4, 1997, Avere Company traded a machine for a similar new machine that has a fair market value of $60,000. These accounts appear on the books of the Avere Company:

	Balance
Machine	$50,000
Accumulated Depreciation--Machine	41,000

   (9,000)

   Required: Give general journal entries to record the trade-in if:

   (1) A trade-in allowance of $5,000 is received on the used asset and the balance is paid in cash.

   (2) A trade-in allowance of $12,000 is received on the used asset and the balance is paid in cash.

	DR	CR
Machine (New)	60,000	
A/D-Machine	41,000	
Loss	4,000	
Cash		55,000
Machine		50,000

	DR	CR
Machine (N)	57,000	
A/D-Mach.	41,000	
Machine(o)		50,000
Cash		48,000

238 Chapter 10

GENERAL JOURNAL

LOSS

Date		Accounts and Explanations	PR	Debit	Credit
(A) JAN	4	Machine (New)		60,000	
		Acc/Dep - Machine		41,000	
		Loss on Disposable Asset			4000
		Cash			55,000
		Machine (Old)			50,000
(B) JAN	4	Machine (New)		57,000	
		A/C/Dep - Machine		41,000	
		Cash			48,000
		Machine (Old)			50,000

4. (LG 7) Compute depletion cost of 30,000 barrels of oil extracted from a well that had an original cost of $12,000,000, no residual value, and is expected to produce 400,000 barrels of oil before it is exhausted.

ANSWERS TO LEARNING GOALS ACHIEVEMENT TEST

1.

GENERAL JOURNAL

Date		Accounts and Explanations	PR	Debit	Credit
1997 Jan.	4	Computer		50,000	
		Cash (or Accounts Payable)			50,000
		To record purchase of computer.			
(a) Dec.	31	Depreciation Expense--Computer		6,000	
		Accumulated Depreciation--Computer			6,000
		1997 depreciation by straight-line method. ($50,000 - $2,000) ÷ 8			
(b) Dec.	31	Depreciation Expense--Computer		12,500	
		Accumulated Depreciation--Computer			12,500
		1997 depreciation by DDB method. $50,000 x (0.125 x 2)			
(c) Dec.	31	Depreciation Expense--Computer		10,667	
		Accumulated Depreciation--Computer			10,667
		1997 depreciation by SYD method. ($50,000 - $2,000) x 8/36			
(d) Dec.	31	Depreciation Expense--Computer		5,250	
		Accumulated Depreciation--Computer			5,250
		1997 depreciation by production unit method. ($48,000 ÷ 32,000) x 3,500			

2. a. capital, Trucks b. capital, Accumulated Depreciation--Trucks c. revenue, Repair Expense--Trucks

3.

GENERAL JOURNAL

Date		Accounts and Explanations	PR	Debit	Credit

1997 (1) Jan.	4	Machine
		Accumulated Depreciation-Machine
		Loss on Disposal of Plant Asset
		    Machine
		    Cash
		To record trade-in for similar asset at a loss.
				60,000
				41,000
				4,000
					
					50,000
					55,000

(2) Jan.	4	Machine
		Accumulated Depreciation-Machine
		    Machine
		    Cash
		To record trade-in for similar asset at a gain. New machine = $9,000 + $48,000.
				57,000
				41,000
					
					50,000
					48,000

4. $12,000,000 ÷ 400,000 barrels = $30 per barrel, and 30,000 barrels x $30 = $900,000 depletion cost.

Chapter 11

CORPORATIONS: PAID-IN CAPITAL

EXPLANATION OF MAJOR CONCEPTS

Corporations   LG 1

A corporation is a "fictitious person" in the eyes of the law. A state creates a legal entity by issuing to a group of incorporators a certificate called a *corporate charter*. A large number of persons may own a corporation. By investing in the corporation, they receive shares of capital stock. The corporation may issue these shares of ownership to any person without obtaining permission from any of its other owners.

Corporations have the ability to raise large sums of money. Another advantage is that the individual owners are not liable for the debts of the corporation. This enables the shareholders (owners) to invest any amount they desire in a business without the risk of losing more than their investment if the business fails. Since corporations are legal entities, they pay federal and state income tax on their earnings.

Paid-In Capital   LG 2

Assets invested in a business by shareholders are known as paid-in capital. A corporation has several sources of paid-in capital, including:

- Cash paid to the corporation in exchange for shares of its stock.
- Assets other than cash given to the corporation in exchange for shares of its stock.
- The value of property such as land donated to a corporation to get it to build a plant in a certain community.

Chapter 11 discusses these types of paid-in-capital and the accounting for transactions that bring paid-in-capital to the corporation.

Key Capital Stock Terms   LG 3

The capital stock terms explained in this chapter are extremely important. You should take time to understand them clearly now rather than be confused by them later.

- *Par value* is an arbitrary amount per share established in the corporate charter. Par value represents the legal capital of the corporation. It is usually set at a

relatively low figure for common stock and is not an indication of the stock's market value.
- *Stated value* is an amount per share assigned by the corporation's directors to take the place of par value. In states that allow the issuance of no-par value stock, a corporation may choose not to have a par value assigned. For accounting purposes, we treat stated value as if it were par.
- *Market value* is the price of a share of stock bought on the stock market. It is in no way related to par value. Market values change daily.

Classes of Capital Stock   LG 4

A corporation typically has two classes of capital stock: *common stock* and *preferred stock*. Common stock represents the residual ownership of the company. If a company has only one class of stock, it is common. Preferred stock represents a type of ownership with certain types of preferences. These preferences normally are in the distribution of earnings and the distribution of assets upon liquidation. In exchange for these preferences, preferred stock often does not carry the right to vote. Preferred stock has certain advantages, such as a stipulated rate of dividends that the corporation must pay before paying any other dividends. However, the residual ownership stock is common stock. Under most circumstances, it is the common stockholders who have the right to vote for election of directors and on other important matters. If a company experiences fast growth, it is the value of common stock that will increase rapidly on the market--not the preferred.

Issuance of Stock   LG 5, 6

The stock of corporations usually has a par value or a stated value. When the corporation issues its stock, most state laws require that the value of assets received in exchange for the stock be equal to or greater than par or stated value. We debit the fair market value of the assets received to the appropriate asset accounts. We credit the amount of the par or stated value to an account called Preferred Stock or Common Stock, whichever is appropriate. We credit amounts received in excess of par or stated value of common stock to an account called Paid-in Capital--Excess over Par Value, Common (or Preferred, if appropriate). Another name for this account is Premium on Common Stock (or Premium on Preferred Stock). It is very important that you bear in mind that the accounts we credit when issuing stock are owners' equity accounts. They show ownership claims generated by investment.

Sometimes, investors subscribe to capital stock. This means that the investor signs a contract agreeing to invest in a specified number of shares at a specified price. Usually they make a down payment, with dates set for payment of remaining installments. In addition to the debit to Cash for the down payment, there is a debit to the current asset account Subscriptions Receivable for the balance due. Subscriptions Receivable is an asset. It is not part of the owner's equity. A stock subscription also increases owner's equity. We credit the amount of new owners' equity equal to par value of the subscribed stock to Common Stock Subscribed (or Preferred Stock Subscribed, if appropriate). This account is a temporary paid-in capital account. It simply shows par value of subscribed but unpaid shares. We will transfer amounts in it to the Common Stock (or Preferred Stock, if appropriate) account when the subscribers pay the subscription in full and the stock issued. If subscriptions are received at a price higher than par or stated value, we credit the excess directly to the Paid-in Capital--Excess over Par or Stated Value account.

Government bodies or people may donate assets to a corporation. When this occurs, we debit the appropriate asset accounts and credit an owners' equity account titled Paid-in Capital--Donations for the fair market value of the donated assets.

Paid-in Capital Section   LG 7

You should take the time to learn the format of the paid-in capital section of a balance sheet.

Stockholders' Equity

Paid-in capital		
Capital stock:		
Preferred stock, x%, $X par value; X shares authorized,		
X shares issued	$XXX	
Common stock, $X par value, X shares authorized,		
X shares issued	XXX	
Total capital stock:		$X,XXX
Additional paid-in capital:		
Paid-in capital--excess over par value, preferred	$XX	
Paid-in capital--excess over par value, common	XX	
Paid-in capital--donation of _____	XX	
Total additional paid-in capital		XXX
Total paid-in capital		$X,XXX

Analyzing Information   LG 8

Financial statement users need to be able to identify information about the paid-in capital of the corporation. Pieces of information that we need to be able to find include

- total number of authorized shares of each class of stock.
- total number of issued shares of each class of stock.
- total number of outstanding shares of each class of stock.
- total paid-in-capital from each class of stock.
- total market value of common shares outstanding.

GUIDED STUDY OF THIS CHAPTER

A. Paid-in Capital Terms
We will first work to understand the meaning of the different types of value attributed to a share of stock.

1. If Kheel Corporation issues 1,000 shares of stock, par value $2.50, to John Smith at $12 a share, its market value at that time is $ _12_ per share.

A1. 12

2. If John Smith sells 100 shares ten months later for $1,950, its market value has risen to $ _19.50_ per share.

A2. 19.50

3. Market value, then, is the _current mkt price_ .

A3. amount that a share of stock sells for in the market

4. If the corporate charter places an arbitrary amount of $2.50 per share as the minimum for which Kheel Corporation can issue its stock, then the $2.50 is ~~stated~~ _par_ value.

A4. par

5. Market value of stock changes daily. Does par value also change? _No_

A5. No.

6. Some states authorize the issuance of no-par value stock. If the Kheel Corporation's stock is no-par, Kheel's directors may assign a _stated_ value.

A6. stated

7. For recording of stock issuances, we treat stated value the same as _par_ value.

A7. par

8. Which of these capital stock values change because of economic conditions, politics, or investors' expectations? _mkt value_

A8. Only the market value.

9. Do we record changes in market value in the corporate accounts? _No_

Corporations: Paid-in Capital 245

A9. No.

A10. total par value, $2,500

A11. 22.50

A12. 22,500, Paid-in Capital--
Excess over Par Value,
Common

B1. 10,000, 40,000

B2. Common Stock

B3. Organization Costs

B4. No; It is an asset.

10. If Kheel Corporation issued 1,000 shares of $2.50 par value common stock, the value recorded in the account Common Stock is $ _2,500 CR_____.

11. Assuming they issue stock at $25 per share, the excess is $ _22.50_ per share.

12. We credit the $22.50 excess x 1,000 shares = $ _22,500_____ to the _Paid-in Cap - Excess Over par-Common._____ account.

B. **Paid-in Capital Transactions**

1. In the February 11 Kheel transaction, owners contributed cash, land, and buildings in exchange for stock. We debited Land for its market value $_____ and debited Buildings for $_____.

2. The total value of the assets received was equal to the par value of the stock issued. Thus, we credited the total amount to _Common Stock_____.

3. Sometimes corporations pay people who help organize the corporation in stock instead of cash for their services. The account debited in such a transaction is _Organization Service Costs_.

4. Is this an expense account? _No_. Explain. _It is an asset._

5. Kheel Corporation's charter authorized it to issue 200,000 shares of $2.50 par value common stock. The organizers charged $10,000 for their services but accepted 4,000 shares of stock. The debit of $10,000 was to _Organization Costs_.

246   Chapter 11

B5. Organization Costs

B6. Common Stock

B7. 12,000

B8. 10,000

B9. Paid-in Capital--Excess over Par Value, Common

B10. No answer required.

B11. Subscriptions Receivable--Common

B12. current asset

B13. Common Stock Subscribed

B14. owners' equity

B15. Common Stock

6. The credit in this transaction was to _Common Stock_.

7. Suppose that this bill was in the amount of $12,000 and they accepted 4,000 shares of stock instead. The amount of debit to Organization Costs would be $ _12000_.

8. The credit to Common Stock would be for $ _10,000_.

9. We would credit the remaining $2,000 to _Paid-in Cap - Excess over par value - common_

10. Corporations also issue stock by the subscription process. A subscription is an agreement to invest in a stipulated number of shares at a specified price. We will use the Kheel Corporation subscription example in the textbook.

11. On December 1, 1997, Kheel received subscriptions for 40,000 shares at $3.00. The first entry records the total subscription and (debits) _Subscriptions Recievable - Common_ for $120,000.

12. Subscriptions Receivable--Common is a ~~receivable~~ _current asset_ account.

13. We credit the par value (40,000 shares x $2.50 = $100,000) to _CR. Common Stock-Subscribed_.

14. Common Stock Subscribed is an _Owner's equity_ account of a temporary nature.

15. When we issue the stock, we will close this account and transfer the $100,000 credit to _Common-Stock_.

16. However, if we should prepare a balance sheet before issuing the stock, we would include Common Stock Subscribed in the _paid-in capital_ section.

B16. paid-in capital

B17. 0.50

B18. Paid-in Capital--Excess over Par Value, Common

B19. Subscriptions Receivable--Common

B20. Common Stock

B21. No; That entry was made on December 1 when the subscription was received.

B22. No answer required.

B23. Paid-in Capital--Donations

17. The subscription price of $3.00 exceeded par value by $ ~~20,000~~ .50 per share.

18. We credited the 40,000 shares x $0.50 = $20,000 to the _Paid-in Cap. Excess over par value - common_ account.

19. Kheel received payment on December 30. The entry reduces the asset _Subscriptions Recievable - Common_ to zero.

20. After subscribers fully paid for the stock, Kheel Corporation issued the stock certificates on December 30. We transfer the amount in Common Stock Subscribed to _Common Stock_.

21. At the time of issuance on December 30, was action necessary to record the excess? _No_. Explain. _It was already recorded when subscription was received._

22. Subscribers who do not complete their payments are said to be in default. Kheel Corporation has several options, depending on state law. One option is to resell the shares and refund to the original subscribers any amounts of paid subscriptions recovered. Another is to issue to subscribers fewer shares at $3.00, up to any amounts they have already paid.

23. To attract industry, cities may donate land or buildings. These assets are a source of paid-in capital, but the donors do not ask for owners' equity. This increases the equity of present owners. To record the donation we credit the account _Paid-in Cap - Donations_.

24. We debit the donated assets in the amount of _FMV_.

248 Chapter 11

B24. fair market value

C1. 1,200,000,000

C2. 564,600,000,
567,000,000

C3. Yes.

C4. 2,400,000 shares.

C5. 524,100,000

C6. No.

C7. Disney held treasury shares.

C8. $44.250

C9. 23,191,425,000

C. **Analyzing Information**
We are using the stockholders' equity section for The Walt Disney Company.

1. What was the total number of common shares authorized on September 30, 1994? _____.

2. On September 30, 1993, there were _____ shares of common stock issued, and on September 30, 1994 there were _____ shares.

3. Did the company issue any new shares of common stock during the fiscal year? _____

4. How many? _____

5. How many shares of common stock did Disney have outstanding on September 30, 1994? _____

6. Was this the same as the number of shares issued? _____

7. Why would the number of shares outstanding be less than the number of shares issued? _____

8. On September 30, 1994, what was the market value per share of stock? _____

9. The total market value of the outstanding shares of common stock was $_____.

10. Did the total market value of Disney's shares increase or decrease during the year? _____

C10. increase

11. Why did this happen? _____
_____
_____
_____

C11. The market price per share increased, and the number of shares outstanding increased.

LEARNING GOALS ACHIEVEMENT TEST

1. (LG 1) List five things that make a corporation different from other forms of business:

    (1) _Has a corporate charter_
    (2) _Has many owners through the investments_
    (3) _Must pay income tax_
    (4) _Ability to raise large sums of money_
    (5) _Owners lies is limited_

2. (LG 2) List three major sources of paid-in capital of a corporation:

    (1) _Paid-in cap par value of capital stock (common + preferred)_
    (2) _Paid-in cap - excess over par value - common + preferred_
    (3) _Paid-in capital - Donations._

3. (LG 3) For each of the following descriptions indicate whether it is most likely to apply to par, stated, or market value:

    a. The value per share set forth in the corporate charter. _Par_
    b. The value per share assigned by directors as a basis for recording stock on the books. _Stated_
    c. The minimum amount per share that buyers must pay in to the corporation on issuance of stock. _Par or Stated Value_
    d. The actual amount per share paid in to the corporation on issuance of stock. _MKT Value_

250   Chapter 11

e. The amount you would pay to buy a share of United Airlines stock on the stock market. __Mkt value__

4. (LG 4) For each of the following descriptions, indicate whether it is more likely to apply to preferred or to common stock:

   a. Has a specified dividend rate. __Preferred__
   b. Votes to elect directors. __Common__
   c. Is usually denied voting rights. __Preferred__
   d. Has first claim on dividends if the corporation pays any dividends. __Preferred__
   e. Is the class that will exist if the corporation issues only one type of stock. __Common__
   f. Is often restricted to a specific dividend rate. __Preferred__
   g. If the corporation is liquidated:
      (1) Has first claim (after creditors) on remaining assets up to a specified amount. __Preferred__
      (2) Has the residual claim against all other assets. __Common__

5. (LG 5-7) Ebony Corporation is authorized to issue 1,000,000 shares of $2 par value common stock and 500,000 shares of $50 par value 10% preferred stock. The following events occurred during July 1997.

   Jul. 7 Issued 5,000 shares of common stock at $14 per share for cash.
   9 Issued 1,000 shares of preferred stock at $52 per share for cash.
   12 Received subscriptions for 10,000 shares of common stock at $18 per share with a 40% down payment.
   20 Collected the unpaid balance due under the subscription contract and issued the stock.
   28 Central City donated land with fair market value of $30,000 for a new plant in their city.

   Required:

   (a) Journalize the transactions.
   (b) Prepare the stockholders' equity section of the balance sheet.

(a)

GENERAL JOURNAL

Date		Accounts and Explanations	PR	Debit	Credit
Jul	7	Cash		70,000	
		Common Stock			10,000
		Paid-in Cap over Par-Comm			60,000
	9	Cash		52,000	
		Preferred Stock			50,000
		Paid-in Cap-Excess over Par-Preferred			2,000
	12	Cash		72,000	
		Subscriptions Receivable		108,000	
		Common Stock Subscribed			20,000
		Paid-in Cap-Excess over Par-Com			160,000
	20	Cash		108,000	
		Subscription Receivable			108,000
	28	Land		30,000	
		Paid-in Cap. Donated			30,000

(b)

Stockholders Equity		
Paid in Capital		
Capital Stock:		
Preferred Stock, 10%, $50 par, 500,000		
shares authorized, 1,000 shares issued	50,000	
Common Stock $2 par, 1,000,000 shares		
authorized, 15,000 shares issued	30,000	
Total Capital Stock:		80,000
Additional Paid-in Cap		
Paid in excess over par, preferred	2,000	
Paid-in-cap excess over par, common	220,000	
Paid-in-cap-donation of land	30,000	
Total additional Paid in Cap		252,000
Total Paid in Capital		$332,000

ANSWERS TO LEARNING GOALS ACHIEVEMENT TEST

1. (1) It is a legal entity.
   (2) The owners' liability for business debts is limited.
   (3) It can raise more capital than other forms.
   (4) Its ownership shares are readily transferable.
   (5) It must pay income tax.

2. (1) Par value paid in for capital stock.
   (2) Excess over par value paid in for capital stock.
   (3) Donated capital.

3. a. Par value   d. Market value
   b. Stated value   e. Market value
   c. Par or stated value

4. a. Preferred stock   e. Common stock
   b. Common stock   f. Preferred stock
   c. Preferred stock   g. (1) Preferred stock
   d. Preferred stock   (2) Common stock

5. (a)

GENERAL JOURNAL

Date	Accounts and Explanations	PR	Debit	Credit
1997 Jul. 7	Cash		70,000	
	Common Stock			10,000
	Paid-in Capital-Excess Over Par Value, Common			60,000
	Issuance of 5,000 shares at $14 per share.			
9	Cash		52,000	
	10% Preferred Stock			50,000
	Paid-in Capital-Excess Over Par Value, Preferred			2,000
	Issuance of 1,000 shares at $52 per share.			
12	Cash		72,000	
	Subscriptions Receivable-Common		108,000	
	Common Stock Subscribed			20,000
	Paid-in Capital-Excess Over Par Value, Common			160,000
	Received subscriptions for 10,000 shares at $18.			
20	Cash		108,000	
	Subscriptions Receivable-Common			108,000
	Collected unpaid subscription.			
20	Common Stock Subscribed		20,000	
	Common Stock			20,000
	Issued stock.			
28	Land		30,000	
	Paid-in Capital-Donations			30,000
	Land donated by Central City.			

(b)

EBONY CORPORATION
PARTIAL BALANCE SHEET
JULY 31, 1997

Stockholders' Equity

Paid-in capital

Capital stock:		
Preferred stock, 10%, $50 par value, 500,000 shares authorized, 1,000 shares issued	$50,000	
Common stock, $2 par value, 1,000,000 shares authorized, 15,000 shares issued	30,000	
Total capital stock		$ 80,000
Additional paid-in capital:		
Paid-in capital-excess over par value, preferred	$ 2,000	
Paid-in capital-excess over par value, common	220,000	
Paid-in capital-donation of land by Central City	30,000	
Total additional paid-in capital		252,000
Total paid-in capital		$332,000

Chapter 12

ADDITIONAL STOCKHOLDERS' EQUITY TRANSACTIONS AND INCOME DISCLOSURES

EXPLANATION OF MAJOR CONCEPTS

As you study stockholders' equity accounts in more detail, keep in mind that they are *sources* of assets on the balance sheet. The things of value are on the asset side of the balance sheet. Many of the titles of stockholders' equity accounts sound as if they are assets, and students often become confused as to their real meaning. Remember that they are merely subdivisions of the owners' equity term in the accounting equation. We subdivide owners' equity in a corporation by source to meet the legal requirements of the various states that charter corporations. The accounts for these subdivisions, however, continue to represent owners' claims against assets of a corporation.

Retained Earnings   LG 1

In a corporation, we close Income Summary to Retained Earnings. We also close amounts of dividends declared to stockholders to Retained Earnings. The balance in the Retained Earnings account represents the total profits minus the total losses and dividends since the corporation began.

In some states, the retained earnings amount is legally a limit to dividends that the corporation can pay. Even if it is not a legal limit, prudent directors do not feel that they should make payouts to owners that amount to more than retained earnings. This would be a return of investment. Therefore, they view retained earnings as a limit on ability to pay dividends. In some situations it is desirable to inform investors of restrictions on the availability of retained earnings for dividends. To do so, the directors may order retained earnings restrictions in specific amounts for specific purposes. This is a way of communicating to financial statement readers the limitations in amounts available for dividends. We usually do this by a note to the financial statements.

A company may make an error in accounting for income and discover the error in a later period. This is called a *prior period adjustment*. We show the correction of this error as an adjustment to beginning retained earnings. Exhibit 12-2 shows the presentation of the statement of retained earnings with this correction.

Dividends LG 2

A corporation may pay dividends out in cash or in property. Corporations pay dividends only if the corporation's board of directors authorizes a dividend (a declaration). When they declare a dividend, the three important dates are: date of declaration, date of record, and date of payment.

- *Date of declaration* is the date the directors declare a dividend. On this date, a legal liability exists to pay the declared dividend. We make the following entry to record the declaration.

	Dr	Cr
Dividends--Common Stock..	XXXXX	
Dividends Payable--Common Stock................ (current Liab)		XXXXX
To record declaration this date of a dividend of X cents a share, payable (date) to stockholders of record (date).		

- *Date of record* is the date that determines who gets the dividend. Any person who buys a share of stock in time to be recorded on the corporation stockholders' record by the date of record will receive the dividend. This is true even if that person buys the share after the dividend has been declared. We make no entry in the corporation's accounts on the date of record.

- *Date of payment* is the date when the checks are to be delivered to stockholders. When we prepare and mail the dividend checks, the journal entry is as follows:

	Dr	Cr
Dividends Payable--Common..................................	XXXXX	
Cash..		XXXXX
To record payment of dividend.		

If a corporation declares quarterly dividends, we debit the Dividends account four times per year with dividend declarations. In the end-of-year closing entries, we close the Dividends account to Retained Earnings since dividends are a distribution of retained earnings. This entry parallels the closing of the withdrawals accounts in proprietorships and partnerships.

Preferred stock usually carries a stipulated dividend rate. If the preferred stock has a par or stated value, we show the rate as a percent of par. If it is no-par value stock, we show the rate in dollars (such as $3.20 preferred). In either case, the rate is an annual rate. Quarterly declarations on preferred would be one-fourth the annual rate. Preferred stock may be cumulative, which means that we must make up dividends not declared in a prior year, dividends in arrears, before the directors can declare current dividends on any stock. Arrearages are not liabilities. We need no journal entries to record them. But we cannot overlook them if we are considering a current dividend.

Usually, preferred stockholders are limited to their stipulated dividend rate, while companies may pay increased dividends (and sometimes extra dividends) to common stockholders. We will work with this further in the Guided Study section of this chapter.

Additional Stockholders' Equity Transactions and Income Disclosures 257

Stock Dividends LG 3

A stock dividend is not just another name for a cash dividend on the corporation's stock. Instead, it is an actual distribution of additional shares of stock to existing shareholders without any additional investment on their part. A stock dividend does not reduce assets or reduce total stockholders' equity. It does reduce retained earnings and increase paid-in capital by the same amount. On the books of the corporation, the result is simply a transfer of some amount of retained earnings to paid-in capital accounts. As in cash dividends, there are three dates. Entries are slightly different. For example, the entries for a small stock dividend (a dividend involving less than 20%-25% of previously outstanding shares) would be:

- Date of declaration.

	DR	CR
Stock Dividends--Common Stock............ (from Retained Earnings)	Market Value	
Stock Dividend to Be Issued-Common.........		Par Value
Paid-in Capital--Excess over Par Value, Common........		Difference

- Date of record. No entry.

- Date of issuance.

Stock Dividend to Be Issued--Common	Par Value	
Common Stock...............................		Par Value

Stock Split LG 3

A stock split is a technique whereby a company forces the price of its stock down. The corporation does this by recalling the current outstanding stock and issuing a multiple number of shares of reduced par value to the owners. For example, assume a company has outstanding 50,000 shares of $10 par value common stock and they declare a 2-for-1 stock split. They will call in all the $10 par stock and reissue to the same owners 100,000 shares of $5 par value common stock. This should cause the market price of the stock to drop about one-half. The purpose of doing this is to make the stock more affordable to a wider group of investors

Treasury Stock LG 4

Treasury stock is the name given to a corporation's own shares that the corporation has reacquired but not canceled. The corporation will hold them temporarily and reissue them. When we purchase the treasury stock, we debit the Treasury Stock account for the cost of the treasury stock purchased. This account is not an asset; it does not represent a thing of value. It does represent a temporary refund of investment to some stockholders. It is a contra account to total paid-in capital and retained earnings. When we reissue treasury stock, we credit the Treasury Stock account for the cost of the shares reissued. Any amounts received upon reissuance in excess of that cost constitute additional paid-in-capital--*not a gain*. If it is reissued below cost, the corporation has suffered a permanent reduction of paid-in capital--*not a loss*. In some cases, we make a restriction of retained earnings equal to the cost of the treasury stock reacquired. We will look at the details of the various entries in the Guided Study.

Book Value of Common Stock LG 5

The book value of common stock is the proportion of stockholders' equity attributable to one share of common stock. If there is only one class of stock outstanding, it is the total stockholders' equity divided by the number of shares of common stock outstanding. If classes of stock other than common are outstanding, we subtract the portion of stockholders' equity attributable to the other classes of stock from total stockholders' equity before dividing by the number of common shares outstanding.

Income Reporting LG 6

Net income is a very important number for users of financial statements. Financial statement users need to know the income from recurring (continuing) operations and from nonrecurring sources. To highlight this number, certain nonrecurring items require special treatment on the income statement. If a business discontinues a significant segment of the business, we show the current period's income and any gain or loss from the disposal of assets separately on the income statement. Extraordinary items are gains and losses from events that are *both* unusual and infrequent. We also show these gains and losses separately. Also, if the company has a change in accounting principle, we report the cumulative effect of the change on past years income separately on the income statement. The general format of the income statement is as follows:

Revenue		$XX,XXX
Cost of goods sold		XX,XXX
Gross margin		$ X,XXX
Operating expenses		XXX
Income from continuing operations before taxes		$ X,XXX
Income tax expense		XXX
Income from continuing operations		$ XXX
Discontinued operations:		
Income from discontinued segment	$XXX	
Gain (loss) on disposal	XX	XXX
Income before extraordinary items		$ XXX

Additional Stockholders' Equity Transactions and Income Disclosures 259

```
Extraordinary items:
    Loss from tornado                              (XX)
  Cumulative effect of change in accounting
    principle:
      Change from double declining to
        straight-line depreciation                   XX
  Net income                                      $ XXX
```

Earnings Per Share   LG 7

Earnings per share is a number of interest to investors. It is exactly what the name implies, the net income per share of common stock. If the corporation has issued no convertible securities, we calculate a single EPS figure by dividing net income by the average number of shares of common stock outstanding during the year. If the corporation has issued convertible securities, *APB Opinion No. 15* requires that we calculate two earnings per share amounts--primary earnings per share and fully diluted earnings per share. Fully diluted earnings per share is equal to the net income available to common stockholders' divided by the weighted average number of common shares plus the number of shares of common stock equivalents.

Analyzing Information   LG 8

After studying all of stockholders' equity, we now begin to work on recognizing differences between two companies. We might look at par values, number of shares issued, number of treasury shares, book value and market value per share. We will also look at cash dividend per share and dividend yield. Other measures we have studied include profit margin percent, return on assets, earnings per share, and price earnings ratio.

GUIDED STUDY OF THIS CHAPTER

A. Retained Earnings

1. Retained Earnings has a normal ___Credit___ (*debit/credit*) balance. Why? _Because it represents owners equity_

A1. credit; Because it is an owners' equity account.

2. ___Net income___ increases the retained earnings balance.

A2. Net income

3. ___Dividends___ and ___Net loss___ decrease its balance.

260 Chapter 12

A3. Net loss, dividends

4. The amount of cash a corporation has limits its ability to pay dividends; _Retained earnings_ also limit its ability to pay dividends.

A4. retained earnings

5. Suppose that a corporation wants to impose a voluntary restriction on dividend payments to retain cash for future plant expansion. Its directors can _restrict_ retained earnings.

A5. restrict

6. When the directors take such action, the action _reduces_ the total amount available for dividend declaration.

A6. reduces

7. Will this action provide money for the plant expansion? _yes_. Explain. _____

A7. No; It limits dividends, but cash can be used for any other purpose.

8. What would be a good way to build up money for plant expansion? _____

A8. Create a special cash fund and make periodic deposits to it.

9. Are the amounts of restricted retained earnings reported in the financial statements? _____

A9. Yes.

10. How? _____

A10. By a note to the financial statements. *We view notes as an integral part of the financial statements.*

11. If we find an error overstating a prior year's computation of net income, we correct it by _DR_ (debiting/crediting) retained earnings and _CR_ the other affected balance sheet account.

A11. debiting, crediting

12. This type of error is called a _____ . We report it at the top of the _____ .

Additional Stockholders' Equity Transactions and Income Disclosures 261

A12. prior period adjustment; statement of retained earnings

B1. May 31, 1995

B2. 150, June 15, 1995

B3. record

B4. The seller; The date of record is past.

B5. Sellor

B6. No effect

B7. Reduces them by $750,000.

B8. reduced

B9. No. It is not an expense.

B. Dividends

1. Pennzoil Company's dividend, illustrated in the textbook, is payable to stockholders of record at the close of business on _____.

2. If you buy 200 shares of Pennzoil common stock on May 25, 1995, you will receive a dividend of $_____ on _____.

3. May 31, 1995, is the date of _____.

4. If you buy 200 shares of Pennzoil common on the stock exchange on June 5, 1995, who gets the dividend (*the buyer /the seller*)? _____. Why? _____

5. Who would get the dividend if you bought the stock after June 15? _____.

6. We used Pennzoil Company to illustrate a dividend declaration and payment. What effect does the declaration of a dividend by Pennzoil have on total assets? *no effect*

7. What effect does the payment on June 15 have on total assets? *reduces them by 750,000*

8. If Pennzoil declares and pays four quarterly dividends in 1995, it will reduce total assets by $3,000,000, and *reduce* stockholders' equity by $3,000,000.

9. Do we close the Dividends account into Income Summary? *no* Why? *it is not an expense*.

10. Then dividends *do not* (*do/do not*) change net income.

262 Chapter 12

B10. do not

B11. We close it into Retained Earnings.

B12. 1,000

B13. 100

B14. 12%.

B15. 100, 12

B16. zero, zero

B17. 12,000, arrearage

B18. 12,000, preferred, current dividend

B19. 28,000

11. Then how does the Dividends account actually reduce stockholders' equity? _we close it into Retained earnings_

12. Move to the illustration of cash dividends on preferred stock in the textbook. Columbia Corporation has outstanding _____ shares of cumulative preferred.

13. The preferred stock has a par value of $_____ per share.

14. What is the dividend rate on preferred? _____

15. The preferred dividend per share of stock is 12% x $_____ par value = $_____ per year.

16. Since the preferred stock was one year in arrears, preferred must have received $_____ in 1996, and common must have received $_____.

17. If the corporation will pay a total of $52,000 in dividends in 1997, we assign the first $_____ to preferred to cover the _____.

18. We must assign the next $_____ to _____ stock to cover the _____ for the year.

19. The remaining amount goes to common stockholders, who would receive $_____.

20. Move to stock dividends. In a stock dividend, the corporation _____ (*does/does not*) distribute assets to stockholders.

Additional Stockholders' Equity Transactions and Income Disclosures 263

B20. does not

B21. additional shares of its own stock

B22. 25

B23. down *(More shares will be available to the same number of buyers.)*

B24. market value of the stock issued

B25. small

B26. 30,000

B27. 10, 10,000

B28. 20

B29. 20,000, Paid-in Capital-- Excess over Par Value, Common

21. In issuing a stock dividend, the corporation distributes _____ _____ _____ .

22. The AICPA defines a small stock dividend as one that will not affect the market value of the stock. A small stock dividend should not be greater than _____ % of the outstanding shares.

23. We expect a large stock dividend to affect the market value of the stock by driving it _____ (*up/down*).

24. When issuing a small stock dividend, a corporation should reduce retained earnings by the _____ _____ _____ .

25. The Topps Corporation 10% stock dividend was a _____ (*small/large*) stock dividend.

26. Since Topps stock is selling for $30 a share, we must move 1,000 shares x $30 = $_____ from retained earnings to paid-in capital.

27. Of this amount, we transfer par value, 1,000 shares x $_____ = $_____, to Common Stock when we issue the dividend.

28. The difference between market value and par value is $_____ a share.

29. We credit this $20 x 1,000 shares = $_____ to the _____ _____ .

30. Suppose Topps Corporation had enough retained earnings and issued a 100% stock dividend. The number of shares outstanding after the dividend would then be _____ shares.

264   Chapter 12

B30. 20,000

31. It would be necessary that Topps have a balance of at least $ _____ in Retained Earnings.

B31. 100,000 *(Note that this is a large stock dividend and we only need to transfer par value .)*

32. The ultimate effect of a 100% stock dividend would be to transfer $100,000 from Retained Earnings to _____.

B32. Common Stock

33. Suppose Topps Corporation were to issue a 2-for-1 stock split instead of a 100% stock dividend. How many shares of stock would then be outstanding after the stock split? _____.

B33. 20,000

34. This gives the same number of shares as a 100% stock dividend. By how much would a 2-for-1 split reduce Retained Earnings? $ _____

B34. None.

35. How much would the 2-for-1 split increase the Common Stock account? $ _____

B35. None.

36. How can we double the number of shares outstanding without increasing the Common Stock account? _____

B36. By reducing Topps' par value from $10 to $5 a share.

37. To summarize, a stock dividend leaves par value per share the same, reduces retained earnings, and increases paid-in capital. Total stockholders' equity is unchanged. A stock split reduces par value per share and increases number of shares. It does not change the Retained Earnings or Capital Stock account balances. Total stockholders' equity is also unchanged.

B37. No answer required.

C. **Treasury Stock and Earnings per Share**

1. In the Ell Corporation example, Ell purchases 1,000 shares of its own stock at $8.00 a share. What is the par value of Ell stock? $ _____

Additional Stockholders' Equity Transactions and Income Disclosures   265

C1. 5 per share.

C2. 8.00.

C3. No; Yes; Since Ell Corporation intends to hold the stock for a temporary period, it will not cancel it. It will record the purchase in Treasury Stock at cost (which is market value).

C4. No; It is a reduction in stockholders' equity.

C5. 10.00

C6. No.

C7. Cost.

C8. Ell did not dispose of an asset. The $200 in excess of cost is additional paid-in capital.

C9. Paid-in Capital from Treasury Stock Transactions, Common

2. What is the market value on August 1, 1997? $ _____

3. Is par value considered when recording the purchase? _____. Is market value? _____. Explain.
   _____
   _____
   _____
   _____

4. Is the Treasury Stock account an asset? _____. Explain. _____
   _____
   _____
   _____
   _____
   _____

5. What is the market value of Ell stock on October 1? $_____ per share.

6. Do we reduce the Treasury Stock account for the current market value when we issue the 100 shares on October 2? _____

7. What is the basis for the credit of $800?
   _____

8. Since Ell sold the 100 shares at $200 above cost, has Ell Corporation made a gain on disposal? _____
   _____
   _____

9. The account credited for the $200 difference is _____
   _____
   _____.

10. If we prepare a balance sheet, how are the 900 shares still held as treasury stock shown on it? _____
    _____
    _____

266 Chapter 12

C10. We deduct their cost from total paid-in capital and retained earnings.

C11. Their cost of $7,200.

C12. Paid-in Capital from Treasury Stock Transactions if it has a balance. *(See entry of Nov. 1.)* If that account cannot absorb the difference, we use other paid-in excess accounts pertaining to the same stock or Retained Earnings.

C13. No answer required.

C14. arrears

C15. actual

11. At what amount? _____

12. If we reissue treasury stock below cost, what account or accounts absorb the difference? _____

13. Book value is not a very meaningful concept because it does not reflect asset market values. To determine book value per common share, we deduct the liquidation claims of preferred stock from total stockholders' equity. We divide the remainder, book value of assets assigned to common stock, by the number of common shares outstanding.

14. Included in liquidation claims of preferred stock are the current dividend and any dividends in _____ if preferred stock is cumulative.

15. Note that we compute book value per share by dividing the stockholders' equity by the _____ (*actual/weighted average*) number of shares outstanding.

D. Reporting Income Information

1. Meaningful income information requires that we report certain items separately. They are _____, _____, and _____.

Additional Stockholders' Equity Transactions and Income Disclosures 267

D1. discontinued operations, extraordinary gains and losses, cumulative effect of a change in accounting principle

D2. income from continuing operations

D3. separately

D4. operating income or loss for the period, gain or loss from the disposal of the assets of the discontinued segment

D5. net

D6. 18,000

D7. 12,000

D8. 30,000

D9. 60,000

D10. unusual, infrequent

D11. income tax

2. The best estimate of future period's net income is _____.

3. When management decides to dispose of a segment, we must report the results for that segment _____.

4. There are two elements in the discontinued operations segment: _____ and _____.

5. We show each of these items _____ of income taxes.

6. For Diversified Corporation, income from operations of the discontinued segment net of income taxes was $ _____.

7. Taxes on the discontinued segment's income were $ _____.

8. Thus, income before taxes must have been $ _____.

9. The before tax gain on the disposal of the assets of the discontinued segment was $ _____.

10. Extraordinary items are gains and losses from events that are both _____ and _____ in the environment of the firm.

11. We also show these losses net of _____.

12. Diversified's total hurricane loss before taxes was $ _____.

268 Chapter 12

D12. 130,000

13. The last item shown separately is the _____ _____ .

D13. cumulative effect of a change in accounting principle

14. Diversified change depreciation methods from _____ to _____ .

D14. straight-line, double declining-balance method

15. Double declining-balance method would have shown $ _____ more in depreciation for past years than straight-line.

D15. 200,000

16. Since double-declining depreciation would have shown expense in prior years, the company would have paid _____ (*more/less*) income tax.

D16. less

17. So the change in accounting principle after taxes would have reduced net income by only $ _____ .

D17. 120,000

E. Earnings per Share

1. Many investors consider earnings per share (EPS) to be an important measure of performance. EPS means earnings per share of _____ stock.

E1. common

2. Before computing EPS, we must deduct dividends to _____ from net income to determine net income _____ .

E2. preferred stockholders, available to common stockholders

3. Then EPS equals net income available to common stockholders divided by the weighted average number of _____ _____ .

E3. common shares outstanding during the year

4. In the textbook example for a simple capital structure, net income was $ _____ .

Additional Stockholders' Equity Transactions and Income Disclosures 269

E4. 60,000

5. Dividends on preferred stock were $_____ . So income available to common stockholders was $_____ .

E5. 12,000; 48,000

6. Weighted average common shares were _____ .

E6. 15,000

7. Earnings per share were $ _____ divided by _____ shares equals $ _____ .

E7. 48,000, 15,000, 3.20

8. Because corporations issue securities that holders can exchange for common stock, it is possible that the number of common shares outstanding could increase suddenly. We would expect an increase in the number of shares outstanding to cause EPS to _____ (*increase/decrease*).

E8. decrease

9. Accordingly, *APB Opinion No. 15* requires companies that have outstanding securities that could dilute the EPS figure to report two amounts for EPS. The amount of EPS without considering the potential conversion of such securities is called _____. When the effect of conversion of such securities into additional shares of common stock is included, the figure is called _____ _____.

E9. primary earnings per share; fully diluted earnings per share

10. When the number of shares of common stock outstanding during the year changes, the end-of-year number of shares _____ (*is/is not*) the same as the weighted average.

E10. is not

11. In the textbook example for fully diluted earnings per share, there are two classes of preferred stock. One is a common stock equivalent and the other is not. For fully diluted earnings per share, we assume that the common stock equivalent ____ (*is/is not*) converted.

270   Chapter 12

E11. is

12. This means that there will be _____ (*more/fewer*) shares of common stock outstanding and _____ (*more/less*) income available to common stockholders than if the preferred were not converted.

E12. more, more

13. The fully diluted earnings per share for Sanders is $_____ .

E13. 1.92

14. This is _____ (*more/less*) than the primary earnings per share.

E14. less

F. **Analyzing Information**
Use Coca-Cola and PepsiCo as of December 31, 1994.

1. Which company has more common stock issued? _____
How many shares does it have outstanding? _____

F1. Coca-Cola, 1,707,627,955

2. Which of the companies have treasury stock? _____

F2. Both

3. How many shares of treasury stock does PepsiCo have? _____

F3. 73,200,000

4. Which company has the higher book value per share? _____
Which company has the higher market value per share? _____

F4. PepsiCo, Coca-Cola

5. Which company has the higher dividend yield? _____
What is it? _____

F5. PepsiCo; 1.93%

6. Which company has the higher profit margin? _____
What is it? _____

F6. Coca-Cola; 15.79%

7. Which company has the higher return on assets? _____
What is it? _____

Additional Stockholders' Equity Transactions and Income Disclosures **271**

F7.   Coca-Cola; 19.73%

8. Which company has the higher earnings per share? _____
    What is it? _____

F8.   PepsiCo; $2.18

9. What might explain why Coca-Cola has the higher profit margin and return on assets, but PepsiCo has the higher earnings per share? _____

F9.   PepsiCo has only half as many shares.

10. Which company is probably the more successful financially? _____

F10. Coca-Cola

LEARNING GOALS ACHIEVEMENT TEST

1. (LG 1, 6) Identify where we would classify or include each of the following accounts on the financial statements: paid-in capital, retained earnings, asset accounts, deductions from stockholders' equity, discontinued operations, extraordinary items, or cumulative effect of a change in accounting principle?

    a. Common Stock.. *Paid-in Capital*
    b. Preferred Stock .... *Paid-in Capital*
    c. Common Stock Subscribed............................... *Paid-in Capital*
    d. Subscriptions Receivable--Common................. *asset*
    e. Gain on the sale of assets of a discontinued segment *Discontinued Operations*
    f. Paid-in Capital--Donations................................ *Paid-in Cap*
    g. Loss from an earthquake.................................. *extraordinary item*
    h. Treasury Stock... *Deductions from Stockholders*
    i. Prior period adjustment .... *retained earnings*
    j. Stock Dividend to Be Issued............................. *Paid-in Cap*
    k. Dividends .... *Retain earnings*
    l. Effect on income of change from straight-line to double declining-balance depreciation..................... *Cummulative effect*
    m. Retained Earnings.. *Retained earnings*

272   Chapter 12

2. (LG 2-4) Vista Corporation had the following data relative to its capital structure on January 1, 1997:

Preferred stock, 8%, $50 par value, 100,000 shares authorized and outstanding	$5,000,000
Paid-in capital-excess over par, preferred	1,000,000
Common stock, $2 par value, 5,000,000 shares authorized, 1,000,000 shares issued	2,000,000
Paid-in capital-excess over par, common	500,000
Retained earnings	3,500,000
Treasury stock, 10,000 shares	100,000

Required:
(1) Prepare a stockholders' equity section as of January 1, 1997.

VISTA CORPORATION

PAID IN CAPITAL		
CAPITAL STOCK:		
Preferred Stock, 8%, $50 par value	5,000,000	
Common Stock, 2 par	2,000,000	
Total Capital Stock:		7,000,000
ADDITIONAL PAID-IN CAPITAL:		
Paid-in Cap-Excess over par, preferred	1,000,000	
Paid-in Cap-Excess over par, common	500,000	
Total additional Paid-in Cap		1,500,000
Total Paid-in Capital		8,500,000
Retained Earnings	3,500,000	
Total Paid-in Cap + Retained Earnings		12,000,000
Deduct Cost of Treasury Stock	100,000	
Total Stockholder's Equity		11,900,000

(2) On March 15, 1997, the directors vote to declare a total quarterly dividend of $760,000. Show computations for this dividend under each of the following possible independent situations. Do not make the entries, but compute the amounts payable to each class of stock.

a. The preferred stock is cumulative with no dividends in arrears.

Dividends Payable - Preferred	100,000	
Remainder to Common		660,000

b. The preferred stock is cumulative with dividends in arrears for 1996.

Dividends Payable - Preferred	500,000	
Remainder to Common		260,000

3. (LG 3) Assume that the Iowa Corporation declared a 10% stock dividend to common on March 15, 1997. The market value of common stock is $20 a share, and the par value is $2 per share. There are 200,000 shares outstanding. Record, in general journal form, the declaration of the dividend.

GENERAL JOURNAL

1997

Date		Accounts and Explanations	PR	Debit	Credit
Mar	15	Stock Dividend - Common		400,000	
		Stock Dividends to be Issued - Com			40,000
		Paid-in Excess over Par - Common			360,000

1997

May 10   Treasury Stock   200,000
           Cash   200,000

Jul 18   Cash   115,000
           Treasury Stock   100,000
           Pd in Cap

Additional Stockholders' Equity Transactions and Income Disclosures   275

4. (LG 4) Assume that Danburg Corporation purchased 10,000 shares of its common stock on the stock exchange at $20 per share on May 10, 1997. On July 18, 1997, the company resold 5,000 of these shares at $23 per share. Record all these transactions.

GENERAL JOURNAL

1997

Date		Accounts and Explanations	PR	Debit	Credit
MAY	10	TREASURY STOCK-COMMON		200,000	
		CASH			200,000
Jul	18	Cash		115,000	
		TREASURY STOCK-COMMON			100,000
		Paid in Cap-Excess over Par-Com			15,000

5. (LG 7) Assume that Vista Corporation's preferred stock (Question 2, part 2a) is convertible into 500,000 shares of common stock, but is not a common stock equivalent. If 1997's net income was $1,250,000, calculate the primary and fully diluted earnings per share.

$$\frac{850,000}{990,000} = \$.86$$

$$\frac{1,250,000}{1,490,000} = \$.84$$

ANSWERS TO LEARNING GOALS ACHIEVEMENT TEST

1.
   a. Paid-in capital
   b. Paid-in capital
   c. Paid-in capital
   d. Asset
   e. Discontinued operations
   f. Paid-in capital
   g. Extraordinary item
   h. Deduction from stockholders' equity
   i. Adjustment to beginning balance in retained earnings
   j. Paid-in capital
   k. Deduction from retained earnings
   l. Cumulative effect of change in accounting principle
   m. Retained earnings

2. (1)

VISTA CORPORATION
PARTIAL BALANCE SHEET
JANUARY 1, 1997

Stockholders' Equity

Paid-in capital
  Capital stock:
    Preferred stock, 8%, $50 par value,
      100,000 shares authorized and issued........ $5,000,000
    Common stock, $2 par value, 5,000,000
      shares authorized, 1,000,000 shares
      issued, 990,000 shares outstanding............. 2,000,000
        Total capital stock... $ 7,000,000
  Additional paid-in capital:
    Paid-in capital-excess over par, preferred........ $1,000,000
    Paid-in capital-excess over par, common.......... 500,000
      Total additional paid-in capital....................... 1,500,000
      Total paid-in capital....................................... $ 8,500,000
Retained Earnings... 3,500,000
  Total paid-in capital and retained earnings.......... $12,000,000
Deduct: Cost of treasury stock (10,000 shares)........ 100,000
Total stockholders' equity $11,900,000

(2)

a.

	Preferred	Common
First quarter to preferred (1/4 x 0.08 x $5,000,000)..................................	$100,000	
Remainder to common...		$660,000
Totals..	$100,000	$660,000

b.

	Preferred	Common
1996 arrears (8% x $5,000,000)............................	$400,000	
First quarter 1997 (1/4 x 8% x $5,000,000)........	100,000	
Remainder to common..		$260,000
Totals...	$500,000	$260,000

3.

GENERAL JOURNAL

Date	Accounts and Explanations	PR	Debit	Credit
1997 Mar. 15	Retained Earnings		400,000	
	Stock Dividend to Be Issued, Common			40,000
	Paid-in Capital-Excess Over Par Value, Common			360,000
	To record declaration of 10% stock dividend to common.			

4.

GENERAL JOURNAL

Date	Accounts and Explanations	PR	Debit	Credit
1997 May 10	Treasury Stock		200,000	
	Cash			200,000
	Purchase of 10,000 shares of common stock at $20.			
Jul. 18	Cash		115,000	
	Treasury Stock			100,000
	Paid-in Capital from Treasury Stock Transactions, Common			15,000
	Reissuance of 5,000 shares at $23.			

5.
Net Income...	$1,250,000
Deduct: Annual preferred dividends	400,000
Net income available to common stockholders	$ 850,000

Primary earnings per share = $850,000 ÷ 990,000 = $0.86

Actual shares of common stock outstanding 990,000
Add: Additional common issuable 500,000
Adjusted shares outstanding 1,490,000

Fully diluted earnings per share = $1,250,000 ÷ 1,490,000 = $0.84

Note that since we assume the preferred stock was converted, there would be no dividends on preferred stock.

Chapter 13

Long-term Liabilities

EXPLANATION OF MAJOR CONCEPTS

Bonds Payable LG 1, 2

A bond has several features which are important to understand:

- The face value is the amount which the borrower will pay back at maturity.
- The stated interest rate is the rate that we multiply by the face value to determine the cash interest payments.
- The maturity date is the date when the borrower must repay the face value, and the term is the time to maturity.
- The interest payment dates determine when the borrower makes the cash interest payments.

The issuance of bonds by a corporation creates a long-term liability. Accounting for bonds differs from the accounting for capital stock in three ways:

- The money received is borrowed, not invested.
- There is a legal obligation to pay interest periodically. Unlike payment of dividends, payment of bond interest is not a matter for the directors to decide. It must be done. Also, interest is an expense; dividends are not.
- The face value of bonds payable is due to be repaid on the maturity date.

Companies use bonds instead of stock to acquire money for several reasons. By the use of bonds, a source of money is available that is not available with stock. For example, many financial institutions buy bonds because the law restricts the amount of stock they may own. Secondly, the issuance of bonds makes use of financial leverage. Third, interest on bonds is deductible for tax purposes, and dividends on stock are not.

Issuance of Bonds LG 3

The issue price of a bond is the sum of two separate elements:

- The present value of the face amount that the issuer will repay to the bond purchaser at maturity.
- The present value of interest payments that the issuer will pay periodically.

We compute the two present values using table factors from the compound interest tables for the present value of an amount (the face value) and the present value of an annuity (the interest) respectively.

If the market interest rate is exactly equal to the stated interest rate on the bonds, this computation will give an amount exactly equal to the face value. In other words, when the market rate and the stated (face) rate are equal the bonds will sell at face value. The entry would debit Cash and credit Bonds Payable.

Corporations often issue bonds at a premium (more than face value) or at a discount (less than face value). The reason for a premium is that the stated rate of interest carried on the bond is higher than the market rate. Because the bond interest rate is higher than the market rate, bond buyers (lenders) bid against each other to get the opportunity to earn this better-than-normal interest. This will force the price of the bond up above face value. On the other hand, if bonds carry a rate of interest that is less than the market rate, the bond buyers (lenders) will refuse to pay face value for the bond, forcing the price down below face value. The compound interest computation determines the exact price--whether above or below face value. It is the price that will bring to the buyers, in true interest, exactly what they believe the correct rate to be. Regardless of the issue price of the bonds, we compute the cash interest with the stated rate on face value. Most corporate bonds pay interest twice a year.

The calculation of the issue price for a $1,000, 10 year, 12% bond with interest payable semi-annually for which the market rate of interest is 11% is as follows:

```
Present value of face     = $1,000 x 0.342729 ..........................  $   342.73
Present value of interest = $60 x 11.950382 ........................       717.02
Actual price of 12% bond issued to yield 11% .......................   $1,059.75
```

The issue price of the bond is the sum of its two elements, in this case, $1,059.75.

Amortization of Premium and Discount LG 4, 5

If an investor buys one $1,000 face value, ten-year, 12% bond at 105 (We rounded this off from the price calculated above to simplify the illustration.), that investor is paying a premium. Since 105 means 105% of face value, the investor will pay 5% (or $50) more than the borrower will repay ten years later. The investor pays in (lends) $1,050 to the corporation. At the end of ten years, the corporation must repay only the face value ($1,000). The $50 premium is not a revenue, because a corporation doesn't earn money by borrowing. Instead it is a reduction in interest expense. (Remember that the investor paid a premium because the stated bond interest rate is higher than the market rate.) It would be contrary to the matching principle to record this $50 reduction in interest expense in any single year. We should spread it across the ten-year life of the bond. Accordingly, each time the corporation records interest expense, it *amortizes* a portion of the premium adjusting the interest expense. Under the straight-line method, we find this portion by dividing the premium, $50, by the number of semiannual interest payments, 20, or $2.50 per payment. The entry to record a semiannual interest payment on the bond would be:

Interest Expense	$57.50	
Premium on Bonds Payable...	2.50	
Cash ($1,000 x 0.12 x 1/2)..................................		60.00

In this way, we divide the interest reduction into an equal amount for each year of the life of the bonds. This method of amortization is the straight-line method. It works in the same way that straight-line depreciation works.

Suppose that they issued the $1,000 bond at 97. This means that the corporation receives only $970 but must repay $1,000 at the end of ten years. The additional $30 that it pays back is, in effect, additional interest expense. Again, it would be wrong to record this extra interest expense against a single year. The semiannual entry to record the interest should include the amortization of a proportionate amount of the discount. We can find the amount of the amortization by dividing the discount, $30, by the number of interest payments in the life of the bonds, 20, or $1.50 per six-month period.

Interest Expense	61.50	
Discount on Bonds Payable...................................		1.50
Cash ($1,000 x 0.12 x 1/2)..................................		60.00

Note in both cases we determined the amount of cash using the face amount of the bond, $1,000, and the stated interest rate, 12%, for one-half year. Also, note that when we reach the maturity date of the bonds, the amortization process has brought the premium or discount account to a zero balance.

To understand the concept of amortization, first concentrate on the straight-line method of amortization. A theoretically more correct way to compute bond interest expense and amortization is called the effective interest method of amortization. The effective interest method is very simple to use if you remember these points:

- The market rate of interest that determined the issue price becomes the *effective interest rate* for the bonds. We use the rate for every six-month period in the life of the bonds.
- We multiply this *effective interest rate* by the *carrying value* of the bonds to get the amount of interest expense for a period of time.
- We calculate the cash interest paid using the face value of the bonds and the stated interest rate.
- The difference between the interest expense and the cash interest paid gives the amount of amortization for a period of time.
- The carrying value of the bonds changes each six months by the deduction of the amount of premium amortized or the addition of the amount of discount amortized.

Go back to the previous examples. A $1,000 bond bought at 105 has a beginning carrying value of $1,050 = (face value + premium). Remember it was a 12% bond, while the true market rate of interest is 11%. The semiannual interest payment is $1,000 x 0.12 x 1/2 = $60. (This is really 6% each six months.) To compute the interest expense and premium amortization for the first six months, use the carrying value times the market rate or:

Interest expense = $1,050 × 0.11 × 1/2 = $57.75.
(*Note: we use the market interest rate to compute interest expense.*)

Interest paid = $1,000 × 0.12 × 1/2 = $60.
(*Note: we use the stated interest rate to compute interest paid.*)

Amortization of premium = Interest paid - Interest expense.
$2.25 = $60 - $57.75.

The entry to record the first interest period's interest expense is then:

Interest Expense	57.75	
Premium of Bonds Payable	2.25	
Cash		60.00

The carrying value for the next six-month period decreases to:

$1,050.00 - $2.25 = $1,047.75.

The interest expense for the second six-month period is:

$1,047.75 × 0.11 × 1/2 = $57.63.

The amortization of premium for the second six-month period is:

$60 - $57.63 = $2.37.

The entry to record the second interest period's interest expense is:

Interest Expense	57.63	
Premium of Bonds Payable	2.37	
Cash		60.00

The total amortization for the first year is $4.62 = ($2.25 + $2.37). Under the straight-line method, it was $5. In each of the remaining nine years, the straight-line amortization will continue to be $5. The effective interest method amortization will increase. In later years, it will be greater than the straight-line amount, but the total amount amortized in ten years will be the same.

Bonds Issued Between Interest Dates   LG 6

We pay bond interest at specified dates each six months--say, for example, April 1 and October 1. The interest paid to each bondholder on those dates is for a full six months.

A bondholder who has owned a bond for only two months before an interest date will still receive a check for six months' interest. (Otherwise, issuers of bonds would have the problem of making payments of interest for partial periods. This would be too expensive, even if it were possible.) To compensate for payments that are greater than interest actually earned, buyers of bonds must buy the interest that has accrued since the last interest date. In the example just used, a bondholder who bought a bond on August 1 must buy four months of accrued interest (April, May, June, and July). On October 1, that bondholder will receive a check for six months' interest, the period April 1 to October 1. The buyer held the bond for only two months (August and September). The check represents interest revenue for those two months plus a refund of the accrued interest for the previous four months that was bought. We follow this practice of buying interest accrued since the last interest date in all cases. We use it when a company issues bonds between interest dates. We also use it is when bondholders sell bonds to each other on the bond market.

Shortened Amortization Periods

When we do not issue a bond issue on the authorization date, the actual life of the bonds will be less than the authorized life. A corporation may be authorized to issue twenty-year bonds. The twenty-year term starts to run at the date of authorization. Assume the company does not issue the bonds (or at least part of them) for a year after authorization. Since these bonds will have only nineteen years of life remaining when issued, we amortize any premium or discount over nineteen years instead of twenty. A good way to compute straight-line amortization is to convert the remaining life into months and determine the amount of amortization per month. Thus,

$$\frac{\text{Premium or Discount}}{\text{19 years}} = \frac{\text{Premium or Discount}}{\text{228 months}} = \text{Monthly amortization}$$

Retirement of Bonds LG 6

When we retire a bond at maturity, the accounting is straightforward. We will have completely amortized the premium or discount. The entry would be a debit to the Bonds Payable account for the face value and a credit to Cash. If we retire a bond issue or part of a bond issue before maturity, we remove the appropriate portion of the Bonds Payable and the same proportion of the Discount or Premium of Bonds. If the cash we pay out is not the same as the carrying value, we experience a gain or loss on the early retirement of the bonds. Bonds are sometimes also retired by conversion into another security of the issuing company.

Mortgage Notes Payable LG 7

Corporations use several other types of long-term liabilities. One is the mortgage note. This is a long-term note with an assignment of a security interest in property. We usually pay mortgages in equal installments. Each installment is part interest and part

284　Chapter 13

principal. Since each payment reduces the outstanding principal, the portion of each payment that is interest goes down each time.

Analyzing Information　LG 8

A statement user must assess whether the company will be able to pay its debt obligations. The notes to the financial statements contain important information. Questions the user might ask include:

- Is the level of total debt manageable?
- Can the company meet interest and principal payments?
- If the company needs additional financing would you recommend investing?

GUIDED STUDY OF THIS CHAPTER

A. Bonds Payable

1. Bonds are a certificate of debt that may not be due for _____ .

A1.　many years

2. Therefore, we show bonds payable, as _____ on the balance sheet.

A2.　long-term liabilities

3. Bonds carry provisions for interest. Interest is commonly paid _____ .

A3.　semiannually (or each six months)

4. A contract between the bondholders and the company is called the bond _____ .

A4.　indenture

5. Before a corporation sells a bond issue, it must obtain approval of the _____ .

A5.　stockholders

6. The denomination of a bond (or amount to be repaid when due) is the _____ value.

A6.　face

7. Cash interest paid is a percent of _____ value.

A7.　face

8. Bonds issued for an amount of money equal to _____ are said to be issued at 100 or at par.

Long-term Liabilities   285

A8. face value

A9. premium

A10. Interest Expense

A11. 200,000

A12. 9, 18,000

A13. November 1, 1997, six, 9,000

A14. May 1, 1998

A15. accrued interest

A16. 12,000

B1. different

B2. lower

9. Bonds issued for more than face value are issued at a _____ .

10. We debit the cost of bond interest to an expense account called _____ .

11. In the Amerson Corporation (bonds issued at face value), the face value of the bonds issued is $ _____ .

12. The interest rate of _____ % means that Amerson Company must pay interest of $ _____ for every 12 months.

13. The first interest payment date is _____ at which time we debit Interest Expense for _____ months of interest = $ _____ .

14. We must prepare financial statements on December 31, 1997, but the next interest payment is not due until _____ .

15. On December 31, 1997, we must make an adjusting entry to record _____ .

16. This makes the total of Interest Expense for the year 1997 $ _____ .

B. Bonds Issued at a Premium or Discount

1. Bonds sell at a premium or discount because the stated interest rate is _____ than the market rate on bonds of similar risk.

2. If the market rate is higher than the stated rate, the issue price of the bonds will be _____ than par.

3. These bonds will sell at a _____ .

286   Chapter 13

B3. discount

4. The issue price of bonds is the sum of the present value of (1) _____ and (2) _____ .

B4. the face value, the interest payments

5. In the textbook example, the company issued $100,000 in five-year 12% bonds at a price to yield _____ %.

B5. 10

6. The present value of the face amount of the bonds was $ _____ .

B6. 61,400

7. The present value of the 10 semiannual interest payments of $ _____ each was $ _____ .

B7. 6,000, 46,332

8. The total of the two present values is equal to the issue price of the bonds. This is $ _____ .

B8. 107,732

9. The first example, Mankato Corporation shows bonds issued at a premium of $ _____ .

B9. 7,732

10. The Mankato Corporation bonds mature in _____ years.

B10. ten

11. Using straight-line amortization, the amount of premium amortized each interest date is $7,732 ÷ 10 = $ _____ .

B11. 773

12. So the straight-line amortization will change expense by $ _____ (rounded).

B12. 773

13. The premium amortization will _____ (*reduce/increase*) 1997 interest expense.

B13. reduce

14. The amount of interest paid by Mankato in 1997 is $ _____ .

B14. 6,000

15. The amortization of premium causes interest expense to be reduced by $773 so that the expense is $ _____ .

Long-term Liabilities 287

B15. 5,227

16. In 1997 Mankato recorded only one-half year's interest expense. How much will they pay in 1998? $ _____ . How much is interest expense in 1998? $ _____ .

B16. 12,000; 10,454

17. Next use the effective interest method to amortize the premium on bonds. The bonds were sold to yield an effective annual interest rate of _____ %.

B17. 10

18. This is the equivalent of _____ % semiannually.

B18. 5

19. Interest expense for the last six months of 1997 is $107,732 x 0.05 = $ _____ .

B19. 5,387

20. Note that we multiplied the _____ _____ of $107,732 by one-half the annual effective interest rate to determine interest expense.

B20. carrying value (face value plus premium)

21. But the amount of interest paid in cash is $ _____ multiplied by one-half the annual stated rate or _____ %.

B21. 100,000, 6

22. Compute it:

B22. $100,000 x 0.06 = $6,000.

23. Now compute the amount of amortization for 1997:

B23. Paid.................... $6,000
      Expense.............. 5,387
      Amortization....... $ 613

24. Compute carrying value used for the first six months' interest computation in 1998:

288   Chapter 13

B24. Old carrying value $107,732
     - Amortization   613
     New value $107,119

25. Use it to compute interest expense for the first six months of 1998:

B25. $107,119 x 0.05 = $5,356.

26. Interest expense in the second six-month period is _____ (*greater/smaller*) than in the first period.

B26. smaller

27. Will it continue to become smaller each six-month period hereafter? _____. Why or why not? _____

B27. Yes; Because we multiply a constant interest rate (5%) by a decreasing carrying value. *See Exhibit 13-5.*

28. Then the amortization will become _____ (*larger/smaller*) each six-month period.

B28. larger (*The interest expense is getting smaller. So the difference between expense and cash increases.*)

29. In the next example (Hastings Corp.), the interest paid on the bonds is at the rate of _____ %.

B29. 12

30. The market rate of interest for this company's bond is _____ %.

B30. 14

31. Since the stated rate on the bonds is lower than the market rate, the bond buyers will compensate for the difference by paying a price resulting in a _____ (*premium/discount*).

B31. discount

32. The carrying value of the Hastings Corporation bonds immediately after issue is $_____ .

B32. 92,944

33. To compute amortization of discount for a six-month period by the straight-line method, we would divide the discount by _____ interest periods.

Long-term Liabilities 289

B33. ten (2 interest payments for each of 5 years)

34. The result is $7,056 ÷ 10 = $_____ .

B34. 706

35. The interest paid each six months is
$_____ x _____ x _____ = $_____ .

B35. 100,000, 0.12, 1/2, 6,000

36. Compute interest expense for the last half of 1997 by straight-line: _____

B36. Interest paid. $6,000
     + Discount amort.   706
     Expense $6,706

37. So discount amortization _____ (*increases/decreases*) interest expense.

B37. increases

38. The Hastings example is for $_____ in bonds issued at a discount of $_____ . This would make the carrying value $_____ .

B38. 100,000, 7,056; 92,944

39. The interest expense for the last six months of 1997 computed by the effective interest method is $_____ x _____ = $_____ .

B39. 92,944, 0.07, 6,506

40. Under the effective interest method of amortization, the amount of cash interest paid in this period is $_____ .

B40. 6,000

41. Amortization of discount is $_____ - $_____ = $_____ .

B41. 6,506, 6,000, 506

42. The new carrying value for computing interest expense in the first period of 1998 is $_____ .

B42. 93,450

43. And the interest expense for the first half of 1998 is $_____ x _____ = $_____ .

B43. 93,450, 0.07, 6,542

44. Is this greater or less than the interest for the first six-month period? _____

290 Chapter 13

B44. Greater.

45. Will it continue to increase each six-month period? _____. Why or why not?
_____
_____
_____

B45. Yes; Because we are multiplying a constant rate of interest (7%) by an increasing carrying value. *See Exhibit 13-9.*

46. Will the amortization of discount also increase? _____

B46. Yes.

47. Look at Exhibits 13-6 and 13-10. Note in both premium and discount situations the amount of amortization under the straight-line method is the same each period. In Exhibit 13-6 the amount of amortization of premium under the effective interest method _____ (*increases/decreases*) with time.

B47. increases

48. In Exhibit 13-10 the amount of amortization of discount under the effective interest method _____ (*increases/decreases*) as time passes.

B48. increases

49. Does this indicate that amortization of both premium and discount increases interest expense? _____

B49. No. (*Look at the lines for "Measured Bond Interest Expense" in Exhibits 136 and 13-10.*)

50. Go back and look at the examples we used. In all cases, amortization of premium _____ interest expense, and amortization of discount _____ it. Don't memorize this. Keep studying these examples until you understand why the above is true.

B50. decreases, increases

C. **Other Bond Topics**

1. When we issue bonds between interest dates, the issuer collects the amount of cash interest which has accrued since the last interest date. In the TennTech example, this was $ _____ .

Long-term Liabilities 291

C1. 2,000

2. This $2,000 is the interest from _____ to _____, the date of issue.

C2. June 30, 1997, September 1, 1997

3. TennTech issued the bonds at a price of $_____, plus the accrued interest of $_____ , for a total cash received of $_____.

C3. 100,000, 2,000, 102,000

4. On the first interest payment date, it will pay _____ months interest. This includes the $2,000 of accrued interest and the interest expense for _____ months.

C4. six, four

5. Why does the company not just pay four months interest the first time? _____
_____
_____
_____
_____

C5. Because the bond contract calls for six months interest to be paid twice each year.

6. When retiring a bond issued at a premium before maturity, we must remove both the Bonds Payable and the _____
_____.

C6. Premium on Bonds Payable

7. In the textbook example, the bonds payable had a face value of $_____ and the premium account had a balance of $_____ on the date of retirement.

C7. 100,000, 3,600

8. Thus, the carrying value on the date of retirement was $_____.

C8. 103,600

9. How much did the company pay to retire the bonds? _____

C9. 104,000

10. Since it paid more to retire the bonds than its records showed it owed, it experienced a _____ (*gain/loss*) on retirement.

292   Chapter 13

C10. loss

C11. the lender had given an assignment of interest in property.

C12. interest, liability balance

C13. 996; 439

C14. The liability balance is decreasing. And a constant percent of a decreasing amount decreases.

D1. 87.6

D2. High.

D3. No.

D4. Yes.

11. Long-term debt sometimes takes the form of a mortgage note payable. This means that _____ _____ _____ .

12. Exhibit 13-12 shows a partial amortization table for a mortgage. We allocate a portion of each monthly payment to _____ and a portion to _____ .

13. For the March 1 payment, how much was interest? $_____ . And how much reduced the liability balance? $_____ .

14. Each month the portion allocated to interest goes down. Why? _____ _____ _____ _____

D. Analyzing Information

1. Looking at L.A. Gear, we see that liabilities are _____ % of total equities.

2. Is this a high or low percentage? _____

3. In Chapters 1 and 2 we saw that revenues for L.A. Gear had declined significantly. Will this give the company large amounts of cash to pay interest and principal? _____

4. In addition to interest payments, in 1996 L.A. Gear must begin to redeem preferred shares. Will this require additional cash? _____

5. Will issuing additional debt to raise cash be a possibility? _____ Why or why not? _____ _____ _____

Long-term Liabilities 293

D5. No. They already have a large amount of debt.

6. Will issuing stock be a possibility? ____ Why or why not? _____

D7. No. The stock price is only $2.00 per share and there are decreasing revenues.

LEARNING GOALS ACHIEVEMENT TEST

1. (LG 1) What are at least three major differences between bonds payable and capital stock?

   NOT represent ownership
   NO Dividends
   Interest

2. (LG 3, 5) Brazoria Corporation issued $100,000 of 12% bonds at a price to yield 14% on April 1, 1997. The bonds mature in ten years. Interest is payable April 1 and October 1.

   Simianually 7% 20 periods — Discount

   a. Show a general journal entry for the issuance. In your explanation, show the computation of the issue price.

GENERAL JOURNAL

1997

Date		Accounts and Explanations	PR	Debit	Credit
April	1	Cash		89,364	
		Disc on Bonds Payable		10,636	
		Bonds Payable			100,000

Present value of face amount of $100,000
20 periods at a mkt rate of 7% = .258   = 25,800
Present value of 20 interest payments of 6,000   = +63,564
7% 10.594
                                                   $89,364

294 Chapter 13

b. Show a general journal entry for payment of interest and straight-line amortization on October 1, 1997.

GENERAL JOURNAL   1997

Date	Accounts and Explanations	PR	Debit	Credit
OCT 1	Interest expense		5468	
	Disc on Bonds Payable			532
	Cash			6000

c. Show a general journal entry for payment of interest and amortization by the effective interest method on October 1, 1997.

GENERAL JOURNAL

Date	Accounts and Explanations	PR	Debit	Credit

3. (LG 6) On April 1, 1999, Brazoria Corporation (Problem 2) made the regular interest payment and straight-line amortization entry on its bonds. It then retired all the bonds by purchase on the market for $90,000 cash. Show a general journal entry for the early retirement.

```
         DISC ON Bonds Payable
         10,636  |  532    ① 10/97
                 |  532    ② 4/98
                 |  532    ③ 10/98
                 |  532    ④ 4/99
                 |  532    ⑤ 10/99
         ─────────
         7979
```

GENERAL JOURNAL

Date	Accounts and Explanations	PR	Debit	Credit
	Bonds Payable		100,000	
	Disc on Bonds Payable			7,979
	Cash			90,000
	Gain on Retirement			2,021
			100,000	100,000

4. (LG 6) Assume that instead of issuing the bonds on April 1, 1997, as was done in Problem 2, they were issued for the same price on June 1, 1997. Record the entry in the general journal.

GENERAL JOURNAL

1997

Date	Accounts and Explanations	PR	Debit	Credit
	Cash		91,406	
	Disc on Bonds Payable		10,594	
	Bonds Payable			100,000
	Interest Payable			2,000
			102,000	102,000

6000 × 2/6 = 2000

Disc 10,594
845

GENERAL JOURNAL

Date	Accounts and Explanations	PR	Debit	Credit

ANSWERS TO LEARNING GOALS ACHIEVEMENT TEST

1. (1) Bonds are debt; preferred stock is owners' equity. (2) Bond interest must be paid each period; preferred stock dividends may be passed (not declared). (3) Bond interest is tax deductible; preferred dividends are not. (4) Bonds have a limited life; preferred stock does not.

2. a.

GENERAL JOURNAL

Date		Accounts and Explanations	PR	Debit	Credit
1997 Apr.	1	Cash Discount on Bonds Payable Bonds Payable Issuance of 10-year, 12% bonds to yield 14% as follows: PV of face: $100,000 x 0.258419 = $25,841.90 PV of interest: $6,000 x 10.594014 = <u>63,564.08</u> Issue price <u>$89,405.98</u>		89,405.98 10,594.02	100,000.00

b.

GENERAL JOURNAL

Date		Accounts and Explanations	PR	Debit	Credit

1997 Oct.	1	Interest Expense
		    Discount on Bonds Payable
		    Cash
		Payment of interest and
		amortization of discount.
		Amortization = $10,594.02 ÷ 20
				6,529.70	529.70
					6,000.00

c.

GENERAL JOURNAL

Date		Accounts and Explanations	PR	Debit	Credit

1997 Oct.	1	Interest Expense
		    Discount on Bonds Payable
		    Cash
		Payment of interest and
		amortization of discount.
		Interest = $89,405.98 x 0.07
				6,258.42	258.42
					6,000.00

3.

GENERAL JOURNAL

Date		Accounts and Explanations	PR	Debit	Credit

1999 Apr.	1	Bonds Payable
		    Discount on Bonds Payable
		    Gain on Retirement of Bonds
		    Cash
		To retire bonds.
				100,000.00	8,475.22
					1,524.78
					90,000.00

4.

GENERAL JOURNAL

Date		Accounts and Explanations	PR	Debit	Credit

1997 Jun.	1	Cash
		Discount on Bonds Payable
		    Interest Payable
		    Bonds Payable
		Issuance of bonds at
		$89,405.98 plus accrued
		interest.
				91,405.98
				10,594.02
					
					2,000.00
					100,000.00

Chapter 14

INVESTMENTS IN STOCKS AND BONDS

EXPLANATION OF MAJOR CONCEPTS

Short-term Investments in Stocks and Bonds   LG 1-4

A business may invest in bonds of governments or corporations. A business may also invest in common and preferred stocks of other corporations. These bonds and stocks all fall under the term securities. If a security is actively bought and sold on the stock exchanges or through securities dealers, it is a marketable security, meaning simply that we can sell it readily.

Short-term investments are investments that are readily saleable and that management intends to sell within one year. If securities meet both of these requirements, they are current assets. Short-term investments may be in bonds or stocks. Short-term investments may fall under any of the three *FASB Statement No. 115* categories:

- Held-to-Maturity — Debt securities only that will be held to the maturity date.
- Trading — debt and equity securities that are purchased and sold for short-term profits.
- Available-for-Sale — All debt and equity securities not classified as held-to-maturity or trading.

We account for the investment in short-term securities by debiting an investment account for the total cost of the security. We do not use a separate premium or discount account for bond investments. The investment account should indicate the category of the security. Some specific techniques you should note carefully are:

- Interest on bonds accrues. We need end-of-period adjusting entries to recognize interest receivable and interest revenue.
- Dividends on stocks do not accrue. We do not record it on the books of an investor before they receive it. For short-term investments in stocks, we record dividends as revenue when the investor receives the dividends.
- Premium or discount on bonds is part of the bond cost. We do not carry it in a separate premium or discount account.
- We do not amortize bond premiums or discounts on trading securities. We do not know how long they will be held and have no specific time period over which to

300   Chapter 14

- compute amortization. (We amortize bond premiums or discounts on available-for-sale securities that will be held for the long-term.)
- For both trading and available-for-sale securities, we mark the security to market at period end. If we classify the security as trading, we show the unrealized gain or loss on the income statement. If we classify the security as available-for-sale, we report the unrealized gain or loss as a separate component of stockholders' equity.
- When we sell the security, we calculate a realized gain or loss. For trading securities, this gain or loss is the difference between the selling price and the adjusted cost. For available-for-sale securities, the realized gain or loss is the difference between the selling price and the original cost.
- When an investor purchases bonds between interest dates, the investor purchases not only the bonds at their market price but also the accrued interest since the last interest payment date. The next interest payment will include the return of this interest. The accounting parallels the accounting for bonds issued between interest dates studied in Chapter 13.

Long-term Investments in Stocks and Bonds   LG 5-7

If we invest in securities that are not marketable or if the intent of management is to hold them for a long term, the securities are long-term investments.

We account for the investment in long-term securities by debiting the investment account for the total cost of the security. We do not use a separate premium or discount account for bond investments. Some specific techniques you should note carefully are:

- Interest on bonds accrues. We need end-of-period adjusting entries to recognize such accruals and the interest associated with them.
- Dividends on stocks do not accrue. We do not record it on the books of an investor before they receive it.
- Premiums or discounts on bonds are part of the bonds' cost. We do not carry them in a separate premium or discount account.
- We amortize premiums or discounts on investments in bonds classified as held-to-maturity. We use the remaining life from the purchase date to the maturity date as the period over which we compute the amortization. In this textbook, we explain the straight-line method and the effective interest method. The mechanics of amortization calculations exactly parallels those covered in Chapter 13 for bonds payable.
- We value investments in held-to-maturity bonds at amortized cost. We do not record changes in the market value.
- We account for long-term investments in stocks by two different methods.
    - If the investor holds less than 20% of the voting stock of a company, we should use the cost method to account for the investment. Under the cost method, we record the receipt of dividends as revenues. We keep the Investment account at its original cost.
    - If the investor holds 20% or more of the voting stock of a company, we use the equity method to account for the investment. Under the equity method,

Investments in Stocks and Bonds 301

==dividends received by the investor reduces the investment account.== At the end of the period, ==the investor picks up his or her share of the investee's income as revenue and as an increase in the investment account.==

Analyzing Information LG 8

The financial statement user wants to assess the extent and type of investments, past successes in generating investment income, current valuation of the investments, and relative maturity dates. The following questions are important to raise:

- What is the percent of total assets invested in securities?
- What is the mix of trading, available-for-sale, and held-to-maturity investments?
- Has the company been successful in generating additional income from investments?
- How does the current market value and cost of the securities compare?
- Are you comfortable with the range of maturity dates for the investments?
- If equity securities are accounted for on the equity method (a) does significant influence exist and (b) how much of the investor's share of income have they received in cash?

GUIDED STUDY OF THIS CHAPTER

A. FASB Statement No. 115.

1. Overall, the statement requires us to value most investments at _____ on the balance sheet date.

A1. market value

2. One of the reasons for the change to mark-to-market was the financial failure of a number of _____ .

A2. banks

3. *FASB Statement No. 115* applies to both _____ and _____ securities.

A3. debt, equity

4. We classify debt securities only that we will hold to the maturity date as _____ .

A4. held-to-maturity

5. We classify debt and equity securities that we purchase and sell for short-term profits as _____ .

302 Chapter 14

A5. trading securities

6. We classify debt and equity securities that we do not classify as held-to-maturity or trading as _____.

A6. available-for-sale

B. Short-term Investments

1. A security is marketable when we can _____.

B1. readily resell it

2. Whether an investment in a marketable security is a current asset or not depends upon _____ and _____.

B2. its marketability, the intent of management

3. In the Nike, Inc. illustration Nike purchased 1,000 shares of IBM stock at $_____ plus a brokerage fee of $_____.

B3. 120, 1,400

4. They debited the Short-term Investments (Trading Securities) account for $_____.

B4. 121,400 (*the total cost*)

5. A dividend on Dec. 1, 1997, brought in cash of $_____.

B5. 1,000

6. We recorded this with a credit to _____.

B6. Dividend Revenue

7. They sold the IBM stock on Dec. 15, 1997, before IBM had declared another quarterly dividend. Was any accrued dividend sold along with the shares of stock? _____ Explain. _____

B7. No; Dividends do not accrue.

8. They received cash of $_____. This was equal to proceeds from the stock of $_____ less a commission of $_____.

B8. 128,500; 130,000, 1,500

9. This was $_____ more than the cost, so Nike had a _____.

Investments in Stocks and Bonds 303

B9. 7,100, realized gain

10. The dividends earned of $_____ plus the realized gain on disposal of $_____ gave a total earnings of $_____ for holding this stock.

B10. 1,000, 7,100, 8,100

11. The FASB has stated that we should value trading securities on the balance sheet at _____.

B11. market

12. In the chapter illustration, we assume that Nike held _____ common stock and _____ common stock.

B12. Coca-Cola, Wendy's

13. The cost of the Coca-Cola stock was $_____ and the market value was $_____.

B13. 80,000, 86,000

14. Thus, there is an unrealized gain of $_____.

B14. 6,000

15. The Wendy's stock has an unrealized _____ of $_____.

B15. loss, 2,000

16. When we record this we actually change the balances in each Short-term Investment account to its _____ _____.

B16. market value

17. We also record $_____ in an account titled _____ _____.

B17. 4,000, Unrealized Gain on Investments

18. We show the unrealized gain on the _____ because these are trading securities.

B18. income statement

19. When we sold the Coca-Cola stock for $84,000, we compared this to the _____ to determine a _____ loss of $_____.

304 Chapter 14

B19. adjusted cost, realized, 2,000

20. The cost of General Motors Corporation's investment in IBM Corporation bonds includes face value of $_____ minus discount of $ _____ plus brokerage fees of $_____ .

B20. 100,000, 2,000, 500

21. Bond interest is a legal liability of the issuer (IBM Corporation). GM Corporation should record an adjusting entry on December 31, 1997, to accrue interest earned of $_____ in 1997 on the IBM bonds.

B21. 2,000

22. Therefore, when they receive payment on May 1, 1998, the entire credit is not to a revenue account but $2,000 is to _____ .

B22. Interest Receivable

23. The remaining $4,000 of the $6,000 receipt is _____ .

B23. Interest Revenue

24. We do not amortize the discount because the investment is _____ .

B24. short-term

25. At the end of 1997, we adjust the value of the bonds to _____ .

B25. market

26. At the same time we record the decline as an _____ of $ _____ .

B26. unrealized loss, 1,500

27. When GM needed cash and sold the bonds on February 1, 1998, they were sold at a gain of $ _____ .

B27. 500

26. Because GM held the bonds another month since recording the last interest, the cash received for the bonds included _____ .

B26. another month's interest earned.

27. Therefore, GM earned interest for two months in 1997 and for one month in 1998 at $1,000 per month, for a total of $ _____ .

Investments in Stocks and Bonds **305**

B27. 3,000

28. The interest of $3,000 minus the unrealized loss of $1,500 plus the gain on disposal of $500 gives a net return of $_____.

B28. 2,000

29. When securities are classified as available-for-sale, the difference from trading is that the unrealized gain or loss is shown as a _____.

B29. separate component of stockholders' equity

30. Thus in the illustration, we adjust the Short-term Investments (Available-for-Sale) account to _____.

B30. market value

31. We also record the $4,000 net gain in _____.

B31. Unrealized Gain (Loss) on Available-for-Sale Securities

32. On January 10, 1998, when Nike sells the Coca-Cola stock for $84,000, we use the original cost of $_____ to determine the realized gain of $_____.

B32. 80,000, 4,000

33. The Short-term Investments (Available-for-Sale) Coca-Cola Stock has a balance of $_____ and the Unrealized Gain (Loss) on Available-for-Sale Securities has a balance of $_____.

B33. 86,000, 6,000

34. In the sale entry, we must close these balances. The realized gain of $_____ then balances the entry.

B34. 4,000

C. Long-term Investments Among the many types of long-term investments that an entity can hold, Chapter 14 focuses on investments in stocks and bonds.

1. Investment in the stock of another company may be for the purpose of earning dividends. A frequent reason to buy shares of voting stock of another company, however, is to gain _____

306 Chapter 14

C1. control

2. *APB Opinion No. 18* states that a company holding less than _____ % of the voting stock of another firm is not assumed to have significant influence.

C2. 20

3. If a company has less than 20% of the voting stock of another, the _____ _____ method of accounting for the investment should be used.

C3. market value

4. Under the market value method, we follow the accounting discussed for available-for-sale securities.

C4. No answer required.

5. When _____ % or more of the voting stock of a company is owned, ability to influence is presumed. *APB Opinion No. 18* then requires the _____ method of accounting for the investment.

C5. 20; equity

6. In the Nike example, Nike purchased 40% of Shoelace's stock. Now accounting standards suggest that Nike _____ (can/ can't) exercise influence over Shoelace.

C6. can

7. Therefore, Nike must use the _____ method.

C7. equity

8. We view the March 1, 1999, dividend as a reduction of Nike's investment (not as revenue). We credit it to Long-term Investment in Stocks, but why only $8,000 of the $20,000 dividend? _____

C8. Nike only owns 40% of Shoelace's stock and received only 40% of the total dividend.

9. Under the equity method, an investor corporation considers that its investment increases as the retained earnings of the investee increases. When Shoelace earned $100,000 in 1998, how much did its retained earnings increase?
$ _____ .

Investments in Stocks and Bonds 307

C9. 100,000

10. Nike should increase its investment account by _____ % of Shoelace's earnings or by $_____ .

C10. 40, 40,000

11. Is this reported as income in Nike's income statement? _____

C11. Yes.

12. In 1999 Shoelace had a loss of $30,000; Shoelace's retained earnings decreased. How does Nike reflect this loss in its books? _____

C12. By a decrease in Long-term Investment in Stocks and a debit to Equity in Investee Loss.

13. Is Nike's share of the loss (_____ % of $30,000 = $_____) reported in its income statement for 1999? _____

C13. 40, 12,000, Yes.

14. Companies also invest in bonds of other companies. The primary reason for an insurance company to do this on a long-term basis is probably to _____ .

C14. earn bond interest

15. If we purchase bonds as short-term investments, premium or discount _____ (is/is not) amortized.

C15. is not

16. When we purchase bonds for a long-term investment, we classify them as _____ and the premium or discount _____ (is/is not) amortized.

C16. held-to-maturity, is

17. The period used for amortization is the _____ .

C17. remaining life to maturity of the bonds

18. In the textbook example, when Trio Corporation paid $107,732 for $100,000 of Mankato Corporation bonds, there was a _____ (premium/discount) of $_____ .

308 Chapter 14

C18. premium, 7,732

C19. does not

C20. 5

C21. 10, 773 (7,732 ÷ 10)

C22. less

C23. decrease, 773

C23. 100,000

C24. 100,000

C25. 12,000

C26. less

19. The investor _____ (*does/does not*) show the premium in a separate account.

20. Trio will amortize this premium over a period of _____ years.

21. Five years = _____ semiannual periods, so the amount of straight-line amortization per semiannual period is $_____.

22. The amortization of premium on investment recognizes that Trio Corporation will receive $7,732 _____ (*more/less*) at maturity than it paid for the bonds.

23. Therefore, amortization should _____ (*increase/decrease*) Interest Revenue by $_____ per semiannual period.

23. At the date of maturity, the Mankato bonds will be worth exactly $ _____ .

24. So, the amortization entry is reducing the carrying value by $773 for six months. On June 30, 2002, the balance in the Long-term Investments in Bonds account will be $ _____ .

25. The Mankato Corporation bonds carry a stated interest rate of 12%, so the investor receives $_____ per year in interest payments.

26. However, because Trio Corporation paid $7,732 more for the bonds than will be repaid to it, its effective rate of interest is _____ (*more/less*) than 12%.

27. Actually, the amount of premium paid was a result of the true market rate of interest for these bonds. It was _____ %.

Investments in Stocks and Bonds 309

C27. 10

C28. discount

C29. 92,944, 7,056

C30. 5,706 ($7,056 ÷ 10)

C31. more, greater

C32. 92,944, 7

C33. effective (or market)

C34. carrying value

C35. Long-term Investments (Held-to-Maturity) Hastings Bonds

C36. 92,944, 506, 93,450

28. When Trio bought Hastings' bonds (the next example), it purchased the bonds at a _____.

29. Trio paid $_____ for the bonds, giving a discount of $ _____.

30. Since there are _____ years remaining to maturity, each six months it will amortize $ _____ of discount.

31. Since Trio Corporation will receive _____ (more/less) back from Hastings at maturity, Interest Revenue will be _____ than the cash received each interest payment date.

32. If we used the effective interest method to amortize the premium, the first amortization entry will credit Interest Revenue with $6,506 = $ _____ x _____ %.

33. The rate of 7% is one-half (or six months) of the _____ rate of interest.

34. The amount $92,944 is the _____ _____ before the first amortization entry.

35. What account does the amortization amount reduce? _____ _____.

36. The carrying value for computing the next interest earned on June 30, 1998, is $_____ + $_____ = $_____.

D. **Investment in Bonds between Interest Dates**

1. If we purchase a bond investment between interest dates, the investor must purchase the _____ in addition to the bond.

310   Chapter 14

D1.   accrued interest

D2.   No; It is repaid to the investor in the first interest payment.

D3.   Yes.

D4.   Recording procedures are the same. The amortization period is only the remaining life of the bond issue.

D5.   58

D6.   86.21

D7.   86.21, 4, 345

D8.   less

D9.   amortized cost

D10. amortized cost, current market value

2. Is the accrued interest amortized? ____ . Explain. _____

3. Are bonds purchased between interest dates subject to premium or discount? _____

4. What is the difference in amortization procedures when bonds are purchased at a premium or discount between interest dates? _____

5. The Trio Corporation investment in TennTech bonds was made when the TennTech bonds had only _____ months of life until the maturity date.

6. We must amortize the $5,000 premium at the rate of $_____ per month.

7. The amortization on December 31 is $_____ x ____ = $_____

8. Trio Corporation's effective rate of interest is _____ (*more/less*) than the stated rate of 12% carried by the TennTech bonds.

9. We value investments in held-to-maturity bonds at _____ .

10. Since the investor intends to hold the bonds to maturity, the _____ is more relevant than _____ .

11. Therefore, we _____ (*do/do not*) record changes in market value, and we _____ (*do/do not*) record any realized or unrealized gains and losses.

Investments in Stocks and Bonds   311

D11. do not, do not

E1. H & R Block, Inc.

E2. 24.4

E3. 8.5

E4. available-for-sale

E5. in stockholders' equity

E6. 7,014,000, 350,000

E7. It is slightly greater.

E8. Yes. Most of the securities are debt and have a contractual maturity within one year.

E. Analyzing Information

1. In this chapter, we use the financial information from _____ .

2. For 1995, what is the percent of total assets that they have invested in current marketable securities? _____ %

3. What is the percent of total assets invested in noncurrent marketable securities?
   _____ %

4. They classify all of the marketable securities as _____ .

5. H & R Block shows any unrealized gains or losses _____
   _____ .

6. For fiscal 1995, gross realized gains were
   $_____
   and gross realized losses were
   $_____ .

7. How does the market value as of April 30, 1995, compare with the amortized cost?
   _____
   _____

8. Is H & R Block minimizing its exposure to interest rate changes? _____
   Why? _____
   _____
   _____

LEARNING GOALS ACHIEVEMENT TEST

1. (LG 1-5) Fill in the blank spaces in the following statements about investments made by the Newport Corporation:

   a. A purchase of 1,000 shares of Exxon Corporation common stock by Newport Corporation as a use of excess cash would be a __Short-term__ investment if Newport's management intends to sell the stock as soon as it needs the cash.
   b. Newport Corporation would use the __Mkt Value__ method to account for the stock investment.
   c. This means that they would credit the dividends received to the __Div Revenue__ account.
   d. If Newton purchased the stock for short-term profits they would classify it as a __Trading Asset__.
   e. If bonds were bought as a short-term investment, we debit the __costs__ to the Short-term Investments in Bonds account.
   f. The premium or discount is __not__ amortized.
   g. We credit interest received to __Int Rev__.
   h. Valuation of short-term investments held as available-for-sale is at __Mkt__.
   i. Suppose Newport Corporation bought 40,000 shares of Alvino Corporation's 100,000 total shares of common stock as a long-term investment. Newport should account for this investment by the __Equity__ method.
   j. In this case, it should credit dividends received to the __INV__ account.
   k. How should Newport record Alvino's reported net income of $60,000 in 1997? __DR INV   CR Equity in INV Income__
   l. If Exxon stock (bought in item a) has a higher market price at the end of the year than Newport paid for it, what adjustment must be made? __DR. Gain to INV + CR gain to uer au__
   m. If Exxon stock is lower at the end of the year then Newport's cost, what adjustment should be made? __DR unrealized loss to acct. + CR- Decrease the INV to Market__
   n. Is Exxon stock a trading security? __No__
   o. Investments in trading securities should be valued on the balance sheet at __market value__

Investments in Stocks and Bonds 313

2. (LG 6) Raccoon River Corporation is offering $10,000 of ten-year, 16% bonds to the public. Interest is paid semiannually. The current market rate for this type of bond is 14%.

   a. Compute the price that ought to be paid by an investor.

   20 at 7%
   10 000 (.258) = 2580
   800 (10.594) 8475.2
   11,055.20

   b. Assume that the bonds are bought as held-to-maturity on the authorization date of March 1, 1997 at the price calculated in part a. Show the general journal entry on the books of the investor to record the purchase.

   1997
   GENERAL JOURNAL

Date		Accounts and Explanations	PR	Debit	Credit
MAR	1	HTM-BONDS INV		11,055.20	
		Premium on			
		Cash			11,055.20

   c. Show a general journal entry to record the receipt of interest and amortization using the straight-line method on September 1, 1997.

   1997
   GENERAL JOURNAL

Date		Accounts and Explanations	PR	Debit	Credit
Sep	1	Cash		800	
		HTM Bonds			52.76
		Int. Rev			747.24

314 Chapter 14

    d. Show a general journal entry to record the receipt of interest and amortization using the effective interest method on September 1, 1997.

GENERAL JOURNAL

Date	Accounts and Explanations	PR	Debit	Credit

(entry crossed out)

3. (LG 5) Raccoon River Corporation purchased 40,000 shares of Des Moines Corporation common stock at $10 per share on March 1, 1997. Des Moines Corp. has 100,000 shares outstanding.

    a. Show the general journal entry on the books of the investor to record the purchase.

GENERAL JOURNAL — 1997

Date	Accounts and Explanations	PR	Debit	Credit
MAR 1	LTI IN STOCKS		400,000	
	Cash			400,000

Investments in Stocks and Bonds   315

b. Show a general journal entry to record the receipt of its share of $10,000 in dividends paid by Des Moines Corp. on September 1, 1997.

GENERAL JOURNAL
1997

Date		Accounts and Explanations	PR	Debit	Credit
Sep	1	Cash		4,000	
		LT-INV -Stocks			4,000

c. Show a general journal entry to record the recognition of investors share of Des Moines Corp.'s $50,000 in net income on December 31, 1997.

GENERAL JOURNAL
1997

Date		Accounts and Explanations	PR	Debit	Credit
Dec	31	Long Term-Inv.		20,000	
		Equity Income Investment			20,000

4. (LG 3) Assume that your company purchased $10,000 in Skunk Corporation 12% bonds on May 1, 1997, as a short-term investment, at a price of 102 plus accrued interest. The bonds pay interest semi-annually on January 1 and July 1. They are classified as trading.

10,200
600   400

a. Record the purchase in general journal form.

GENERAL JOURNAL
1997

Date		Accounts and Explanations	PR	Debit	Credit
May	1	Short Term Invest Bonds		10,200	
		Int. Receivable		400	10,800
		Cash			10,600

316 Chapter 14

b. Record the receipt of the first semiannual interest on July 1, 1997.

GENERAL JOURNAL

1997

Date		Accounts and Explanations	PR	Debit	Credit
Jul	1	Cash		600	
		Int Rec			400
		Int Rev			200

c. At December 31, 1997, the market value of the bonds were $10,700. Record the adjustment to market.

GENERAL JOURNAL

1997

Date		Accounts and Explanations	PR	Debit	Credit
Dec	31	Short-Term Inv		500	
		unrealized gain			500

5. (LG 4) Goldstein Company purchased three short-term investments in marketable securities in 1997. All three securities are classified as available-for-sale. On December 31, 1997, values were as follows:

	Cost	Market Value
Krypton common stock	$8,000	$7,500
Xenon common stock	6,000	7,000
Neon common stock	6,000	4,700

a. Compute the net amount of unrealized loss or gain on these stocks. Is the unrealized gain or loss shown on the income statement or the balance sheet? Why?

Krypton —(500)   Balance sheet Now
Xenon   1000
Neon   (1300)

        (800)

b. On December 31, 1998, the investment values were:

	Cost	Market Value
Krypton common stock	$8,000	$7,600
Xenon common stock	6,000	7,200
Neon common stock	6,000	5,600

What is the unrealized gain or loss for 1998?

again $1,200

ANSWERS TO LEARNING GOALS ACHIEVEMENT TEST

1.
   a. short-term
   b. market value
   c. Dividends Revenue
   d. trading
   e. cost
   f. not
   g. Interest Revenue
   h. market
   i. equity
   j. Long-term Investment in Stocks
   k. Forty percent ($24,000) should be debited to Long-term Investment in Stocks and credited to Equity in Investee Income
   l. Increase the investments account to market and credit an unrealized gain account.
   m. Decrease the investments account to market and debit an unrealized loss account.
   n. Yes
   o. market

2.
   a. PV of face ($10,000 x 0.258) .... $ 2,580.00
      PV of interest ($800 x 10.594) 8,475.20
      Price to be paid $11,055.20

318 Chapter 14

b.

GENERAL JOURNAL

Date		Accounts and Explanations	PR	Debit	Credit

1997
Mar.
	1	Long-term Investments (Held-to-Maturity) Raccoon River
		    Cash
		    Investment in 16% bonds to yield 14%.
				11,055.20	11,055.20

c.

GENERAL JOURNAL

Date		Accounts and Explanations	PR	Debit	Credit

1997
Sep.
	1	Cash
		    Long-term Investments (Held-to-Maturity) Raccoon River
		    Interest Revenue
		Receipt of interest and amortization with straight-line method.
		($1,055.20 ÷ 20 = $52.76)
				800.00	52.76
					747.24

d.

GENERAL JOURNAL

Date		Accounts and Explanations	PR	Debit	Credit

1997
Sep.
	1	Cash
		    Long-term Investments (Held-to-Maturity) Raccoon River
		    Interest Revenue
		To record interest and amortization with interest method.
		($11,055.20 × 0.07 = $773.86)
				800.00	26.40
					773.86

Investments in Stocks and Bonds 319

3. a.

GENERAL JOURNAL

Date		Accounts and Explanations	PR	Debit	Credit

1997 Mar.	1	Long-term Investment in Stocks-- Des Moines Corp.
		    Cash
		        To record purchase of 40% of stock of Des Moines Corp.
				400,000	400,000

b.

GENERAL JOURNAL

Date		Accounts and Explanations	PR	Debit	Credit

1997 Sep.	1	Cash
		    Long-term Investment in Stock--Des Moines Corp.
		        To record receipt of dividends.
				4,000	4,000

c.

GENERAL JOURNAL

Date		Accounts and Explanations	PR	Debit	Credit

1997 Dec.	31	Long-term Investment in Stock-- Des Moines Corp.
		    Equity in Investee Income
		        To record investor share of investee net income.
				20,000	20,000

4. a.

GENERAL JOURNAL

Date		Accounts and Explanations	PR	Debit	Credit

1997 Apr.	1	Short-term Investment (Trading Securities) Skunk Bonds
		Interest Receivable
		    Cash
		        Purchase of bonds as a short-term investment.
				10,200
				400
					10,600

320 Chapter 14

b.

GENERAL JOURNAL

Date		Accounts and Explanations	PR	Debit	Credit

1997 Jul.	1	Cash
		    Interest Receivable
		    Interest Revenue
		Purchase of bonds as a short-term investment.
				600	400
					200

c.

GENERAL JOURNAL

Date		Accounts and Explanations	PR	Debit	Credit
1997 Dec.	31	Short-term Investment (Trading Securities) Skunk Bonds Unrealized Gain on Investments To revalue trading securities to market value and recognize holding gain.		500	500

5. a. Total cost $20,000
        Total market value end of 1997................... $19,200
        Unrealized loss .... $ 800

We show the unrealized loss as a separate component of stockholders' equity because the investments are available-for-sale securities. If the investment had been a trading security, we would have shown it on the income statement.

   b. Total market value end of 1998................... $20,400
       Total market value end of 1997................... $19,200
       Unrealized gain in 1998............................... $ 1,200

The unrealized gain is $1,200 because the investment account was adjusted at the end of 1997 and an unrealized loss was recognized on the income statement in 1997.

Chapter 15

STATEMENT OF CASH FLOWS

EXPLANATION OF MAJOR CONCEPTS

What the Statement Is   LG 1

The three major financial statements that we have studied up to now do not completely explain where a company received its financial resources and what it did with them. The fourth major financial statement--the statement of cash flows--completes the set of major financial reports by reporting on the flow of cash in and out of the firm. It shows what caused cash to increase and what caused cash to decrease in a given period. Exhibit 15-1 shows how the statement of cash flows fits into the set of financial statements.

The statement of cash flows answers such questions as: why is there a difference between net income and cash from operations, how has the entity financed the purchase of new plant assets, and why has the balance of cash increased or decreased from one balance sheet to the next?

The FASB has specified that the statement of cash flows should explain the change in cash and cash equivalents. Cash includes currency plus demand deposits such as checking accounts. Cash equivalents include highly liquid, short-term investments, such as Treasury Bills and money market funds.

Classification of Cash Flows   LG 2

We classify the cash inflows and outflows into three categories (see Exhibit 15-2):

- *Operating activities* are events that generally involve the producing and selling of goods and the providing of services. We usually report these events on the income statement.
- *Investing activities* are events that include the buying and selling of plant assets, buying and selling securities that are not cash equivalents, and making of loans and collecting the principal.
- *Financing activities* are events that obtain resources from owners or creditors, that pay a return to owners on their investment, or that repay creditors the principal.

Some investing and financing events affect assets and liabilities but do not result in cash flows. We term these *noncash investing* and *financing activities*. The statement of cash flows discloses them in either narrative form or in a supplementary schedule.

322 Chapter 15

Preparation of the Statement LG 3-7, 9

The chapter presents a five-step approach to preparing the statement of cash flows. If you study this closely you will understand the basics of the preparation of the statement of cash flows. The five steps include:

1. *Compute the net change in cash and cash equivalents.*

   List the balances for cash and cash equivalents for the beginning and end of the period. Then determine the difference between the beginning and ending amount. One of the purposes of the statement of cash flows is to explain the change in cash and cash equivalents during a period of time.

2. *Compute the amount of the net cash provided by (used in) operating activities by the direct method.*

   Convert each income statement item from the accrual basis to the cash basis. To do this relate the change in a current balance sheet account to appropriate income statement item. Then add to or subtract the change in the balance sheet item from the income statement item as appropriate. For example, sales go through accounts receivable, so we must combine the change in accounts receivable with the amount of accrual basis sales shown on the income statement. If accounts receivable increased during the year, we collected less accounts receivable than we recognized as sales revenue. Thus, we must subtract the increase in accounts receivable from accrual basis sales to get cash collections from customers. On the other hand, if accounts receivable decreased, we must have collected more cash from customers than we made sales. We add the decrease in accounts receivable to accrual sales to get cash sales. We must make a similar adjustment to each item on the income statement that relates to a current asset or liability on the balance sheet. Exhibit 15-6 summarizes these adjustments. Take some time now to review this exhibit. Also, if a revenue or an expense does not cause a cash flow in the same period, leave that item out of the calculation of net cash from operating activities. For example, depreciation expense is an example of a noncash expense. It does not cause a cash outflow. So, we do not list depreciation expense as an operating activity that causes a cash flow. We will review this step in more detail in the Guided Study section.

3. *Prepare the reconciliation of net income to net cash provided by (used in) operating activities by the indirect method.*

   Reconcile net income to cash provided by operating activities by starting with accrual net income. First, adjust for noncash charges and credits. Second, adjust for changes in operating current assets and operating current liabilities. Step 1 in Exhibit 15-8 summarizes the treatment of noncash charges and credits. Step 2 summarizes the treatment of operating current assets and liabilities. Again spend some time reviewing Exhibit 15-8. The figure below summarizes this computation. We will review this step in more detail in the Guided Study section.

Add	Deduct
Decreases in Current Assets	Increases in Current Assets
Increases in Current Liabilities	Decreases in Current Liabilities

4. *Compute the amount of net cash provided by (used in) investing activities and financing activities.*

    Analyze all of the changes in the remaining balance sheet accounts for the period. These accounts are primarily noncurrent accounts. We must determine the reason for the change in each account and use the change to identify whether the cash flow was for investing or financing activities. For example, if the Automobiles account increased by $8,500, the most likely cause would be the purchase of a new vehicle. Thus, there would be a cash outflow for an investing activity of the purchase an automobile. Or if the Common Stock account increased, the most likely cause would be the issuance of stock, a cash inflow from a financing activity. We also will study this type of analysis in more detail in the Guided Study section.

5. *Prepare the statement of cash flows.*

    Once we have identified all of the cash flows, we use them to prepare the statement of cash flows in proper format. The format of the statement using the direct approach to compute cash provided by (used in) operating activities is as follows:

Increases (Decreases) in Cash and Cash Equivalents
Cash flows from operating activities
    Cash receipts from customers .... $ XXX
    Cash payments to suppliers .... (XXX)
    Cash payments to employees .... (XX)
    Cash payments for *"name of service"* .... (XX)
        list each separately .... (XX)
        Net cash provided by (used in) operating activities .... $XXX
Cash flows from investing activities
    Purchase of *"asset"* .... $(XXX)
    Proceeds from sale of *"asset"* XXX
        Net cash provided by (used by) investing activities   XXX
Cash flows from financing activities
    Proceeds of *"issuance of debt or stock"* .... $XXX
    Dividends paid .... (XX)
        Net cash provided by (used by) financing activities   XXX
Net increase (decrease) in cash and cash equivalents .... $ XX
Cash and cash equivalents at beginning of period   XX
Cash and cash equivalents at end of period .... $ XX

Reconciliation of net income to cash provided by (used in) operating activities
Net income .... $XX
Add: Items providing cash or not requiring cash:
    Depreciation expense .... $XX
    Loss on sale of *asset* XX
    Decreases in *current assets* XX
        list separately XX
    Increases in *current liabilities* XX
        list separately XX
Deduct: Items requiring cash or not providing cash:
    Gain on sales of *asset* .... (XX)
    Increases in *current assets* .... (XX)
        list separately .... (XX)
    Decreases in *current liabilities* .... (XX)
        list separately .... (XX)
        Total adjustments   XX
Net cash provided by (used in) operating activities .... $XX

Supplemental schedule of noncash investing and financing activities
    Security issued directly for purchase of *asset* .... $XX
    list separately   XX
        Total .... $XX

Interpreting Statement of Cash Flows LG 8

Overall, we want to know how successful management has been in generating and investing cash flows. Questions that we might ask are:

- How does accrual basis net income compare with cash basis net income?
- What uses of cash has the management made for investing activities?
- To what extent has cash from operations been sufficient to pay for investments?
- What sources and uses of cash have come from financing activities?

The answers to questions like these will help us more completely analyze the financial results of a company.

Work Sheet Approach (Appendix 15A) LG A1

Chapter 15 describes a simple step-by-step approach to the preparation of the statement. This method will work in the simple cases. However, as noncurrent accounts have additional transactions affecting them, it becomes more difficult to keep track of account changes. Another method shown in Appendix 15A is the work sheet approach. It essentially utilizes the same reasoning as the simple analytical approach, but in a more organized manner. Exhibits A15-1 and A15-2 illustrate the preparation of the work sheet. Follow along on these figures as we review the mechanics.

The work sheet approach begins by setting up a four-column work sheet. The first column is for the beginning balance sheet account balances. We use the second and third columns to reconstruct the transactions that changed the account balances. We use the fourth column for the ending balance sheet account balances. Then divide the work sheet vertically into three parts. The top part lists the debit and credit balance sheet account balances at the beginning and end of the period. The second part lists the income statement account balances for the period, and the third part lists the cash flows as we complete the work sheet.

The first step in the preparation is to enter the beginning and ending balances of the balance sheet accounts in the first and fourth columns, respectively. We do not enter all accounts on the balance sheet. We combine the totals of cash and cash equivalents and enter them as the first debit amount. We then enter the rest of the accounts.

The second step is to enter the balances for the income statement accounts below the balance sheet accounts and in one of the center two columns depending on whether each is a debit or credit balance. Since the debits do not usually equal the credits in the income statement accounts, we must enter a balancing amount in one of the center columns of the income statement section. This amount is net income. Also enter this amount in the opposite column on the Retained Earnings line of the balance sheet area. We must enter the balancing amount twice to maintain the equality of debits and credits. It is also logical to enter it on the Retained Earnings line since in closing entries we close the net income to Retained Earnings. We will use these income statement amounts to compute the cash provided by (used in) operating activities.

Divide the bottom section of the work sheet into four categories for cash flows from operating, investing, financing, and noncash investing and financing activities. As we analyze each change in a balance sheet account and enter in the top section, we enter the cash flow effect in the bottom section. If the balance sheet account relates to an income statement account, combine the balance sheet change with the income statement amount, and enter the net cash flow effect in the operating activities section of cash flows at the bottom. If the transaction required a credit to explain the change in a balance sheet account, it will require a debit in the bottom section to maintain equality of debits and credits. Debits in the cash flow section represent cash inflows. On the other hand, if a transaction required a debit to explain the change in the balance sheet account, we would enter a credit in the bottom half of the work sheet as an outflow of cash.

When we have entered all of the changes in the individual accounts, subtotal the debit and credit columns for the bottom section of the work sheet. These subtotals are the total inflows and outflows of cash. The difference between the two subtotals should be the same as the change in cash and cash equivalents. Place an entry (z) on the first line of the balance sheet accounts to explain the change in that item, and the offsetting debit or credit should cause the subtotals in the bottom section of the work sheet to balance.

GUIDED STUDY OF THIS CHAPTER

A. Purpose and Content of the Statement of Cash Flows

1. The primary purpose of the statement of cash flows is to provide information about cash __Receipts__ and __Payments__.

A1. receipts(inflows), payments(outflows)

2. Cash includes not only currency on hand but also __Demand Deposits__.

A2. cash equivalents

3. Cash equivalents are __short__-term, __highly liquid__ investments that are readily converted into __cash__ and so near their maturity that they are not likely to change __in value__ due to changes in interest rates.

A3. short, highly liquid, known amounts of cash, value

4. We categorize cash receipts and payments by type of activity into __Operating__, __Investing__, and __Financing__ activities.

A4. operating, investing, financing

5. Operating activities include _Producing or delivering goods for sale + providing services_. They generally involve events that we report on the _income statement_.

A5. producing or delivering goods and providing services; income statement

6. Investing activities include buying and selling _plant assets_ and _acquiring + selling securities_ that are not cash equivalents and _lending money + collecting on the principal amounts of these loans_.

A6. plant assets, securities, making loans and collecting them

7. Financing activities include _obtaining resources from owners_ and providing them with a _return on their investment_ and obtaining resources from _creditors_ and repaying _the principal amounts borrowed_.

A7. obtaining resources from owners, return, creditors, principle amounts owed

8. Study Exhibit 15-2 for examples of these types of activities.

A8. No answer required.

9. Some activities affect assets and liabilities but do not result in cash receipts or payments. We call these _noncash investing + financing activities_.

A9. noncash investing and financing activities

B. **Generalized Approach to Preparing the Statement of Cash Flows** Refer to the illustration beginning with the Expo Company financial statements shown in Exhibits 15-10 and 15-11.

1. The first step is to compute the net change in _cash + cash equivalents_.

B1. cash and cash equivalents.

2. On December 31, 1997, Expo's total cash and cash equivalents were $ _23,000_ , and on December 31, 1998, they were $ _76,000_ .

B2. 23,000, 76,000

B3. increased, 53,000

B4. net cash provided by (used in) operating activities by the direct method

B5. accrual, cash

B6. balance sheet, income

B7. No answer required.

B8. 360,000; 180,000, 136,000; decreased, 44,000

B9. more; add; 360,000, 44,000, 404,000

3. Thus, cash and cash equivalents _increased_ (increased/decreased) by $ _53,000_ during 1998.

4. The second step is computing the _amount of net cash provided by (used in) operating activities by the direct method_

5. To do this, we convert each income statement item from the _accrual_ basis to the _cash_ basis.

6. This process involves analyzing the changes in _balance sheet_ accounts that relate to each item on the _income_ statement.

7. Review Exhibit 15-6 for the generalized approach to converting accrual basis items to cash basis items.

8. Sales for 1998 on the accrual basis were $ _360,000_. Accounts receivable on 12/31/97 was $ _180,000_, and on 12/31/98 $ _136,000_. Therefore, accounts receivable _decreased_ (increased/decreased) by $ _44,000_.

9. Accounts receivable decreased because Expo collected _more_ (more/less) from customers than it sold during the year. Thus, we would have to _add_ the decrease in accounts receivable to sales on an accrual basis to get the cash inflow from customers. For Expo the cash inflow from customers would be $ _360,000_ + $ _44,000_ = $ _404,000_.

10. The conversion of cost of goods sold to cash payments to suppliers must take into consideration the change in both _inventory_ and _accounts payable_.

Statement of Cash Flows 329

B10. merchandise inventory, accounts payable

11. Inventory __increased__ during the year by $ __20,000__ . This happened because the company bought __more__ (*more/less*) goods than it sold during the year.

B11. increased, 20,000; more

12. Since Expo bought more inventory than it sold, purchases from suppliers must be __more__ (*more/less*) than cost of goods sold.

B12. more

13. Since accounts payable also relates to payments to suppliers for merchandise, we must consider the change in it. It __decreased__ by $ __10,000__ during the year. For this to happen we must have paid __more__ (*more/less*) to suppliers than we purchased.

B13. decreased, 10,000; more

14. Since it paid out more to suppliers than it bought, we must __add__ the decrease in accounts payable to get cash paid to suppliers.

B14. add

15. Thus, we would calculate the cash payments to suppliers by (adding) the increase in inventory of $ __20,000__ and decrease in accounts payable of $ __10,000__ to cost of goods sold from the income statement of $ __193,000__ to get cash payments to suppliers of $ __223,000__ .

B15. 20,000, 10,000, 193,000 223,000

16. Salaries Expense appeared on the accrual basis income statement as $ __70,000__ . However since the balance in salaries payable changed, the amount actually paid to employees was different than the amount shown as accrual expense.

B16. 70,000

17. On 12/31/97, salaries payable was $ __4,000__ , and on 12/31/98 $ __7,000__ . This increase in the liability would mean that we paid __less__ (*more/less*) to employees than we showed as expense on the accrual basis.

330   Chapter 15

B17. 4,000, 7,000; less

18. Therefore, we must __Subtract__ (*add/subtract*) the increase in salaries payable from(to) the accrual basis expense to get cash paid to employees.

B18. subtract

19. The computation would be salaries expense of $__70,000__ minus the increase in salaries payable of $__3,000__ is equal to cash paid to employees of $__67,000__.

B19. 70,000, 3,000, 67,000

20. Look at rent expense. It involves a prepaid amount. Rent expense on the income statement was $__36,000__. Prepaid rent on 12/31/97 was $__18,000__ and on 12/31/98 $__9,000__.

B20. 36,000; 18,000, 9,000

21. Since prepaid rent decreased, the company must have paid out ~~more~~ __less__ (*more/less*) cash for rent during the year than it showed as expense.

B21. less

22. Thus, to convert rent expense on the accrual basis to rent paid out, we must __Subtract__ the decrease in the asset prepaid rent from the accrual basis rent expense.

B22. subtract

23. The computation would be the rent expense of $__36,000__ minus the decrease in prepaid rent of $__9,000__ is the rent paid in cash of $__27,000__.

B23. 36,000, 9,000, 27,000

24. When we have converted all of the accrual basis items on the income statement to cash basis, we calculate the net cash provided by (used in) operations. Exhibit 15-15 shows the cash flows from operating activities section. Expo Company had __cash provided by operating activities__ of $__71,000__.

B24. cash provided by operations, 71,000

25. When we use the direct method of calculating cash provided by operating activities, as in Exhibit 15-15, *FASB 95* requires a reconciliation of net income with cash provided by operating activities.

B25. No answer required.

B26. net income; providing cash or not requiring cash, requiring cash or not providing cash

B27. add, deducted

B28. 34,000, 37,000, 71,000

B29. balance sheet accounts, investing, financing

B30. 0, 122,000

B31. outflow

26. Exhibit 15-8 shows a two-step generalized approach to the indirect method. The starting amount is __net income__. To this, we add items __providing cash or not requiring cash__ and subtract items __requiring cash or not providing cash__. The indirect method serves as a reconciliation of net income to cash provided by (used in) operations.

27. For the Expo Company for 1998, Exhibit 15-13 shows the reconciliation. We __add__ depreciation expense to net income because we __Deduct__ it in calculating net income but it did not require any cash payment during this period.

28. Study the reconciliation in Exhibit 15-13. Note that it starts with net income from the income statement of $ __34,000__ and adds adjustments of $ __37,000__ to get net cash provided by operating activities of $ __71,000__. This is the same as derived by the direct method.

29. The fourth step is to analyze the changes in all remaining __Balance sheet accts__ to determine the net cash provided by __Investing__ and __Financing__ activities.

30. For example, the balance in the land account on 12/31/97 was $ __0__ and on 12/31/98 was $ __122,000__.

31. This increase occurred because Expo purchased land, causing an __outflow__ (inflow/outflow) of cash.

32. Since the purchase of a long-term asset such as land is a(n) __investment__ activity, we would show this cash outflow of $ __122,000__ as an __investing activity__.

332 Chapter 15

B32. investing, 122,000, investing activity

33. The machinery account has two changes occurring during the period. Expo sold machinery. We removed the original cost of the machinery of $_____ from the account causing a(n) _____. Also Expo purchased a new machine with a cost of $_____ causing a(n) _____ in the machinery account.

B33. 20,000, decrease; 50,000, increase

34. The sale of the machinery produces a cash _____. We find the amount by combining the change in Machinery with the related change in _____ and the loss on the sale.

B34. inflow, Accumulated Depreciation

35. The decrease in Machinery of $_____ minus the $_____ reduction of Accumulated Depreciation, minus the $_____ loss equals a cash inflow of $_____.

B35. 20,000, 5,000, 1,000, 14,000

36. Consider next the 12% Bonds Payable account. It increased by $_____ during the year. This was caused by the _____ of bonds.

B36. 100,000; issuance

37. Issuing bonds would have caused a cash _____ from a _____ activity.

B37. inflow, financing

38. Lastly, we will study the change in the Retained Earnings account. The balance on 12/31/97 was $_____ and on 12/31/98 $_____ , or an increase of $ _____.

B38. 17,000, 41,000, 24,000

39. Two items caused the change, the closing of net income of $ _____ increased the account, the declaration of a dividend of $ _____ decreased it.

B39. 34,000, 10,000

B40. 10,000; 10,000

B41. prepare the statement of cash flows

B42. 71,000; 108,000; 90,000

B43. 53,000

B44. 23,000, 76,000

B45. reconciliation, operating activities

40. We have already explained the change due to net income as a part of cash provided by operating activities. The declaration of dividends caused the $_____ decrease. Since there were no dividends payable at either the beginning or the end of the year, the cash payments for dividends must have been $_____.

41. The fifth step is to use the information determined in the analysis to _____.

42. Exhibit 15-15 shows the statement. The first section shows net cash provided by operating activities of $_____. The second shows net cash used by investing activities of $_____. The third shows net cash provided by financing activities of $_____.

43. The three sections combined show a net increase in cash and cash equivalents of $_____. This is the same amount calculated in step 1.

44. When we add the beginning of the year cash and cash equivalents of $_____ to this, we get the ending total cash and cash equivalents of $_____.

45. The next portion of the statement shows the _____ of net income to net cash provided by _____. This is in essence the indirect method. Study this section.

46. The bottom portion of the statement of cash flows is a supplemental schedule of _____.

334　Chapter 15

B46. noncash investing and financing activities

B47. common stock issued for machinery, 50,000

B48. No answer required.

C1. Cash collections from customers.

C2. Accounts receivable decreased indicating that Expo collected more than it sold.

C3. Salaries expense. Salaries payable increased during the period indicating that Expo did not pay all of their expense.

C4. Rent expense. Prepaid rent decreased indicating that Expo did not pay all of the rent that they incurred this period.

C5. 15,000, 1,000, inflow, 14,000

47. The only item that shows here is _____ _____ of $_____. This means that Expo issued common stock directly for a machine and they exchanged no cash

48. Study Exhibit 15-16. The numbers in boxes are cross references to discussion in the textbook. Take time to study each of these as a review of the chapter.

C. **Analysis and Interpretation of the Statement of Cash Flows**

1. Was sales revenues or cash collections from customers greater? _____

2. Why? _____

3. Was salaries expense or cash payments for salaries higher? _____
   Why? _____

4. Which was higher rent expense or cash payments for rent? _____
   Why? _____

5. Expo sold machinery with a book value of $_____ at a loss of $_____. Thus, there was a cash _____ (*inflow/outflow*) of $_____.

6. The payment of a cash dividend caused a cash_____ (*inflow/outflow*) of $_____.

Statement of Cash Flows   335

C6. outflow, 10,000

C7. noncash investing and financing activity

C8. 37,000

C9. reduced Accounts Receivable

C10. issuance of bonds payable

C11. purchase of land, 122,000

C12. 53,000

C13. 161,000, 108,000

D1. calculate the net change in cash and cash equivalents.

7. The common stock issued for machinery is a example of a _____.

8. In 1998, cash provided by operating activities was $ _____ greater than net income.

9. The increase in operating cash flows in 1998 is primarily because Expo _____.

10. In additional to operating activities, the major source of cash was _____.

11. The major use of cash was _____ for $ _____.

12. The net increase in cash during 1998 was $ _____.

13. This occurred because the net cash inflows from operating and financing activities of $ _____ exceeded the net cash outflow from investing activities of $ _____.

D. **Work Sheet (Appendix 15A)**
Follow the illustration beginning with Exhibit A15-1.

1. The first step is the same as in the step-by-step approach, and that is _____.

2. The work sheet has _____ columns and is divided into _____ sections. In the top section, we list the balances in the _____ accounts at the end of the previous year in the _____ column, and the balances in the _____ _____ accounts at the end of the _____ year in the _____ column.

336   Chapter 15

D2. four, three; balance sheet, first, balance sheet, current fourth

3. In the second section, we list the balances in the _____ accounts in the _____ _____.

D3. income statement, center (analysis) columns

4. Since the credits exceed the debits, the income statement requires an additional _____ amount to balance the middle section. To maintain equality of debits and credits, we also need a _____. We enter this on the _____ line.

D4. debit; credit; Retained Earnings

5. This is logical because when we close net income to Retained Earnings, we _____ Retained Earnings.

D5. credit

6. The bottom section is set up with captions for each of the categories of _____ _____.

D6. cash flows

7. We create four areas. They are _____, _____, _____, and _____.

D7. From operating activities, From investing activities, From financing activities, Noncash investing and financing activities

8. Exhibit A15-2 shows completion of the work sheet, the first step is determining the cash operating flows. We do this by combining each revenue and expense account with the related change in a _____ or _____ account.

D8. current asset, current liability

9. For example, we combine sales with _____, cost of goods sold with _____ and _____, rent expense with _____ _____ and salaries expense with _____ _____.

D9. accounts receivable, merchandise inventory, accounts payable, prepaid rent, salaries payable

D10. credit, 360,000

D11. decrease, 44,000

D12. credit, 44,000; debit, 404,000

D13. inflow; from customers

D14. 193,000, debit, 20,000, debit, 10,000

D15. credit, 223,000

D16. outflow, payments to suppliers

10. Look first at sales. The sales amount appears as a _____ of $ _____ .

11. We must combine this amount with the _____ (*increase/decrease*) in accounts receivable of $ _____ .

12. We make an entry in the analysis columns. Since accounts receivable decreased, we must enter a _____ of $ _____ on that line. We combine this with the $360,000 credit in sales that is already on the work sheet. To balance the entry, a _____ of $ _____ is necessary.

13. Since this is a debit, it represents a cash _____ . We enter it in the operating activities section as cash receipts _____ .

14. Cost of goods sold is a little more complicated. We combine the debit of $ _____ on the cost of goods sold line with the change in merchandise inventory which requires a _____ entry of $ _____ and the change in accounts payable, which requires a _____ entry of $ _____ .

15. To complete this entry, we enter a _____ of $ _____ in the cash flow section.

16. Since it required a credit, it represents a cash _____ and we label it as "Cash _____ ."

17. We combine the salaries expense debit of $ _____ , already entered, with the change in salaries payable which requires a _____ of $_____ .

338   Chapter 15

D17. 70,000, credit, 3,000

18. We enter the balancing entry in the amount of $_____ under operating activities as a _____, and label it "Cash _____ _____."

D18. 67,000, credit, payments to employees

19. We combine the rent expense entry of $_____, already entered, with the change in _____ which we must enter as a _____ of $_____. We enter the balancing amount as a _____ of $_____ and label it "Cash _____ _____."

D19. 36,000, Prepaid Rent, credit, 9,000; credit, 27,000, payments for rent

20. We analyze the remaining income statement accounts and enter them the same way. Next we explain the changes in the remaining _____ accounts except cash and cash equivalents.

D20. balance sheet

21. For example, the Land account increased. This would require a _____ entry of $_____ on the Land line.

D21. debit, 122,000

22. We enter the balancing amount as a _____ in the cash flow section as an _____ activity.

D22. credit, investing

23. Since it requires a credit in the cash flow section, it would represent a cash _____, and we would label it "_____."

D23. outflow, Purchase of land

24. Entry (g) is for the disposal of machinery. It combines the loss on sale of machinery of $1,000 in the income statement debit column with a decrease in the machinery account of $_____ entered as a _____ and the decrease in accumulated depreciation of $_____ entered as a _____ to get the cash flow of $_____ entered as a _____ in the cash flow section to balance the entry.

Statement of Cash Flows   339

D24. 20,000, credit, 5,000, debit, 14,000, debit

25. Since the disposal of equipment is an _____ activity, we enter the balancing amount in that area of the cash flow section.

D25. investing

26. Since the cash flow portion of the entry required a debit, it represents a cash _____ and we label it "_____ _____."

D26. inflow, Proceeds from sale of machinery

27. When we have explained all of the changes in balance sheet accounts, we balance the cash flow section of the work sheet. We do this by subtotaling the center columns. The debits exceed the credits by $_____. We enter this amount as a _____ to make the cash flows section balance. We enter the offsetting _____ on the _____ line. This should also explain the change in that line of the balance sheet section.

D27. 53,000; credit; debit, cash and cash equivalents

28. When we have completed the work sheet, the information necessary to prepare the statement of cash flows is in the Cash Flows (bottom) section.

D28. No answer required.

LEARNING GOALS ACHIEVEMENT TEST

1. (LG 2) For each of the following transactions, indicate in the spaces provided whether it would be a cash inflow, outflow or neither and whether it would be an operating, investing or financing activity, or none of these.

	Cash Flow	Type of Activity
a. Sale of used delivery van.............................	_____	_____
b. Issuance of bonds.......................................	_____	_____
c. Payment of wages.	_____	_____
d. Declaration of a cash dividend.....................	_____	_____
e. Sale of merchandise on account..................	_____	_____
f. Payment of an account payable...................	_____	_____
g. Payment for purchase of a building..............	_____	_____
h. Collection of an account receivable.............	_____	_____
i. Recording amortization expense for the year...	_____	_____
j. Payment of cash dividend that was declared last year..	_____	_____
k. Collection of a 90-day note receivable.........	_____	_____
l. Recording of depreciation expense for the year...	_____	_____
m. Purchase of treasury stock for cash..............	_____	_____

2. (LG 1, 2-4) Pierre Corporation had the following amounts on its financial statements (all normal balances) for the year ended December 31, 1997 and 1996:

	1997	1996
Cash	$ 90	$ 70
Temporary investments	15	25
Accounts receivable	60	70
Merchandise Inventory	200	180
Prepaid expenses	15	20
Equipment	570	350
Accumulated depreciation	60	50
Accounts payable	40	50
Notes payable (due in 60 days)	80	100
Accrued payables	20	15
Common stock	400	300
Retained earnings	350	200
Sales	900	
Cost of goods sold	600	
Operating expenses (includes depreciation of $10)	80	

a. What is the amount of cash and cash equivalents at the end of 1997? (Temporary investments qualify as cash equivalents.) $_____ .
1996? $_____ .

b. What is the net change in cash and cash equivalents during 1997?
$ _____ .

c. What was the amount of the cash inflow from sales during 1997?
$ _____ .

d. What were net purchases for 1997? $ _____ .

e. How much cash was paid to suppliers during 1997?
$ _____ .

f. The change in notes payable would be shown as a(n) _____ activity.

g. How much cash was paid for operating expenses during 1997?
$_____ .

3. (LG A1) Using the data in Problem 2, prepare a work sheet for the statement of cash flows for the year ended December 31, 1997. Assume that the company declared and paid cash dividends of $70.

PIERRE CORPORATION
WORK SHEET FOR STATEMENT OF CASH FLOWS
FOR THE YEAR ENDED DECEMBER 31, 1997

	Balances December 31, 1996	Analysis of Transactions for Current Year Debit	Credit	Balances December 31, 1997

4. (LG 3-5, 7, 8) Using the data in Problem 2, prepare a complete statement of cash flows for the year ended December 31, 1997, using the direct method for cash from operations. Assume that the company declared and paid cash dividends of $70.

344   Chapter 15

5. (LG 4) During 1997 Anarc purchased merchandise for resale in the amount of $200,000. At the beginning of the year the balance in the merchandise inventory account was $35,000, and at the end of the year it was $30,000. Accounts payable at the beginning of 1997 was $35,000, and at the end of the year $20,000. What was cost of goods sold for 1997? What were the cash payments to suppliers during 1997?

ANSWERS TO LEARNING GOALS ACHIEVEMENT TEST

1.

	Cash Flow	Type of Activity
a.	inflow	investing
b.	inflow	financing
c.	outflow	operating
d.	neither	none
e.	neither	none
f.	outflow	operating
g.	outflow	investing
h.	inflow	operating
i.	neither	none
j.	outflow	financing
k.	inflow	financing
l.	neither	none
m.	outflow	financing

2. a. 105, 95   b. 10   c. 910   d. 620   e. 630   f. financing
   g. 60 (80 - 10 deprec. exp. - 5 prepaid exp. decrease - 5 acc. pay. increase)

3.

PIERRE CORPORATION
WORK SHEET FOR STATEMENT OF CASH FLOWS
FOR THE YEAR ENDED DECEMBER 31, 1997

	Balances December 31, 1996	Analysis of Transactions for Current Year Debit		Credit		Balances December 31, 1997
Debit Balance Sheet Accounts						
Cash & Cash Equivalents	95	(z)	10			105
Accounts Receivable	70			(a)	10	60
Merchandise Inventory	180	(b)	20			200
Prepaid Expenses	20			(c)	5	15
Equipment	350	(d)	220			570
Totals	715					950
Credit Balance Sheet Accounts						
Accumulated Depreciation	50			(c)	10	60
Accounts Payable	50	(b)	10			40
Notes Payable	100	(e)	20			80
Accrued Payables	15			(c)	5	20
Common Stock	300			(f)	100	400
Retained Earnings	200	(g)	70		220	350
Totals	715					950
Income Statement Accounts						
Sales				(a)	900	
Cost of Goods Sold		(b)	600			
Operating Expenses		(c)	80			
			680		900	
Net Income			220			
			900		900	
Cash Flows						
From Operating Activities						
Cash receipts from customers		(a)	910			
Cash payments to suppliers				(b)	630	
Cash payments for operations				(c)	60	
From Investing Activities						
Purchase of equipment				(d)	220	
From Financing Activities						
Paid off notes payable				(e)	20	
Issued common stock		(f)	100			
Dividends paid				(g)	70	
			1,010		1,000	
Net increase in cash & cash eq.				(z)	10	
			1,010		1,010	

4.

PIERRE CORPORATION
STATEMENT OF CASH FLOWS
FOR THE YEAR ENDED DECEMBER 31, 1997

Increase (Decrease) in Cash and Cash Equivalents
Cash flows from operating activities
    Cash receipts from customers... $ 910
    Cash payments to suppliers.. (630)
    Cash payments for operations... (60)
        Net cash provided by operating activities......................... $ 220
Cash flows from investing activities
    Purchase of equipment... (220)
Cash flows from financing activities
    Payment on note payable... $ (20)
    Proceeds from issuance of common stock............................ 100
    Dividends paid.. (70)
        Net cash provided by financing activities.......................... 10
Net increase in cash and cash equivalents................................. $ 10
Cash and cash equivalents at beginning of year........................ 95
Cash and cash equivalents at end of year.................................. $105

Reconciliation of net income to net cash provided by operating activities
Net income.. $220
Add: Items providing cash or not requiring cash:
    Depreciation.. $ 10
    Decrease in accounts receivable.. 10
    Decrease in prepaid expenses.. 5
    Increase in accrued payables... 5
Deduct: Items requiring cash or not providing cash:
    Increase in merchandise inventory... (20)
    Decrease in accounts payable... (10)
        Total adjustments... 0
Net cash provided by operating activities................................... $220

5.   Accrual purchases... $200,000
    Add: Decrease in merchandise inventory................................. 5,000
    Cost of goods sold... $205,000

    Accrual purchases... $200,000
    Add: Decrease in accounts payable... 15,000
    Cash paid to suppliers... $215,000

Chapter 16

ANALYSIS AND INTERPRETATION OF FINANCIAL STATEMENTS

EXPLANATION OF MAJOR CONCEPTS

Objectives and Process of Analysis LG 1

Financial statement analysis is the application of analytical tools and techniques to financial statement data. Users of accounting information want to predict future financial results of an organization. They use these predictions as an aid in decision making. External users rely on the general-purpose financial statements that companies publish and the explanatory notes that are an integral part of the financial statements.

In decision making, users constantly try to balance the risk and expected return. Generally the greater the risk the greater the return. Financial statement analysis is one source of information for assessing risk and return. Exhibit 16-1, in the textbook, summarizes the types of decisions and the sources of information for those decisions.

Sources of Information LG 2

The primary sources of information include:

- *Published Reports* Published annual reports include a letter by the CEO reviewing the past year and discussing future plans; the financial statements; explanatory notes; management's discussion and analysis; and the report of the independent accountant.

- *Government Reports* The Securities and Exchange Commission requires periodic reports of public companies. These include the 10K, 10Q, and 8K that are public information.

- *Financial Service Information* Several companies publish financial information for businesses. These include Moody's Investor's Service, Standard and Poor's, Dun and Bradstreet, Inc., and Robert Morris Associates.

♦ *Financial Newspapers and Periodicals* Knowledge of current financial events comes from such publications as *The Wall Street Journal, Barrons, Forbes, Fortune,* and *Business Week.*

Horizontal Analysis   LG 3

Comparative financial statements are statements in which we present two or more periods' data in parallel columns. Current practice shows two years data for balance sheets and three years data for income statements. This style of reporting permits better identification of changes and trends.

It is difficult to make useful comparisons of financial statement data when we show only dollar amounts. A way to overcome this problem is to change the dollar amounts to percentages. Then we can compare several years in a single entity (or could compare several companies in the same year). In horizontal analysis, we use data from a designated year, called the base year, as a measure against which to judge all other years. For the chosen base year, we designate each statement item as 100%. We express the same item for other years as a percentage of the base-year item. We call this type of horizontal analysis *trend percentages*. In another type of horizontal analysis, we express the amount of change from one year to the next as a percent of the earlier (or base) year. This type of analysis is called *percent of change*. In both cases, we compute the percentages for the same item across a span of years; this is why we use the term horizontal analysis.

Vertical Analysis   LG 4

In the preparation of common-size statements or vertical analysis, we select a financial statement amount as the base (that is, 100%). We then express all other amounts in that statement as a percent of the base. We use net sales as the base for vertical analysis of an income statement. In the balance sheet, there are two bases, but both are the same amount. We express each dollar amount in the assets section as a percent of total assets (the base). In the other half of the balance sheet, total liabilities and stockholders' equity is the base amount. We express each item as a percent of total liabilities and stockholders' equity.

In either horizontal or vertical analysis, remember that you are expressing some amount as a percent of a base amount. The resulting percent is always equal to the designated item divided by the base amount.

Percentage analysis helps comparative statements take on real meaning. Look for changing relationships. Ask questions such as: What items changed? Is the change favorable or unfavorable in terms of operating results? What could be the causes of the change? Is corrective action in order? Is the change temporary or permanent?

Ratio Analysis LG 5

A ratio is a fraction or the relationship of one number to another. Ratio analysis is another tool, which we can use to make financial statements more useful. It is best to aim for understanding of the meaning of a ratio rather than simply to memorize the formula to compute the ratio. To say that the working capital ratio equals current assets divided by current liabilities, doesn't mean much. But to say that the current ratio tells us how many times the current assets could cover (or liquidate) the current liabilities, helps us comprehend what it means.

There is an important key to remember in computing ratios. Whenever one part of the ratio is an income statement number, and the other part is a balance sheet number, we must express the balance sheet number as the average-for-the-period amount. For example, if we express net income in ratio to total assets, we should use the average total assets. The easy way is to add the beginning-of-the-period assets to the end-of-the-period assets and divide by two. Remember that no one ratio or set of ratios gives the final answer. Each is just one of several pieces of evidence of the financial performance of an entity, and points to the need for further investigation and analysis.

Exhibit 16-7 summarizes the ratio formulas and meanings of the ratios covered in Chapter 16. Take the time to study these now. We will review their application in the Guided Study section.

Limitations LG 6

In using financial statement analysis, you should always be careful of the limitations. In doing financial statement analysis remember:

- Accounting information is historical.

- Economic conditions in the future may be very different than in the past.

- Make comparisons with industry averages.

- Be aware of the effect of seasonal factors.

- The accounting methods selected will affect the "quality" of the information.

Exhibit 16-8 summarizes the effect on reported net income of accounting methods and estimates that we have studied. For each method or estimate, it references the chapter where we studied that item. As a part of the study of financial statement analysis, study this exhibit carefully.

350   Chapter 16

GUIDED STUDY OF THIS CHAPTER

A. Objectives and Process

1. The overall objective of financial statement analysis is _____ _____ _____.

A1.	to make predictions as an aid in decision making	2. External users rely on _____ _____ financial statements.
A2.	general-purpose	3. The process of financial statement analysis is the _____ _____.
A3.	application of analytical tools and techniques to financial statement data	4. In making decisions, users evaluate the _____ of an investment and its expected _____.
A4.	risk, return	5. (Refer to Exhibit 16-1) Decisions made by short-term credit grantors include _____ _____ _____.
A5.	the ability to pay accounts payable and short-term notes payable	6. The accounting information used includes _____ _____.
A6.	current resources on the balance sheet and cash flows from operations	7. Long-term credit grantors _____ _____ _____.
A7.	evaluate prospects for future earnings	8. They use _____ _____ _____.
A8.	profitability and debt equity relationships	9. Stockholders _____ _____ _____.
A9.	evaluate the company's future earnings prospects and dividend policies	10. The four sources of external information are _____, _____, _____, and _____.

Analysis and Interpretation of Financial Statements   351

A10. published reports, government reports, financial service information, financial newspapers and periodicals

A11. letter to stockholders, financial statements, explanatory notes, management's discussion and analysis, report of independent accountants

A12. compare

A13. current developments

B1. prior year amount, current year amount

B2. 33,000, 36,000

B3. 15,000, 17,000, (2,000)

B4. the amount of change

B5. 1,000, 3,000

11. A corporate annual report includes the _____, _____, _____, _____, and _____.

12. We can use financial service information to _____ the information with other firms in similar lines of business.

13. Newspapers such as *The Wall Street Journal* keep users knowledgeable about _____.

B. Horizontal Analysis

1. In horizontal analysis, we compute the change amount by subtracting a _____ from the _____.

2. Using the Amy Company balance sheet shown in Exhibit 16-2, we find the $3,000 change in cash by subtracting $_____ from $_____.

3. The dollar change in notes payable is equal to $_____ - $_____ or $_____.

4. We can compute the percentage change by dividing _____ by the dollar amount in the base, earlier, year.

5. For wages payable the 33.3% increase is equal to $_____ divided by $_____.

6. The largest percentage change on the balance sheet is in _____.

352 Chapter 16

B6. long-term notes payable

B7. Amy Company issued notes to finance the purchase of plant assets

B8. 84,600, 70,800, 70,800

B9. interest expense

B10. issuance of bonds to finance plant and equipment

B11. net income increased

C1. total amount for that statement

C2. total amount

C3. total assets or total liabilities and owners' equity

C4. net sales

7. The explanation for this change is: _____ _____ _____ .

8. We compute the percentage change on the income statement in the same way. We would compute the 19.5% increase in net income as $_____ minus $_____ divided by $_____ .

9. The largest change on the income statement is in _____ .

10. The reason for this change was the _____ _____ .

11. Although this was an increase in interest expense, the effect was positive in that _____ .

C. Vertical Analysis

1. Vertical analysis shows how each item in a financial statement compares to a _____ .

2. To calculate the common-size amounts, we divide each amount on the statement by the appropriate _____ .

3. For the balance sheet the total amount used is _____ .

4. On the income statement the total amount used is _____ .

5. To calculate the 1997 common-size amount for Amy Company's total current liabilities, we divide $_____ by $_____ giving _____ %.

Analysis and Interpretation of Financial Statements 353

C5. 102,000, 570,600, 17.9

6. We then calculate the percents for each of the individual current liabilities. For accounts payable we divide $_____ by $_____ giving _____%

C6. 83,000, 570,600, 14.5

7. We rounded the 14.5% to 14.6% so that the total of the individual percentages for current assets would sum to the 17.9% calculated for total current liabilities. The percents for the subtotals must add to 100%, and the details that make up a subtotal must add to the subtotal.

C7. No answer required.

D. **Ratio Analysis** Use the Amy Company balance sheet, Exhibit 16-4, and income statement, Exhibit 16-5 to study ratio analysis.

1. Ratio analysis shows the relative size of _____.

D1. one financial statement component to another

2. We calculate and interpret ratios to evaluate (1) _____,
(2) _____,
(3) _____, and
(4) _____.

D2. short-term solvency, long-term solvency, profitability, market performance

3. We compute the current ratio by dividing _____ by _____.

D3. current assets, current liabilities

4. For 1997, this is $ _____ divided by $ _____.

D4. 231,600, 102,000

5. A ratio of 2.27 means that Amy had _____.

D5. $2.27 in current assets for every $1.00 in current liabilities

6. Did Amy's current ratio increase during 1997? _____. What does this indicate? _____

D6. Yes; It indicates an increase in liquidity.

7. The numerator of the quick ratio includes _____.

354 Chapter 16

D7. cash, short-term investments, and net current receivables

8. For 1997, Amy's quick ratio was _____ . This means it had $_____ in quick current assets for every $1 in _____ .

D8. 1.14; 1.14, current liabilities

9. Accounts receivable turnover measures how many times we turn receivables into _____ during a period.

D9. cash

10. We compute Amy's 1997 accounts receivable turnover by dividing $ _____ by $_____ .

D10. 940,000, ($60,000 + $80,600) ÷ 2

11. The ratio of 13.37 means that Amy is collecting its average accounts receivable balance 13.37 _____ .

D11. times per year.

12. Days' sales in receivables shows how many day's sales remain _____ .

D12. uncollected in accounts receivable

13. The computation is a two-step process. First, compute _____ . Then, divide _____ by _____ .

D13. net sales per day; average net accounts receivable, net sales per day

14. Amy's 1997 net sales per day was $_____ and its average accounts receivable was $_____ .

D14. 2,575, 70,300

15. Thus it has _____ days sales uncollected.

D15. 27.3

16. We compute inventory turnover by dividing _____ by _____ .

D16. cost of goods sold, average inventory

17. Note that since inventory is from the balance sheet and cost of goods sold is from the income statement, inventory must be an _____ .

Analysis and Interpretation of Financial Statements 355

D17. average

18. We calculate Amy's inventory turnover by dividing $ _____ by $ _____ that equals _____ times.

D18. 545,000, 97,500, 5.59

19. This means that Amy is selling and _____ its inventory 5.59 times per year.

D19. replacing

20. Now let's turn to long-run solvency. The debt ratio measures the _____ _____ _____.

D20. portion of total assets creditors contribute

21. For 1997, Amy's debt ratio was $ _____ divided by $ _____ which equals _____ %.

D21. 182,000; $570,600; 31.9

22. During 1997 Amy's debt ratio _____ (increased/decreased). This means that there was more _____.

D22. increased; risk

23. Times interest earned measures the _____ _____.

D23. number of times the company earned interest expense with current income

24. The numerator is equal to _____ + _____ + _____.

D24. net income, tax expense, interest expense

25. We divide this by _____ _____.

D25. interest expense

26. For 1997, this is $ _____ + $ _____ + $ _____ divided by $ _____.

D26. 84,600, 36,200, 9,500, 9,500

27. A _____ (higher/lower) ratio is more favorable.

D27. higher

28. Now look at profitability ratios. Profit margin is equal to _____ divided by _____.

356   Chapter 16

D28. net income, net sales.

29. For Amy Company in 1997, this was $ _____ divided by $ _____, which is equal to _____ %.

D29. 84,600, 940,000, 9

30. This means that every $1.00 in sales generated $ _____ in net income.

D30. 0.09

31. Asset turnover is a measure of the _____ of the company in using its assets to generate _____ .

D31. efficiency, sales

32. Amy's total asset turnover in 1997 was _____ times. We found this by dividing $ _____ by $ _____.

D32. 1.87; 940,000, 503,300

33. This means that Amy generated $ _____ in sales for each $1.00 of _____ .

D33. 1.87, average total assets

34. Return on total assets measures the amount a company _____ _____ .

D34. earns on each dollar of investment

35. We calculate this by dividing _____ _____ by _____ .

D35. net income, average total assets

36. Return on owner's equity measures the _____ _____ .

D36. return on owner's investment in the company

37. The numerator is _____ minus _____ . And the denominator is _____ _____ .

D37. net income, preferred dividends; average common stockholders' equity

38. For Amy in 1997, this is $ _____ - $ _____ divided by $ _____, that equals _____ %.

D38. 84,600, 0, 357,300, 23.7

39. Earnings per share is equal to _____ _____ - _____ divided by _____ _____ .

Analysis and Interpretation of Financial Statements 357

D39. net income, preferred dividends, average number of common shares outstanding during the year

D40. number of times earnings per share the stock is currently selling for

D41. 15, 0.85

D42. 17.6

D43. receive cash dividends, sell the stock at a higher price

D44. dividend paying performance of the company

D45. 1.5, 0.22, 15

E1. decisions affect the future

E2. economic conditions.

E3. Yes; They may be taking advantage of a situation

E4. distort the ratio

40. The price/earnings ratio is the _____ _____ _____ _____.

41. On December 31, 1997, Amy Company stock was selling for $_____ and their EPS was $_____.

42. The price/earnings ratio was _____ times.

43. Investors buy stock for two reasons. They _____ and _____.

44. Dividend yield is a measure of the _____ _____.

45. Amy's dividend yield was _____ %. We calculated this by dividing $_____ by $_____.

E. **Limitations**

1. The fact that financial statement information is historical limits the user in that _____ _____.

2. When we compare ratios for different periods, we must consider the changing _____.

3. Often we compare ratios to the industry averages. Should a company ever deviate from the average? _____. Why? _____ _____.

4. If an account balance is higher or lower when we calculate the average, it may _____.

5. The accounting methods a company uses

358   Chapter 16

                            affects the reported net income. Accounting methods that minimize net income give a net income number that is higher _____ .

E5.   quality   6. Evaluating the underlying accounting methods and estimates a company uses is an important part of analyzing financial statements. Exhibit 16-8 summarizes the accounting methods that you have studied.

E6.   No answer required.

LEARNING GOALS ACHIEVEMENT TEST

1. (LG 1, 2) The following pertain to the use of financial statements by both internal and external users. Opposite each financial statement user, indicate a type of decision to be made based on the financial statements.

User	Decision
An officer of a bank................	_____
	_____
	_____
	_____
	_____
An Amy stockholder	_____
	_____
	_____
	_____
	_____
A vendor that is accepting a large order from Amy	_____
	_____
	_____
	_____
	_____

User	Decision
The vice-president for production planning	_____
	_____
	_____

The board of directors
as a group .... _____
                                        _____
                                        _____
                                        _____
                                        _____

2. (LG 3-5) Following are some selected figures from income statements and balance sheets of an industrial company:

	Figures in Thousands of Dollars			
	1997	**1996**	**1995**	**1994**
Sales....................................	$330,195	$285,659	$247,113	$178,664
Net income..........................	10,439	9,385	8,598	5,867
Total assets.........................	138,684	122,477	111,457	88,693
Stockholders' equity...........	65,407	57,152	49,956	41,193

a. Using 1996 as the base year, compute the percent of change in 1997 for each item.

b. Using the earliest year as the base year, convert sales, net income and stockholders' equity items to trend percentages. Round to the nearest percent.

c. Compute a common-size percent for net income, for stockholders' equity, and for total liabilities for 1997 and 1996. Carry each percent to two decimal places.

d. Compute the rate of return on stockholders' equity for 1997, and 1996.

e. Explain why sales and net income both increased in total dollars from 1996 to 1997 but net income as a percent of sales decreased.

3. (LG 6) Write out the formula for computing each of the following:

   a. Merchandise inventory turnover.

   b. Average number of days' sales uncollected.

   c. Acid-test ratio.

   d. Current ratio.

   e. Price-earnings ratio.

   f. Number of times bond interest earned.

   g. Sales to property, plant, and equipment.

h. Earnings per share of common stock.

4. (LG 6) List five limitations users should remember in doing financial statement analysis.

1. _____

2. _____

3. _____

4. _____

5. _____

ANSWERS TO LEARNING GOALS ACHIEVEMENT TEST

1. (These are some possible decisions.)

User	Decision
An officer of a bank	Whether to make a specific loan to Amy, whether to grant an extended line of credit, the limits to be placed on the loan or line of credit, what collateral to require, and what interest rate to charge.
An Amy stockholder	Whether to hold, buy more, or to sell his or her shares.
A vendor that is accepting a large order from Amy	Whether to require total payment in advance, a partial down payment, a note, or to sell on open account to Amy.
The vice-president for production planning	Which products shall be produced in greater quantity, cut back, or discontinued. What capital equipment or plant expansion projects should be undertaken.
The board of directors as a group	Whether to make changes in the management, declare a dividend (and, if so, how much), or propose a bond issue to the stockholders.

2. a.

Sales in 1997	$330,195	$44,536 / $285,659	= 15.59%
Sales in 1996	285,659		
Increase	$ 44,536		
Net income in 1997	$10,439	$1,054 / $9,385	= 11.23%
Net income in 1996	9,385		
Increase	$ 1,054		
Total assets in 1997	$138,684	$16,207 / $122,477	= 13.23%
Total assets in 1996	122,477		
Increase	$ 16,207		
Stockholders' equity	$65,407	$8,255 / $57,152	= 14.44%
Stockholders' equity	57,152		
Increase	$ 8,255		

b.

	1997	1996	1995	1994
Sales	185 %	160 %	138 %	100 %
Net income	178	160	147	100
Stockholders' equity	159	139	121	100

c.

	1997	1996
Net income	3.16%	3.29%
Stockholders' equity	47.16	46.66
Total liabilities	52.84 *	53.34 *

* Total liabilities and stockholders' equity is equal to total assets. Then the common-size percent for total liabilities plus the common-size percent for stockholders' equity equals 100%.

d. 1997: $\dfrac{\text{Net income}}{\text{Average SE}} = \dfrac{\$10{,}439}{(\$65{,}407 + \$57{,}152) \div 2} = 17.04\%.$

1996: $\dfrac{\$9{,}385}{(\$57{,}152 + \$49{,}956) \div 2} = 17.52\%.$

e. The sales have increased each year. Although net income also increased in total dollars each year, it has increased less on a percentage basis than sales. (See answer to Part b.) This is due to a decrease in the ability to control costs and expenses.

3. a. Merchandise inventory turnover = $\dfrac{\text{Cost of goods sold}}{\text{Average inventory}}$

b. Average number of days' sales uncollected = $\dfrac{\text{Average accounts receivable}}{\text{Net credit sales per day}}$

c. Acid-test ratio = $\dfrac{\text{Quick current assets}}{\text{Current liabilities}}$

d. Current ratio = $\dfrac{\text{Current assets}}{\text{Current liabilities}}$

e. Price-earnings ratio = $\dfrac{\text{Market price per share}}{\text{Earnings per share}}$

f. Number of times bond interest earned = $\dfrac{\text{Net income + Income taxes + Annual bond interest expense}}{\text{Annual bond interest expense}}$

3. g. Sales to property, plant, and equipment $=\dfrac{\text{Net sales}}{\text{Average property, plant, and equipment (net)}}$

   h. Earnings per share of common stock $=\dfrac{\text{Net income - Annual preferred dividend}}{\text{Weighted average outstanding common shares}}$

4.
   1. The historical nature of accounting information
   2. Changing economic conditions
   3. Comparisons with industry averages
   4. Seasonal factors
   5. The quality of reported net income

Chapter 17

BUSINESS CONSOLIDATIONS AND INTERNATIONAL ACCOUNTING

EXPLANATION OF MAJOR CONCEPTS

Parent/Subsidiary Relationships   LG 1

A business acquires a controlling interest in other companies for many reasons. One is to obtain control of either the supply or distribution of the company's products. A second is to develop a market for the company's products. A third is to diversify by acquiring control of companies with different product lines.

When an investor owns more than 50% of the stock of an investee corporation, a *parent-subsidiary* relationship exists. We assume that the investor can control the investee. When a parent-subsidiary relationship exists, the companies are known as *affiliates*. Each of the corporations is still a legally separate entity and each maintains a totally separate set of accounting records. However, from an external reporting perspective, it is often more informative to combine the records and present consolidated financial statements. In such a case, we are viewing the economic entity as more important than the legal entity.

Prepare Consolidated Financial Statements   LG 2-6

We must eliminate reciprocal accounts when we consolidate the amounts (combine them) for reporting. The Investment account on the parent's books and the stockholders' equity accounts on the subsidiary's books is one set of reciprocal accounts. The investment represents an interest in all or part of the subsidiary's equity which shows in the subsidiary's stockholders' equity accounts. Thus, the balances are measuring the same element and we must eliminate them in order not to double count the item.

Other reciprocal accounts may exist if the two companies engage in transactions with one another. For example, if the parent loans the subsidiary money, the parent's books would show a receivable and the subsidiary's books would show a payable. From a legal perspective, this is accurate because they are separate legal entities. But from an economic perspective, an entity cannot owe itself money. Thus we must eliminate the reciprocal accounts for consolidated statements. Other types of reciprocal amounts can arise. For example, if the subsidiary sells to the parent, some of the sales on the subsidiary's records measure the same event as some of the purchases on the parent's books. And since we cannot sell to ourselves, we must eliminate them.

If the parent owns less than 100% of the outstanding stock of the subsidiary, the outside owner's share of the stockholders' equity of the subsidiary is termed *minority interest*. We show this proportion of the stockholders' equity of the subsidiary on the consolidated balance sheet as a separate item between liabilities and stockholders' equity and title it minority interest.

In many cases, the investing company pays more than book value for the subsidiary. We first assign the excess paid to undervalued assets or overvalued liabilities. If there is an additional excess, we assign the excess to a new account called Goodwill.

International Accounting   LG 7

Many companies today operate in more than one country. When they do, they must account for the fluctuations of one currency in relation to another. Two basic financial reporting issues occur when international transactions involve dealings in more than one national currency. One of these issues is the accounting for foreign currency exchange transactions. These are transactions that involve an agreement to receive or make payment in the currency of a foreign country. When we exchange the foreign currency, the amount received or paid may be more or less than the amount shown as an account receivable or payable. This difference is a foreign currency exchange gain or loss.

The other is the translation of financial statement items from foreign currencies into the reporting currency used in the consolidated statements. A functional currency is the currency in which a foreign entity generates revenues and expends cash. When the functional currency is the local currency of the foreign subsidiary, the accounting information of the foreign subsidiary will be in a different currency than the parent's. In this case, we first measure all elements of the financial statements in the local currency. We then translate these amounts to the parent's currency to prepare consolidated statements. We use the current exchange rate to translate balance sheet items. We generally translate income statement items at the weighted average exchange rate for the period. We accumulate gains and losses on translation and show them in the stockholders' equity section of the balance sheet.

When the functional currency of the subsidiary is the reporting currency of the parent, we follow the current/historical method. Monetary assets and liabilities are translated at the current exchange rate. We translate other assets and liabilities at the rate in effect when we recorded the balances. We translate revenues and expenses at the weighted average rate for the period. However, we translate expenses (such as cost of goods sold and depreciation expense) related to specific balance sheet items at the same historical rate as the balance sheet item. Under this approach, we report translation gains and losses on the income statement.

GUIDED STUDY OF THIS CHAPTER

A. Parent-Subsidiary Relationships

1. When an investor owns more than 50% of the outstanding stock of the investee, we presume that the investor has the ability to _____ the investee.

A1. control

2. The investor is known as the _____, and the investee is a _____.

A2. parent, subsidiary

3. The group is known as _____.

A3. affiliates

4. In these cases, the operating results and financial position is often more meaningful if we present it for the _____ entity instead of the _____ entity.

A4. economic, legal

5. We call statements presented for the economic entity _____ financial statements.

A5. consolidated

B. Consolidated Financial Statements

1. In a parent-subsidiary relationship, reciprocal accounts exist. On the parent's books, one reciprocal account is entitled _____.

B1. Investment in Sub Company

2. On the subsidiary's books, the reciprocal accounts would be the _____ account and the _____ account.

B2. Common Stock, Retained Earnings

3. When the parent owns 100% of the subsidiary's outstanding stock, we will eliminate the _____ account against the stockholders' equity of the subsidiary.

370 Chapter 17

B3. Investment

4. The eliminations which we make on the worksheet for consolidated statements _____ (are/are never) journalized on the books of either corporation.

B4. are never

5. Exhibit 17-3 shows the consolidated work sheet at acquisition, when we acquire _____ % of the subsidiary's stock.

B5. 100

6. The work sheet first eliminates the _____ accounts. Then, it _____ the remaining balances.

B6. reciprocal; combines

7. Since the Investment in Sub Company account has a debit balance, the elimination entry _____ it.

B7. credits

8. The investment account is reciprocal to _____ and _____ .

B8. Common Stock, Retained Earnings

9. Then we combine the remaining account balances. The consolidated amount for Cash is $_____ + $_____ = $_____ .

B9. 50,000, 40,000, 90,000

10. The consolidated amount for Common Stock is $_____ + $_____ - $_____ = $_____ .

B10. 175,000, 80,000, 80,000, 175,000

11. We eliminated the subsidiary's common stock because it was _____ .

B11. reciprocal to the parent's investment account

12. If the parent purchases less than 100% of the subsidiary, a _____ interest exists.

B12. minority

13. In Exhibit 17-4, the elimination entry still eliminates all of the subsidiaries _____ _____ and _____ .

B13. common stock, retained earnings

B14. Minority Interest

B15. the ownership interest of the remaining stockholders in the assets of the subsidiary

B16. adjust the assets and liabilities; goodwill

B17. 10,000

B18. 10,000

B19. 10,000

B20. Goodwill

B21. equity

B22. stockholders' equity

14. The difference between the credit to Investment in Sub Company and the debits to Common Stock and Retained Earnings is a credit to _____ .

15. Minority interest represents _____ .

16. When a company pays more than book value of the subsidiary, GAAP requires that we first _____ to fair value. We show the remaining excess as _____ .

17. In Exhibit 17-5, the parent paid $_____ more than the book value.

18. If we assume that the subsidiary's assets and liabilities are valued at fair value, the minority interest is $ _____ .

19. In the elimination entry, the credit to Investment in Sub Company is $ _____ more than the debits to Common Stock and Retained Earnings.

20. We debit this to _____ .

21. When the parent owns more than 50% of the outstanding stock of the subsidiary, it will use the _____ method.

22. This means that the parent's investment changes proportionally to the subsidiary's _____ .

23. In the textbook example, Par Company's investment account and Sub Company's stockholders' equity both increased by $_____ since the date of acquisition.

372   Chapter 17

B23. 30,000

24. Since Par owns 100% of Sub, the elimination entry eliminates _____ of Sub's stockholders' equity.

B24. all

25. In many cases the parent and the subsidiary have transactions between themselves called _____ transactions.

B25. intercompany

26. In consolidated financial statements, we must eliminate intercompany transactions so that we do not double count _____.

B26. revenues, expenses, assets, and liabilities

27. For example, if a parent makes a loan to the subsidiary, we must eliminate notes receivable and _____ and we must eliminate interest revenue and _____.

B27. notes payable, interest expense

28. In Exhibit 17-7, Pop Company had sold $_____ in merchandise to Son Company.

B28. 60,000

29. Since Son had sold the merchandise, the $60,000 is in Pop's _____ and in Son's _____.

B29. Sales, Sales

30. In order not to double-count the $60,000, we must eliminate these _____ from Sales and from _____.

B30. sales, Cost of Goods Sold

C. International Accounting

1. Currencies from different countries are actively traded. The foreign exchange rate is the price of one currency stated in terms of _____.

C1. another currency

2. In an international sale by a U.S. company, if the buyer pays in a foreign currency, the seller then must use the foreign currency to purchase dollars. The transaction in which they purchase dollars is called a _____ transaction.

C2. foreign currency exchange

C3. French, francs

C4. dollars

C5. dollars, 0.15

C6. 2,000,000, 0.15, 300,000

C7. 0.18

C8. 0.18, 360,000

C9. gain, 60,000

C10. 0.17

C11. loss

C12. 340,000

3. In the textbook example of the foreign currency exchange transaction, Alabama Corporation made a sale to a _____ company and agreed to accept _____ in payment.

4. Alabama Corporation's reporting currency was _____.

5. We must translate the 2,000,000 franc sale on December 16 into _____ for recording on Alabama's books. We did this by multiplying the number of francs by the number of dollars that a franc would buy, $ _____.

6. Thus we record the sale at _____ francs x $_____ or $ _____.

7. As of December 31, 1997, the exchange rate had risen so that one franc will buy $ _____.

8. Therefore, the 2,000,000 francs that Alabama will receive will buy more dollars. 2,000,000 francs x $_____ equals $_____.

9. Thus, Alabama has experienced a foreign currency exchange _____ of $ _____.

10. When Alabama collected the receivable on January 15, 1998, the exchange rate had dropped to $_____ per franc.

11. Since December 31, 1997, Alabama has experienced a foreign currency exchange _____ , because the 2,000,000 francs they will receive will buy fewer dollars.

12. The 2,000,000 francs will now buy only $ _____.

LEARNING GOALS ACHIEVEMENT TEST

1. (LG 1) List four reasons for business acquisitions.

   (1) _____
   (2) _____
   (3) _____
   (4) _____

2. (LG 2-6) On December 31, 1997, the accounts of the Catalina Corporation and its wholly owned subsidiary, Capri Corporation, showed the following balances:

Account Title	Catalina	Capri
Cash	$ 50,000	$10,000
Accounts Receivable from Capri	4,000	0
Accounts Receivable--Other	12,000	6,000
Investment in Capri	94,000	0
Property, Plant, and Equipment	120,000	90,000
Accounts Payable to Catalina	0	4,000
Accounts Payable--Other	30,000	8,000
Common Stock	150,000	60,000
Retained Earnings	100,000	34,000

   Enter the balances on the work sheet to prepare consolidated financial statements on the next page and complete the work sheet. Also prepare the consolidated balance sheet.

CATALINA CORPORATION AND SUBSIDIARY CAPRI
WORK SHEET FOR CONSOLIDATED STATEMENTS
DECEMBER 31, 1997

Account Title	Catalina	Capri	Eliminations Debit	Eliminations Credit	Consolidated Trial Balance

Consolidated Balance Sheet

3. (LG 7) The Iowa Grain Marketing Co-op sold a load of grain to a Japanese importer for 5,000,000 yen on September 10, 1997, when the exchange rate was $0.007 = 1 yen. On October 28, 1997, it received payment in yen. The exchange rate on that date was $0.008 = 1 yen. Prepare general journal entries to record the sale and collection, assuming that the reporting currency of Iowa Grain is the dollar.

GENERAL JOURNAL

Date	Accounts and Explanations	PR	Debit	Credit

ANSWERS TO LEARNING GOALS ACHIEVEMENT TEST

1. Possible answers include:

   Opening new markets
   Establish a fair market share in new products
   Achieve growth
   Complement existing operations
   Diversify into nonrelated fields
   Improve overall profitability

2.
CATALINA CORPORATION AND SUBSIDIARY CAPRI
WORK SHEET FOR CONSOLIDATED STATEMENTS
DECEMBER 31, 1997

Account Title	Catalina	Capri	Eliminations Debit	Eliminations Credit	Consolidated Trial Balance
Debit Accounts					
Cash	50,000	10,000			60,000
Accts. Rec. - Capri	4,000	0		(b) 4,000	0
Accts. Rec. - Other	12,000	6,000			18,000
Investment in Capri	94,000	0		(a) 94,000	0
Property, plant, & Equipment	120,000	90,000			210,000
Totals	280,000	106,000			288,000

Credit Accounts					
Accts. Pay. - Catalina	0	4,000	(b) 4,000		0
Accts. Pay. - Other	30,000	8,000			38,000
Common Stock	150,000	60,000	(a) 60,000		150,000
Retained Earnings	100,000	34,000	(a) 34,000		100,000
Totals	280,000	106,000	98,000	98,000	288,000

CATALINA CORPORATION
CONSOLIDATED BALANCE SHEET
DECEMBER 31, 1997

Assets

Current
Cash	$60,000	
Accounts receivable	18,000	
Total current assets		$ 78,000
Property, plant, and equipment		210,000
Total assets		$288,000

Liabilities

Current
Accounts payable		$ 38,000

Stockholders' equity
Common stock	$150,000	
Retained earnings	100,000	
Total Stockholders' equity		250,000
Total liabilities and stockholders' equity		$288,000

3.
GENERAL JOURNAL

Date		Accounts and Explanations	PR	Debit	Credit
1997 Sep.	10	Accounts Receivable		35,000	
		Sales			35,000
		Sale of grain for 5,000,000 yen. Exchange: $0.007 = 1 yen.			
Oct.	28	Cash		40,000	
		Foreign Currency Exchange Gain			5,000
		Accounts Receivable			35,000
		Collection of 5,000,000 yen. Exchange: $0.008 = 1 yen.			

Chapter 18

FINANCIAL REPORTING ISSUES

EXPLANATION OF MAJOR CONCEPTS

Standard-Setting Bodies   LG 1

Three authoritative bodies have had a significant influence on the establishment of accounting standards: the American Institute of Certified Public Accountants, the Financial Accounting Standards Board, and the Securities and Exchange Commission. The AICPA was very active in the setting of standards until 1973 when the FASB came into existence. The principal pronouncements of the AICPA which affected financial reporting were the *Accounting Research Bulletins* and the *Accounting Principles Board Opinions.*

In 1973, the accounting profession created the FASB as an independent, standard setting body. Through their staff, the FASB researches financial reporting issues and makes pronouncements regarding reporting practices. Today the FASB is the primary non-governmental body which establishes the practices and procedures of financial reporting in the United States. The FASB established many of the accounting methods which you are studying in this course.

The SEC also plays a role in the establishment of accounting standards. The SEC alone has the legal authority to set accounting methods for firms that sell their stocks and bonds on the stock exchanges. In most cases, the SEC has relied on the FASB to issue financial accounting reporting standards. The primary concern of the SEC is the fairness and accuracy of public disclosure in external financial reports. To this goal, the SEC has required additional notes and disclosures to the financial statements of publicly held companies in order to provide full and fair disclosure.

Generally Accepted Accounting Principles   LG 2

Over the years the accounting profession has developed a set of standards which are called generally accepted accounting principles. The principles discussed in the chapter are:

- Entity--keep separate accounting records for each business.
- Going Concern--an entity will continue to operate indefinitely.
- Consistency-- follow the same procedures every period.
- Conservatism--choose the procedure which produces the least favorable immediate result on the financial statements.

- Periodicity--prepare financial statements for regularly specified time periods.
- Objective Evidence--amounts recorded in accounting records should be supported by source documents.
- Materiality--accounting treatment of an item too small to influence a decision need not follow prescribed standards.
- Full Disclosure--financial statements should report all significant information.
- Historical Cost--record assets at the actual cost incurred.
- Stable Dollar--use the dollar as the unit of measure without adjustment for changes in price levels.
- Revenue Realization--generally recognize revenue in the accounting records according to one of the following methods:
  - Point of Sale
  - Collection Method--cost recovery or installment basis
  - Percentage of Completion
- Matching Expense and Revenue--match expenses incurred in the generation of revenue against those revenues.

The Conceptual Framework of Accounting   LG 3

Recently, the FASB has worked on a project to create an overall "Conceptual Framework of Accounting." This project has resulted in the issuance of several Concept Statements to provide the framework within which the FASB will set accounting standards.

The first concept statement presents the overall objectives of financial reporting. It states that financial reporting should provide (1) information useful in making investment and credit decisions, (2) information useful in judging future cash flows, and (3) information about the resources, claims to the resources, and changes in resources of an organization.

Concepts Statement 2 examined the characteristics that make accounting information useful. Exhibit 18-1 presents these qualities in a diagram. The two primary qualities that make accounting information useful are relevance and reliability. Accounting information is relevant if it is timely, helps make predictions, and provides feedback. It is reliable if it is verifiable, neutral, and has representational faithfulness.

Inflation Impact   LG 4

Current accounting standards require that we base external financial reporting on historical cost. From 1979 through 1987, the FASB required certain large companies to include supplemental information on the effects of changes in price levels on selected income statement information. During the period of experimentation, they required two alternative methods. The first adjusts for general price-level changes, and the second adjusts to the current cost of the specific item.

On the balance sheet, inflation will mean that GAAP shows assets at a lower value than their current market price. On the income statement, historical cost will mean that expenses such as depreciation are stated at an amount lower than the current cost of using those assets. Thus net income is higher.

Financial Reporting Issues 381

Management's Discussion and Analysis (MDA) LG 5

The SEC requires management to prepare a detailed explanation of any favorable or unfavorable trends and significant events. They include this in a special section of the annual report called management's discussion and analysis (MDA). The MDA must include a discussion of each of three areas: operating results, capital resources, and liquidity.

Report of the Independent Accountant LG 6

An important point to remember is that the financial statements are the representations of management not of the independent accountant. The role of the independent accountant is to provide a check on the financial reporting of management. The end result of the audit examination is the report of the independent accountant that expresses an opinion on the fairness of the presentation of the financial statements.

GUIDED STUDY OF THIS CHAPTER

A. Authoritative Bodies and Generally Accepted Accounting Principles

1. The authoritative body that published statements entitled *Opinions* is the _APB_.

A1. Accounting Principles Board of the AICPA

2. The current nongovernmental standard setting body is the _FASB_.

A2. FASB (*Financial Accounting Standards Board*)

3. The major pronouncements of the FASB are the _Statements of Financial Standards_.

A3. Statements of Financial Accounting Standards

4. The major governmental body that makes accounting rules governing external reporting is the _SEC_.

A4. Securities and Exchange Commission

5. The accounting principle which suggests that the alternative accounting procedure chosen should present the least favorable result is the _conservatism_ principle.

382 Chapter 18

A5. conservatism

A6. Going concern

A7. Full disclosure

A8. entity

A9. consistency

A10. Historical cost

A11. materiality

A12. point of sale

A13. percentage of completion

6. _Going Concern_ assumes that the entity will continue indefinitely.

7. _Full Disclosure_ dictates that all significant financial and economic information should be reported.

8. The principle which requires that we keep a separate set of books for each business is the _Entity_ principle.

9. The principle which requires that we follow the same accounting procedures each period is the _consistency_ principle.

10. _Historical Cost_ requires that we record assets at their incurred cost.

11. The _Materiality_ principle suggests that we may treat an item in a manner different from prescribed accounting if the item is small enough that it does not influence a decision based upon the statements.

12. The revenue realization method which dictates that we record revenue when we perform the service or deliver the goods is the _Point of sale_ method.

13. The revenue recognition method that uses the current proportion of the total costs incurred to determine the revenue recorded is the _% of completion_ method.

14. A method of revenue recognition often used by retail stores recognizes a portion of each dollar collected as a return of cost and a portion as gross margin. This is the _Installment basis_.

Financial Reporting Issues 383

A14. installment basis

A15. matching

B1. useful in making investment and credit decisions, in judging future cash flows, and in reporting on resources, claims to resources, and changes in resources

B2. benefits should be greater than cost, materiality

B3. relevance, reliability

B4. historical cost

B5. independent appraisals

B6. $22,000

15. Under the _Matching Principle_ principle, we should record the expenses incurred to generate revenue in the same period as the revenues.

B. Conceptual Statement and Price-level Accounting

1. The first *Statement of Financial Accounting Concept* lists as the basic objectives of financial reporting the fact that financial information should be _useful in making investment + credit decisions, useful in judging amounts future cash flows, useful resourses of the business - claims + changes in Resources_.

2. *Concept Statement No. 2* lists two overall constraints on accounting information. They are _Benefits > Cost_

   and _must be material_.

3. The two primary qualities that make accounting information useful are _Relevance_
   and _Reliability_.

4. Considering the impact of inflation on the balance sheet, users must remember that most assets are stated at _Historical Cost_.

5. If we are making decisions that require information on asset values, we may need _Independent appraisals_.

6. If a company bought two identical cars, one in 1995 at $10,000 and one in 1997 at $12,000, we would show total assets of $ _22,000_.

7. Would this represent the current value of the two cars? _No_

384 Chapter 18

B7. No.

B8. 2,500, 3,000

B9. No.

B11. overstate

C1. Management Discussion and Analysis (MDA)

C2. operating results, capital resources, liquidity

C3. independent accountant

C4. specifies the financial statements audited, the auditor's responsibility, expresses an opinion

8. If each of the cars has an estimated useful life of 4 years and no residual value and we used straight-line depreciation, the depreciation expense on car one in 1998 would be $ _2500_ and on car two $ _3000_ .

9. If the cars were identical, do these depreciation amounts reflect the current cost of using the cars? _No_

10. Will we overstate or understate the net income by using these depreciation amounts? _overstate_

C. Other Reporting Issues

1. The SEC requires that the annual report contain an explanation of favorable and unfavorable trends. Companies include this in the _MDA_ .

2. The MDA explains trends and significant events or uncertainties in the areas of _Operating results_, _Financial position_, and _liquidity of the company_.

3. The annual report also contains a report of the _Independent accountant_.

4. This report includes three paragraphs which _specifies the financial statements audited_, states _auditor's responsibility_, and _expresses an opinion_.

LEARNING GOALS ACHIEVEMENT TEST

1. (LG 1-3, 5,6) Complete the following statements by filling in the blank.

   a. Currently, the primary private sector standard setting body is the ___FASB___.

   b. The series of statements that have dealt with the objectives of financial reporting, the qualitative characteristics of accounting information, and the elements of financial statements are known as ___Statements of Financial accounting concepts___.

   c. According to these statements accounting information should be ___relevant___ and ___Reliable___.

   d. The part of the annual financial report where management is required by the SEC to explain trends, significant events, and uncertainties is called ___MDA___.

   e. The financial statements of a company are the representations of ___management___.

2. (LG 2) Match the letter of the description with the proper generally accepted accounting principle.

_C_	Entity	a.	Financial statements are prepared at regular intervals.
_I_	Going concern		
_B_	Consistency	b.	The same accounting procedures should be followed each year.
_K_	Conservatism		
_A_	Periodicity	c.	A separate set of records is kept for each business.
_J_	Objective evidence		
_D_	Materiality	d.	Small dollar amounts need not follow generally accepted accounting principles.
_F_	Full disclosure		
_H_	Historical cost		
_G_	Stable dollar	e.	Expenses incurred in generating revenues should be recorded in the same period as the revenues.
_E_	Matching		
		f.	Financial statements should report significant financial and economic events.
		g.	The dollar is significantly free from changes in purchasing power.
		h.	A transaction is recorded at the amount incurred.
		i.	A business is assumed to operate indefinitely.
		j.	Amounts used in recording transactions should be based on source documents.
		k.	Using the alternative which will give the least favorable immediate results.

3. (LG 2) The Bargain Basement sold a television set for $400 which had cost them $300. For each of the following months calculate the amount of gross margin that will be recognized on the installment basis given the amount received from the customer.

   a. March, $50.

   b. April, $75.

   c. May, $100.

ANSWERS TO LEARNING GOALS ACHIEVEMENT TEST

1. a. Financial Accounting Standards Board
   b. Statements of Financial Accounting Concepts
   c. relevant, reliable
   d. management's discussion and analysis (MDA)
   e. management

2. c, i, b, k, a, j, d, f, h, g, e.

3. a. $50.00 x [($400 - $300)/$400] = $12.50.
   b. $75.00 x .25 = $18.75.
   c. $100.00 x .25 = $25.00.

Appendix A

FEDERAL INCOME TAXES

EXPLANATION OF MAJOR CONCEPTS

The Federal Income Tax System

Under our federal income tax system each taxpayer makes an annual report to the Internal Revenue Service (IRS). This report, made on standardized forms, is called an income tax return. Each individual taxpayer must file (mail a report of) his or her return for a given year with the IRS by April 15 of the following year. Married couples may combine their information into one return called a joint return, or they may elect to file separate returns. In addition to individuals, there are three other classes of taxpayers: corporations, estates, and trusts.

We partially pay federal income tax month by month during the tax year. The most common method to do this is withholding. In this method, the laws requires an employer to withhold a portion of each employee's paycheck and remit it to the IRS. Individuals who have income other than salary (and thus have income not subject to withholding) must file a declaration of estimated tax on such amounts and make quarterly payments of those estimates. Corporations must also make prepayments based on estimated income. The IRS credits amounts withheld and amounts prepaid with estimates to the taxpayer's account during the year. Then, when the taxpayer files their return with the actual tax due computed, they may take credit for these prepaid amounts against the total tax due. Many taxpayers each year find that their prepayments are greater than the tax due and receive a refund check from the IRS.

Computing the Tax Due   LG 1-3

Exhibit A-1 shows the steps that an individual (or joint return) taxpayer takes to compute the amount of tax due. You should refer to this Exhibit constantly as you study Appendix A. Read Exhibit A-1 from top down. Note that it splits into two paths just below the determination of adjusted gross income. Each taxpayer takes only one of these two paths. The path chosen by the taxpayer will depend upon whether or not they have itemized deductions in excess of the standard deduction amount. If they do not, they will follow the nonitemizer path. If they follow the itemizer path, they will list all of their qualifying deductions. Both the itemizer and nonitemizer then deduct their exemptions to arrive at their taxable income. At this point, they compute the gross tax using the appropriate tax rates. To determine the net taxes payable, subtract tax credits and prepayments from the gross tax.

To determine the amount of tax due, a taxpayer reports the gross amount of income for the year--usually on a cash basis. They may exclude only a few specified items (listed in Exhibit A-2) from reporting. Although it may appear that taxpayers are on an "honor system" to report all income items, the IRS has many ways to check the accuracy of reporting. Every employer reports to IRS the amount of wages and salaries paid; corporations report dividends and interest paid; savings institutions report the amount of interest paid, and so on. With an enormous computer network, the IRS can match this information with a taxpayer's return to ensure that the taxpayer has reported all items of gross income.

Many taxpayers use provisions within the tax laws to adjust their gross incomes downward. For example, the law allows a taxpayer to deduct reimbursed employee business expenses, payments into IRAs and Keogh Plans for certain individuals, and other like items to determine adjusted gross income. Adjusted gross income (AGI) is a key amount in most tax returns because it serves as a basis for other computations. For example, we use AGI to compute limitations on amounts of deductions for medical expenses. Exhibit A-3 illustrates the AGI computation.

The law allows a taxpayer to deduct certain items from AGI to determine the amount of taxable income. The textbook discuss these items. They fall into six major categories.

- Contributions to religious, educational, or charitable institutions.
- Allowable medical and dental expenses in excess of 7 1/2 % of AGI.
- State and local income taxes, and real estate and personal property taxes.
- Interest paid on home mortgages.
- Limited nonbusiness casualty losses.
- Employee expenses such as union dues, special work clothes, or dues to professional societies, and expenses of producing income such as tax return preparation in excess of 2% of AGI.

The law allows a personal exemption for the taxpayer, for the spouse (if a joint return is filed), and for each person who qualifies as a dependent. In 1996, the exemption is $2,500 per exemption. The IRS will increase the personal exemption each year for inflation.

The final step is computation of the amount of tax due and the application of certain credits against that tax. The allowable tax credits include: elderly and permanently disabled, child and dependent care, earned income credit, and targeted job credits. The taxpayer then files the return with a check for the amount due or an indication on the return form that a refund is due.

Corporate Income Taxes LG 4

The income of a corporation is subject to tax. In general, we compute the taxable income of a corporation in the same manner as for an individual. A few differences exist. Personal exemptions and adjusted gross income are not applicable. A corporation may only deduct charitable contributions up to 10% of net income. They may deduct 80% of dividends received from domestic corporations.

Interperiod Tax Allocation   LG 5

The income tax expense of a business based on net income computed with generally accepted accounting principles and the income tax actually paid by a company may differ for several reasons. Sometimes, these differences are only temporary and will cancel each other in a few years. The *FASB Statement No. 96* concluded that we must allocate income tax expense among the relevant periods and that we should use the liability method of tax allocation. We must base income tax expense reported on the income statement on book net income. This practice is known as *interperiod income tax allocation.*

Tax Planning

It is illegal to fail to report income or, in some other manner, to evade the payment of income taxes that are legally due. It is perfectly proper, however, to make business decisions in a way that will have the most favorable income tax effect. Suppose an individual (a cash basis taxpayer) incurs a medical expense in late December but has not yet been billed for it. If that person has already accumulated enough medical expenses to qualify for a deduction, he or she would want to pay before receipt of the bill to ensure that they include this expense in a year that has excess medical expenses. On the other hand, if the taxpayer will not have enough medical expenses to qualify, he or she will want to wait until January to pay (even if billed by the end of December) because there is a chance that medical expenses may qualify as excess in the following year. Business managers, while not on a cash basis, do a similar type of tax planning. The use of LIFO to place a valuation on inventory usually produces a lower reported net income to the stockholders, but it also provides a lower taxable income to be reported to the IRS. The important point is that a manager should consider the effect that a decision will have on income taxes before making decisions to purchase more equipment, hire additional people, or other actions that could affect the taxes of the business.

390   Appendix A

GUIDED STUDY OF THIS APPENDIX

A. The Federal Income Tax System

1. Individuals in the United States are subject to payment of tax on their income. Are proprietorships also required to pay income tax? _____ Explain.
   _____
   _____
   _____
   _____
   _____

A1. No. The individual proprietor (*owner*) includes business earnings on his or her personal income tax return.

2. Is a partnership a taxpaying entity? _____ Explain. _____
   _____
   _____
   _____
   _____
   _____

A2. No. We allocate the shares of partnership income to partners who report them on their individual returns.

3. Is a corporation a taxpaying entity? _____ Explain. _____
   _____
   _____
   _____
   _____

A3. Yes. A corporation is a legal entity (*as well as an accounting entity*) and pays income taxes in its own name.

4. Each taxpayer files an income tax return once per _____ .

A4. year

5. The law does not allow taxpayers to wait until the end of a tax year to make tax payments. Persons whose income comes from salaries must pay a part of their income tax each payday through the _____ system.

Federal Income Taxes 391

A5. withholding

6. Persons with income amounts not subject to withholding must also pay taxes during the year by _____ _____ _____.

A6. filing an estimate of such taxes and making quarterly payments

7. At the end of the year, a taxpayer whose total of withholdings and other payments is less than actual tax due will _____ _____.

A7. send a check to the IRS for the difference

8. Conversely, a taxpayer who has overpaid may _____ _____.

A8. receive a refund

9. Individuals compute their personal tax liabilities on a(n) _____ (*cash/accrual*) basis.

A9. cash

10. Business income is determined on a(n) _____ basis.

A10. accrual

B. Tax Computation
Exhibit A-2 shows the flow of computations for determining the amount of an individual's gross income.

1. All items of income are taxable unless they are _____ _____.

B1. specifically excluded by the tax law

2. Some people are not aware of the status of tips. Are tips taxable income? ____

B2. Yes.

3. What is the status (*taxable/nontaxable*) of gifts? _____.
GI bill educational benefits? _____ _____. Interest on municipal bonds? _____.

B3. These items are generally nontaxable.

4. Exhibit A-3, shows deductions to arrive at _____ _____.

B4. adjusted gross income (AGI)

5. Deductions to arrive at adjusted gross income include _____
_____
_____
_____ .

B5. reimbursed employee business expenses, certain IRA deposits, self-employed health insurance, Keogh deduction, and alimony paid

6. For example, reimbursed travel expenses of employees _____ (are/are not) deductible to arrive at AGI.

B6. are

7. But travel reimbursement by employers is included in gross income. This means that an employee who travels is taxed on travel reimbursements if they _____
_____ .

B7. are greater than the actual expenses

8. On the other hand, if expenses are greater than reimbursement, the employee will end up with a _____ (lower/higher) adjusted gross income.

B8. lower

9. Certain deductions shown in Exhibit A-4 are deductible from AGI. Contributions, to be deductible, must be to a religious, educational, or charitable organization. Does a contribution to a college fraternity qualify? _____

B9. No.

10. Suppose a fraternity or sorority holds a walkathon with all proceeds going to the Heart Fund. May sponsors of individual walkers deduct as contributions the amounts they donate? _____

B10. Yes.

11. Charitable contributions are one type of itemized deduction. Another category is allowable medical expenses.

B11. No answer required.

12. In 1996, what was the limitation on the inclusion of medical expenses in itemized deductions? _____
_____
_____

Federal Income Taxes 393

B12. Only costs in excess of 7 1/2% of AGI were deductible.

B13. They were not deductible.

B14. various employee expenses and expenses of producing income

B15. 2% of AGI

B16. itemizer

B17. nonitemizer

B18. exemptions

B19. taxable income

B20. gross income tax before tax credits

B21. tax credits, payments against tax

13. What was the tax-deductible status of the sales taxes and the state tax on gasoline? _____

14. Another category of deductions is home mortgage interest. The last category of deductions, called miscellaneous, includes _____ _____ _____ .

15. We may deducted only if they exceed _____ _____ .

16. We call a taxpayer who lists and reports deductions in these categories a(n) _____ taxpayer.

17. A taxpayer whose itemized deductions are less than the standard deduction would not claim itemized deductions but would take the standard deduction and would be called a(n) _____ taxpayer.

18. After deducting the standard deduction or itemized deductions whichever is greater, we deduct _____ .

19. At this point, the amount computed is the _____ .

20. We use taxable income to compute the _____ _____ .

21. From this amount, we subtract _____ _____ and _____ _____ to get the tax due or refund.

394   Appendix A

C1. gross income with certain earnings related deductions subtracted

C2. Yes.

C3. 2,000 ($2,250 with a nonworking spouse), IRA

C4. They may be claimed by either an itemizer or nonitemizer taxpayer to determine AGI.

C5. When personal deductions are greater than the standard deduction.

C6. that a nonitemizer may deduct in computing taxable income

C. Tax Terms Study the meaning of some specific tax terms.

1. Adjusted gross income is _____ _____ _____ _____ _____.

2. Business travel to and from one's job is not deductible. Is the reimbursed cost of business travel (for example, from your place of work to attend a meeting and back to the place of work) deductible to determine AGI? _____

3. A taxpayer not covered by an employer pension plan may set aside $ _____ in an _____ each year.

4. How are these deductions from gross income different from itemized deductions? _____ _____ _____

5. When should an individual decide to be an itemizer taxpayer? _____ _____ _____ _____

6. The standard deduction is the amount _____ _____ _____.

7. Are personal deductions and personal exemptions the same thing? _____

C7. No.

C8. charitable contributions, allowable medical expenses, mortgage interest, state and local taxes, and some miscellaneous items

C9. No. Medical must exceed 7 1/2% of AGI, and miscellaneous must exceed 2% of AGI.

C10. An amount for each person who qualifies as a dependent, $2,500 in 1996, that a taxpayer deducts in calculating taxable income.

C11. Deductions from the amount of computed income tax.

D1. book net income

8. Personal deductions from AGI cover such things as _____
_____
_____
_____
_____
_____
_____ .

9. May we deduct total itemized deductions? _____ Why or why not?
_____
_____
_____
_____

10. What is a personal exemption? _____
_____
_____
_____
_____
_____
_____
_____

11. In general, what are tax credits?
_____
_____
_____
_____
_____

D. **Tax Allocation** Temporary differences arise when a company has income on its books that is different from taxable income for a reason that will reverse over a period of time.

1. We base income tax expense for the current year under the matching concept on _____ .

2. When differences exist between book net income and taxable income due to _____ differences, the accepted practice is to _____ income taxes among the relevant periods. We refer to this practice as _____
_____ .

396 Appendix A

D2. temporary, allocate; interperiod income tax allocation

3. One type of temporary difference arises when we recognize revenue in one accounting period for book purposes, but do not pay _____ until later periods.

D3. tax

4. Another type of temporary difference occurs when the MACRS deduction exceeds the _____ reflected on the income statement.

D4. depreciation expense

5. When the MACRS deduction exceeds the depreciation expense, accounting income will be _____ (*higher/lower*) than taxable income.

D5. higher

6. Thus income tax based on accounting income will be _____ (*higher/lower*) than income tax based on taxable income.

D6. higher

7. When we record this, the debit to Income Tax Expense will be _____ (*more/less*) than the credit to Income Taxes Payable.

D7. more

8. To balance the entry, we will need an additional credit. This will be to _____.

D8. Deferred Income Taxes

9. When the temporary difference reverses itself, we will _____ Deferred Income Taxes.

D9. debit

LEARNING GOALS ACHIEVEMENT TEST

1. Indicate whether the following are true or false.

   ____ a. The types of entities subject to federal income tax are (1) individuals, (2) corporations, (3) income-producing estates, and (4) income-producing trusts.
   ____ b. Employee reimbursed business expenses are deductible from gross income to calculate AGI.
   ____ c. Gross income for tax purposes includes every dollar that an individual receives in a tax year.
   ____ d. After AGI has been determined, there are additional amounts that may be deducted to determine taxable income if a person is an itemizer taxpayer.
   ____ e. Persons are allowed a personal exemption for their spouse if the return is joint, and for each dependent.
   ____ f. Partnerships are taxable entities and pay income taxes on total partnership net income before it is divided among partners.
   ____ g. Corporations are taxable entities and pay income taxes on corporate net income before it is paid out to the stockholders as dividends.
   ____ h. All taxpayers are allowed to deduct contributions to charitable organizations.
   ____ i. The fact that the law does allow a corporation to report greater depreciation on its tax return than on its income statement can cause the income tax expense to be greater than the tax actually paid.
   ____ j. Any difference between income tax expense on the income statement and the tax actually paid caused by using different methods of depreciation for the two purposes is a permanent gain or loss and will never be repaid or recovered.
   ____ k. Because the difference described in Question j is self-reversing it is called a temporary difference.
   ____ l. The fact that a temporary difference exists means that the corporation should use interperiod tax allocation in the accounting records.

ANSWERS TO LEARNING GOALS ACHIEVEMENT TEST

1. a. T f. F k. T
   b. T g. T l. T
   c. F h. F
   d. T i. T
   e. T j. F

Appendix B

UNDERSTANDING PUBLISHED ANNUAL FINANCIAL REPORTS

EXPLANATION OF MAJOR CONCEPTS

Using Accounting Concepts and Methods   LG 1

Appendix B contains the two sets of financial statements, notes and report of the independent auditor. The first is for a hypothetical company, Starr Home Products. These are simplified statements designed to present a clear and concise review. Boxed references highlight important items and explain their significance. Study these box references carefully.

The second set of statements is from the 1995 Annual Report of the Procter & Gamble Company. The appendix includes two questions covering the material in each chapter. These questions require the use of the financial statements and notes for 1995 for Procter & Gamble. We have designed these questions to help you in understanding and using actual financial statements. You can use them after completing each chapter, after each unit, or at the end of each semester. Consult your instructor on how he or she plans to use them in your class.

Appendix C

APPLICATION OF COMPOUND INTEREST AND TABLES

EXPLANATION OF MAJOR CONCEPTS

A Comparison of Simple Interest and Compound Interest LG 1

Simple interest is interest computed only on the principal. Compound interest is interest computed on the principal plus prior period's interest. With compound interest, we do not pay the interest in each period but add it to the principal. The next period the new sum earns interest. A simple illustration will help show the difference. Assume that we invested $1,000.00 in an account for four months at 12%. If it earned simple interest, the calculation of the interest would be as follows:

$1,000.00 x 0.12 x (4/12) = $40.00

If we had invested the amount in an account at the same rate of interest, but the interest compounded monthly, the interest calculation would have been as follows:

$1,000.00 x .12 x (1/12)	=	$10.00	$1,000.00 + $10.00 = $1,010.00
$1,010.00 x .12 x (1/12)	=	10.10	$1,010.00 + $10.10 = $1,020.10
$1,020.10 x .12 x (1/12)	=	10.20	$1,020.10 + $10.20 = $1,030.30
$1,030.30 x .12 x (1/12)	=	10.30	$1,030.30 + $10.30 = $1,040.60
Total		$40.60	

When we loan or invest money at compound interest, the interest accumulated for a period is not paid but is added to the principal amount. For the next period, we apply the same interest rate to the greater principal, yielding a larger amount of interest than in the prior period. We again add this interest to the principal, creating a greater amount that we multiply by the same rate. The cycle continues period after period until the end of the specified term. We can see in this illustration that simple interest at 12% for four months on $1,000.00 was $40.00. Interest compounded monthly at 12% for four months gave $40.60 in interest or $0.60 more interest. The important concept here is that interest is constantly being added back to the principal. Thus we are calculating interest on the original principal plus the periodic interest additions. We refer to this concept as *compound interest*.

Banks compound interest in savings accounts. Certain other types of investments can earn compound interest. For this reason, business people compare simple interest investments with their equivalents in compound interest yields to make decisions. Although bonds issued by corporations to borrow money actually carry simple interest at an annual rate, investors make a compound interest calculation to determine where to invest. Choices among investments in plant or in equipment are often made on the basis of comparisons of their compound interest returns to the company. If you are to understand these topics, you must master compound interest techniques first.

Types of Compound Interest Calculations   LG 2-6

In Appendix C, we use the time value of money in connection with five basic computations. We will briefly review each of the five in this section.

Future Amount of a Single Sum   LG 2

When we add the $1,000.00 principal to the interest shown in the previous section, the amount becomes $1,040.60 = ($1,000.00 + $40.60), or the *future amount of a single sum*. This compound amount is the dollar value to which a single sum of $1,000.00 will grow in four months at a given interest rate (12%) and a given frequency of compounding (monthly). The more frequent the compounding, the faster the amount will grow. Thus, $1,000.00 compounded daily at the annual rate of 12% will grow to a future sum greater than $1,040.60 in four months because we add the interest back more times.

Present Value of a Single Sum   LG 3

We can work any computation that allows us to determine a compound future amount backward. The process of working backward from a known future sum to find what earlier amount we compounded to produce it is called discounting. The amount that we used to begin the compounding (the original principal) we call the *present value*. In our example, we know that the present value (today) of $1,040.60 four months from today is $1,000.00 if the annual interest rate is 12% and the compounding is done monthly. If we know only the future amount, we can compute the present value for any given annual interest rate and number of compounding periods.

Future Amount of an Ordinary Annuity   LG 4

An annuity is a type of investment in which we add periodic deposits to an original sum in addition to the compound interest. Thus, an annuity grows in two ways: (1) by the addition of compound interest and (2) by the addition of periodic additional deposits. Of course, an annuity will grow to a much greater amount than a single sum given the same interest rate and compounding periods. We call the additional deposits rents. When we deposit the rents at the end of each period, the annuity is called an *ordinary annuity*. The amount the periodic deposits and compound interest grow to is the *future amount of an ordinary annuity*.

Present Value of an Ordinary Annuity LG 5

There are instances in which a person (or business) would like to invest a single sum now and withdraw periodic amounts from the investment over a period of time. We make the withdrawals at the end of each compounding period. The amount invested now to allow us to make these withdrawals is called the *present value of an ordinary annuity*. For example, a company may buy a machine now for $100,000 that will increase net income by $5,000 per month over its estimated useful life. The monthly earnings are really periodic withdrawals instead of deposits. We still call them rents. The $100,000 investment required to earn them is the present value of the investment in an ordinary annuity. Often we know the amounts of withdrawals (as is the case with interest on corporate bonds) but we do not know the present value. We can compute it for any given rate of interest, amount of each rent, and frequency of withdrawals.

Present Value of an Annuity Due LG 6

An annuity due is similar to an ordinary annuity except that we deposit or withdrawal each rent at the beginning of the period instead of the end. In this case, we invest the *present value of an ordinary annuity* and immediately begin making the withdrawals. We can find the present value of an annuity due using the present value of an ordinary annuity. The factor for the present value of an annuity due of 6 rents is equal to the factor for the present value of an ordinary annuity of 5 rents plus 1.0. Multiplying this factor by the amount of the rent gives the present value of an annuity due.

Compound Interest Tables

As explained in Appendix C, there are formulas for the computation of each of the four compound interest amounts. You should understand the idea that underlies each formula, but it is not necessary to memorize them. The tables in the back of the appendix provide factors for each of the four basic computations. The factors in each of these tables represent the formula applied to $1. Accordingly, you can use the tables in two steps as follows:

1. Determine the appropriate table to use. Which of the five above situations are you working with? (This isn't easy. Students find it useful to draw time lines or other diagrams and label them to see exactly what type of situation exists.)

2. When you have selected the proper table, multiply (or divide) by the factor for *n* and *i* for the given situation. In doing this, remember that *n* is the number of periods in the future amount of a single sum or present value of a single sum and the number of rents for an annuity. The variable *i* represents the interest rate per compound period, not the annual rate. In the case of 12% compounded monthly, $i = 1\%$.

404 Appendix C

GUIDED STUDY OF THIS APPENDIX

A. Simple and Compound Interest

1. In the formula for simple interest ($I = PRT$), P is the _____ .

A1. principal amount

2. R is the interest rate per _____ .

A2. year

3. And T is the time at interest stated as a fraction (or multiple) of a _____ .

A3. year

4. To apply the formula, the textbook uses an example of K. Wait and D. Orlando. When the term of the loan is 90 days, T = _____ .

A4. 90/360 or 1/4

5. The principal amount of this note is $_____ .

A5. 10,000

6. The simple interest for 90 days is $_____ .

A6. 300

7. Compound interest is interest earned on a principal sum we increase at the end of each period by the _____ .

A7. interest for that period

8. Exhibit C-1 shows a compound interest computation. For the first quarter, the amount of interest is $_____ .

A8. 300

9. Is this the same as it would be under simple interest for 1/4 year? _____ . Why or why not? _____

A9. Yes; Because it is original principal x rate x time.

10. In the second quarter at the same rate, the interest is now $_____ instead of $300. How is this possible? _____

Application of Compound Interest and Tables 405

A10. 309; Because we added last quarter's interest to the principal making it larger.

A11. 10,300

A12. For the total term of the loan.

A13. $10,000 + ($10,000 x 0.12 x 1) = $11,200.

A14. the future accumulated amount at the end of each quarter becomes the new principal

B1. four

B2. 12; 4

B3. 3; 16

11. In the second quarter, we multiply $_____ 12% x 1/4 to equal $309.

12. Each quarter the principal becomes larger. How long will this continue? _____
_____
_____

13. In Exhibit C-1, the future amount at the end of a year is $11,255.09. Compute the amount it would be (its maturity value) at the end of a year using simple interest.
_____
_____

14. At compound interest the loan has earned $55.09 more than it would at simple interest because _____
_____
_____ .

B. **Compound Interest Techniques**

1. The first example is of the future amount of a single sum of $10,000 compounded annually at 12% for _____ years.

2. Since each compounding period is exactly one year, *i* is the same as the annual rate of _____ % and *n* is _____ periods.

3. If compounding were quarterly for this four-year period, *i* would become _____ percent and *n* would be _____ .

4. Exhibit C-2 shows a partial table for the future amount of $1. To use any table determine the values of *n* and *i*. Then go down the *n* column to the desired number of periods and across the table on that row to the column for the desired amount of _____ .

406 Appendix C

B4. *i* (interest)

B5. 1.574

B6. 10,000, 1.574, 15,740

B7. end

B8. 15,735.19, 2001

B9. 1997, four

B10. 0.635518

B11. 10,000.00 (rounded)
     ($15,735.19 x 0.635518)

B12. a series of equal payments
     or rents made at the end
     of regular intervals with
     interest compounded

B13. equal, compound, future
     amount of an ordinary
     annuity

5. The factor for 12% compounded annually for four years is _____ .

6. Thus the future value of $10,000 at 12% for four years is $_____ x _____ = $_____ .

7. In the present value of a single given sum, the known amount is the amount that will be on deposit at the _____ of the time period.

8. In the textbook illustration on page C-7, $_____ is to be in the fund on December 31, _____ .

9. We are to determine the present value as of December 31, _____, or for a period of _____ years.

10. The present value of $1 for 4 periods at 12% is $_____ .

11. If the present value of $1.00 is 0.635518 then the present value of $15,735.19 is $_____ .

12. An ordinary annuity is _____ .

13. If a person made _____ deposits to an account at the end of each period and the account earns _____ interest, the amount that would be in the the account five years from now would be called the _____ .

14. In the future amount of an ordinary annuity illustration, the amount deposited at the end of each period is $_____ . The interest rate per period is _____ %, and the number of rents is _____ each _____ apart.

Application of Compound Interest and Tables   407

B14. 10,000; 12, 4, one year

15. The future value of an ordinary annuity of $1 for four years at 12% compounded annually is $_____ .

B15. 4.779328

16. Thus, the future value of an annuity of $10,000 at 12% for four years is $_____ .

B16. 47,793.28

17. In the present value of an ordinary annuity, the amount of each rent is _____ (known/unknown) and we want to calculate the _____ .

B17. known, amount which is on deposit one period before the first rent

18. In the illustration, we want to know the amount which must be on deposit on _____ to permit four withdrawals of $_____ each on December 31, 199 __ through December 31, _____ .

B18. January 1, 1997, 10,000, 7, 2001

19. The amount that satisfies these conditions is $_____ . We found it by _____ $10,000 by the factor_____ .

B19. 30,373.49; multiplying, 3.037349

20. An annuity due differs from an ordinary annuity in that the rent occurs at the _____ instead of the end of the period.

B20. beginning of the period

21. We calculate the present value of an annuity due _____ .

B21. immediately before the first rent

22. In the textbook example, the first rent occurs on _____ and we calculate the present value as of _____ .

B22. January 1, 1997, January 1, 1997

23. We can find the table factor for an annuity due using the _____ _____ table.

B23. present value of an ordinary annuity

24. For an annuity due of 4 rents at 12%, we look up the factor for an ordinary annuity of _____ rents at 12% and add _____ .

408 Appendix C

B24. 3, 1.0

25. Thus the factor for an annuity due of 4 rents at 12% compound annually is _____ .

B25. 3.401831

C. Use of Compound Interest Tables

1. Tables exist for each of the four basic types of compound interest situations and various values of n and i. The next several frames will explore the use of these tables.

C1. No answer required.

2. A person wants to have $18,000 available five years from today. She can do so by depositing a single amount today that will grow to $18,000. We call that deposit made today the _____ of a single sum.

C2. present value

3. If money is worth 16% compounded quarterly, i is _____ %.

C3. 4

4. Remember that 16% is the annual rate; i is the rate per compounding period, so we must divide the annual rate by _____ periods per year.

C4. four

5. Because the total term is five years, n is _____ .

C5. 20 (5 X 4)

6. Look up the table factor in the table for the present value of a single future amount for $n = 20$ and $i = 4\%$; the factor is _____ .

C6. 0.456

7. This is the amount that will grow to a future amount of _____ .

C7. $1

8. But she needs $18,000 or $18,000 times 0.456= $ _____ .

C8. 8,208

9. This seems unbelievable; let's check it. To determine the future amount to which $8,208 would grow in five years if compounded quarterly at an annual rate of 16%, we would use the table for _____
_____ .

Application of Compound Interest and Tables   409

C9. the future amount of a single sum

10. In Table C-1, the factor for $n = 20$ and $i = 4\%$ is _____.

C10. 2.191

11. And $8,208 × 2.191 = $_____.

C11. 18,000 (rounded)

12. Jane wants to deposit an amount now to make 20 withdrawals of $1,000 at the end of each quarter for the next five years. Are we viewing a present value or a future amount situation? _____.

C12. Present value

13. Is this a single sum an ordinary annuity or an annuity due? _____.

C13. An ordinary annuity

14. So we need the table for the _____.

C14. present value of an ordinary annuity

15. Assume that money is still worth an annual rate of 16% compounded quarterly. The values of n and i are _____ and _____ %.

C15. 20, 4

16. In this case (an ordinary annuity), n is the _____.

C16. number of rents (withdrawals)

17. Look up the table factor; it is _____.

C17. 13.590

18. This, in dollars, is the amount that Jane must deposit now to withdraw $_____ per period for 20 periods.

C18. 1

19. To withdraw $1,000 per period, Jane must deposit 1,000 times that amount or $_____.

C19. 13,590

20. The steps in dealing with compound interest situations require that we first determine whether we are seeking an unknown _____ amount or _____ value.

410   Appendix C

C20. future, present

21. Then we must determine whether we are dealing with a single sum or an _____.

C21. annuity

22. These two steps lead us to the correct table. Now it is necessary to determine the values of _____ and _____ .

C22. n, i

23. Having found the correct table and determined the values of n and i, we locate the factor in the i th column on the n th row and apply it to our known amount.

C23. No answer required.

24. Usually, we must multiply--but sometimes it is necessary to divide--by the table factor. For example, if we know the present or future values of an annuity but we do not know the amount of each rent, we must _____ by the table factor.

C24. divide

D. Applications of Compound Interest

1. When we make installment payments, the amount borrowed or the price of the item purchased represents the _____ value of _____ .

D1. present, an annuity

2. To determine the amount of the installment payments, you would _____ the purchase price by the appropriate factor.

D2. divide

3. In recording the payment of cash, the accountant would split each payment between _____ and _____ .

D3. principal, interest

LEARNING GOALS ACHIEVEMENT TEST

1. (LG 1) Compute the maturity values of the following loans at simple interest:

    a. $1,000 loaned on January 4, 1997, for 90 days at 14%:

    b. $3,000 loaned on April 11, 1997, for 120 days at 15%:

    c. $10,000 loaned for 180 days at 18%:

2. (LG 2-6) Using the compound interest tables, solve the following problems (show *n* and *i* in each case):

   a. Determine the amount to which $1,000 will grow in three years at 18% per year compounded monthly.

   b. Determine the amount you must deposit now to allow 20 quarterly withdrawals of $3,000 each with money worth 20% per year compounded quarterly.

   c. Shelly Lair began to receive a Christmas bonus of $2,000 a year at the end of 1997. She invested each bonus in a savings plan that pays 12% per year compounded annually. How much was in her fund immediately after she deposited her 2001 bonus?

d. The town of Sibley must pay off a debt of $500,000 on December 31, 2006. The town council voted to accumulate a fund by making semiannual deposits into a plan that will earn 12% per year compounded semiannually. The first deposit is to be made on July 1, 1997. What is the amount of each deposit?

e. You have decided to take to take two years off work and volunteer for Operation Greenpeace. You believe that you will need $2,000 per month to travel and promote the environmental movement. You have an investment that will earn 18% compounded monthly. How much will you have to invest now to begin making withdrawals immediately?

ANSWERS TO LEARNING GOALS ACHIEVEMENT TEST

1. a. $1,000 x 0.14 x 90/360 = $35.00 interest; and $1,000.00 + $35.00 = $1,035.00.

   b. $3,000 x 0.15 x 120/360 = $150.00 interest; and $3,000 + $150.00 = $3,150.00.

   c. $10,000 x 0.18 x 180/360 = $900.00 interest; and $10,000.00 + $900.00 = $10,900.00.

2. a. $n = 36 \quad i = 1.5\%$ (Use Table C-1)
   $1,000 x 1.709 = $1,709.

   b. $n = 20 \quad i = 5\%$ (Use Table C-4)
   $3,000 x 12.462 = $37,386.

414 Appendix C

2.   c. $n = 5$ $i = 12\%$ (Use Table C-3)
$2,000 × 6.353 = $12,706.

     d. $n = 20$ $i = 6\%$ (Use Table C-3)
$500,000 ÷ 36.786 = $13,592.

     e.   ordinary annuity factor
$n = 23$ $i = 1.5\%$ (Use Table C-4)

annuity due factor = 19.331 + 1.000 = 20.331
$2,000 × 20.331 = $40,662

Appendix D

SPECIAL JOURNALS AND ACCOUNTING SYSTEMS

EXPLANATION OF MAJOR CONCEPTS

Transaction Processing System LG 1

An accounting system is the set of forms and business papers, journals and ledgers, accounting equipment, and the rules and procedures that tie all of them together to:

1. Capture information about transactions.
2. Record it in an organized and understandable way.
3. Use it to prepare reports that are useful for making decisions.

There is no ideal accounting system. For each entity, the accountant must design a system that suits the unique needs of that organization. Sometimes a simple system with only a general journal and ledger accounts will be adequate. As the entity becomes larger and more complex, the accounting system must contain more journals and equipment.

Exhibits D-1 and D-2 of the textbook diagram and explain the flow of documents through a typical purchases system and sales system. You should take the time to study these flow charts and their explanations. You do not need to memorize these exhibits. Instead, use them as a reference throughout the text.

We divide systems into 3 parts--input, processing, and output. In an accounting system, source documents form the input. They are the basis for the entries into the accounting system. The processing consists of the operations performed to record and classify the input data for use in accounting reports. The output from the accounting system includes the financial statements and management reports.

Subsidiary Ledgers LG2

In order to keep track of what individual customers owe, use a separate Accounts Receivable account for each customer. As we do this the general ledger becomes unwieldy. Avoid this problem by removing the individual customer accounts receivable from the general ledger and placing them in a **subsidiary ledger**. In order to keep the general ledger in balance, replace these individual accounts in the general ledger by a controlling account titled Accounts Receivable. When posting the journal entry for a sale on account, post the debit to accounts receivable twice. One posting is to the controlling account in the general ledger. The second is to the specific customer's account in the Accounts Receivable Subsidiary Ledger. Thus, we keep the general ledger in balance by the debit to the controlling account and credit to revenue. We keep the detail necessary to send out monthly statements and manage accounts receivable in the subsidiary ledger.

At the end of any accounting period, test the accuracy of the general ledger by using the trial balance. Test the accuracy of the subsidiary ledger by making a listing of the individual subsidiary ledger account balances. Since we have posted only one-half of each transaction to the subsidiary ledger, we don't have the self-balancing feature (debits equal credits). But the total of the accounts in the subsidiary ledger must be equal to the balance in the Accounts Receivable Controlling account in the general ledger.

We can use subsidiary ledgers for any general ledger account for which management desires the additional detail. We normally find them for Accounts Receivable and Accounts Payable. But often accounts such as Merchandise Inventory, and Equipment also employ subsidiary ledgers.

Special Journals LG 3-5

Special journals are an addition to, not a replacement for, the general journal. An accounting system can operate without special journals, but it must always include a general journal. Because the special journals illustrated in Appendix D are clearly illustrated and explained, there is no need to repeat explanations here. The Guided Study section will include a detailed study of their use. These suggestions will help you understand their use.

- Regardless of its name or special nature, a journal is still a book of original entry. We first record a transaction in one (*and only one*) of the journals. From there we post it to ledger accounts.
- Ledger accounts receive postings directly from all of the journals.
- So that we can accurately trace ledger account entries back to the journals, it is important to use correctly the symbols, S, P, CR, CP, and J, when posting to accounts in the general ledger and in the subsidiary ledgers.
- Introducing special journals into the system does not destroy the journal/ledger relationship that you have already learned, nor does it affect the use of a work sheet. It simply expands and makes the use of the special journals more efficient in recording transactions from business papers.
- To determine which journal to use for any transaction, a specific decision process is suggested. Ask the questions indicated in the flow chart on the next page. Whenever the answer is yes, you have found the proper journal.

A summary of the posting of special journals is as follows:

Special Journal	Posting
Special columns provided for a single account (with no subsidiary ledger).	Post the *total* to the appropriate *general ledger* account. Do not post the individual amounts.
Special columns provided for an account with a subsidiary ledger.	Post the *total* to the appropriate *general ledger* account and the *individual amounts* to the appropriate *subsidiary ledger* account.
"Other accounts" columns.	Post the *individual* amount to the appropriate *general ledger* account, and do not post the total.

Computerized Accounting Systems LG A1-A4

With the significant decreases in the cost of computer systems, more and more businesses are able to afford computerized accounting systems. Owners of the smallest retail stores are finding that they are able to computerize their accounting with the use of a micro-computer. Thus, today we find computerized accounting systems in the very smallest to the very largest businesses. The principles of accounting which you are learning in this text are just as appropriate to these computerized systems as they are to the manual systems. Instead of the records being in human readable form as they are in the textbook, they are recorded magnetically on disk or tape. The computer simplifies the recording process, eliminates all of the mathematics, and speeds up the preparation and dissemination of accounting reports. But, the fundamentals which you are learning still apply. (You may be using one or more of the computerized practice sets or software for end-of-chapter problems that accompany the text to achieve a basic understanding of what the computer can accomplish.)

GUIDED STUDY OF THIS APPENDIX

A. **Special Journals** We must first understand how to determine the journal to use. Refer to the flow chart on the prior page of the Study Guide, if necessary.

1. Use the cash receipts journal to record every transaction that involves _____ _____ .

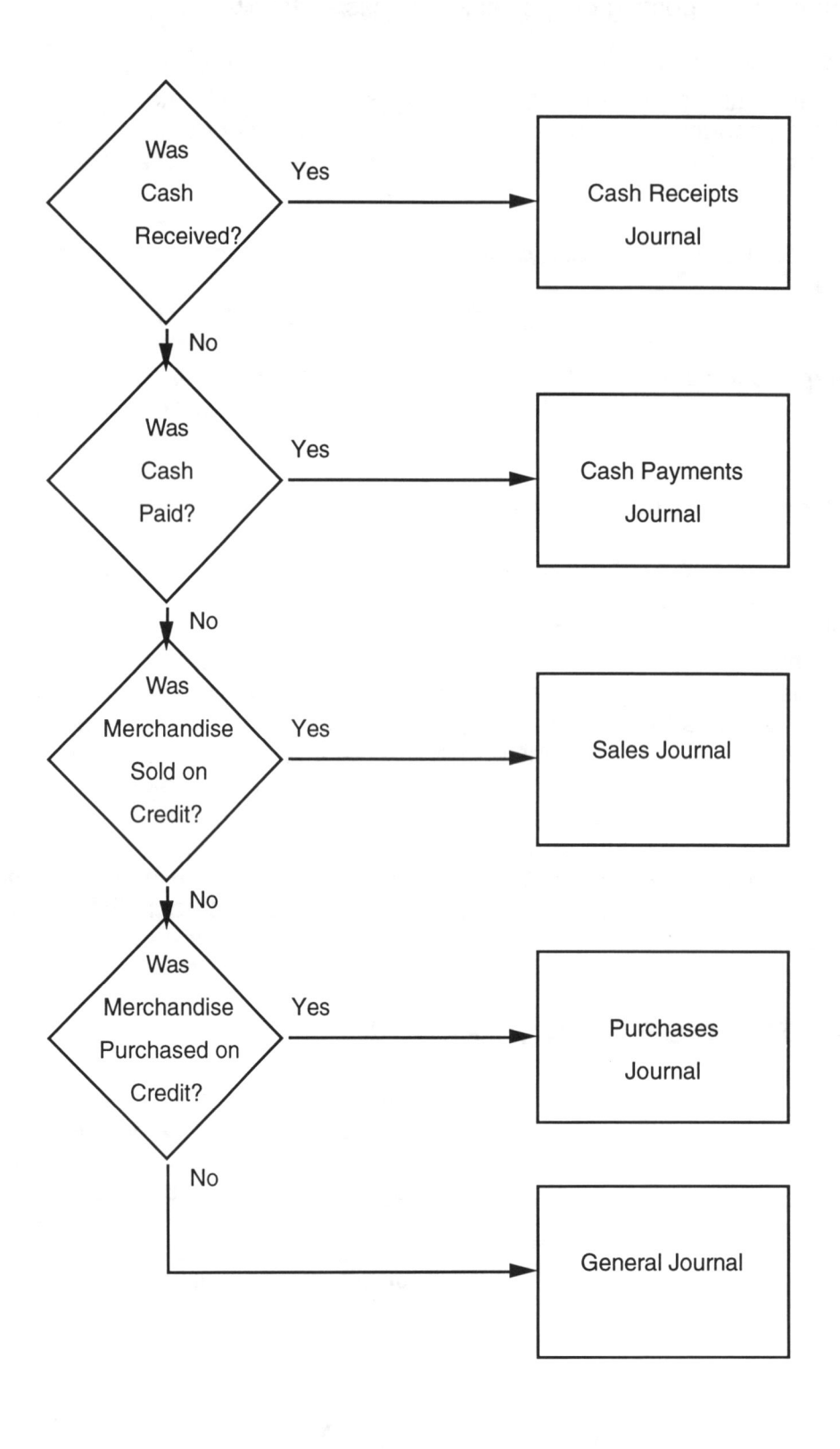

```
                    ┌─────────────┐
           Was      │             │
          Cash      │Yes          │  Cash Receipts
        Received?  ─────────────▶ │    Journal
                    │             │
                    └─────────────┘
            │ No
            ▼
                    ┌─────────────┐
           Was      │             │
          Cash      │Yes          │  Cash Payments
          Paid?    ─────────────▶ │    Journal
                    └─────────────┘
            │ No
            ▼
           Was
        Merchandise  Yes           Sales Journal
         Sold on   ─────────────▶
         Credit?
            │ No
            ▼
           Was
        Merchandise  Yes           Purchases
        Purchased on ────────────▶  Journal
         Credit?
            │ No
            ▼                       General Journal
```

(Flowchart of transaction routing to special journals: Was Cash Received? → Yes: Cash Receipts Journal. Was Cash Paid? → Yes: Cash Payments Journal. Was Merchandise Sold on Credit? → Yes: Sales Journal. Was Merchandise Purchased on Credit? → Yes: Purchases Journal. No → General Journal.)

Special Journals and Accounting Systems 419

A1. a receipt of cash

2. If the cash receipt is for a sale of merchandise, record the entry in the _____ journal.

A2. cash receipts

3. However, record a sale of merchandise for credit in the _____ journal.

A3. sales

4. If we sold a piece of office equipment on account, enter it in the _____ journal.

A4. general (It is not a sale of merchandise.)

5. Collections of accounts receivable follow credit sales. Enter such collections in the _____ journal.

A5. cash receipts

6. If the collection is only a partial payment (not payment in full) for a sale, enter it in the _____ journal.

A6. cash receipts

7. Enter a purchase of office equipment on credit in the _____ journal.

A7. general

8. Enter a purchase of merchandise for credit in the _____ journal.

A8. purchases

9. If we pay cash for a purchase of merchandise, we should enter the transaction in the _____ journal.

A9. cash payments

10. If we pay cash for office supplies, we should make the entry in the _____ journal.

A10. cash payments

11. Enter a return of faulty merchandise from a customer in the _____ journal.

A11. general

12. Enter payment of rent in advance in the _____ journal.

420 Appendix D

A12. cash payments (Payment in advance has no bearing on the journal used.)

A13. general

A14. general

A15. cash receipts

A16. general

A17. cash payments

A18. No. (Only credit purchases of merchandise for resale.)

A19. No. (If cash is involved, the entry goes in a cash journal.)

A20. fewer, divide

13. Make adjusting entries in the _____ journal.

14. Make closing entries in the _____ journal.

15. If an owner invests cash in a business, enter it in the _____ _____ journal.

16. If an owner invests store equipment in a business, enter the transaction in the _____ journal.

17. Enter a $10,000 contribution by a business to a college in the _____ _____ journal.

18. Is it true that we should enter every credit purchase in the purchases journal? _____

19. Would we enter any transaction involving a payment or receipt of cash in any journal other than cash? _____

20. Special journals will strengthen internal control. The general ledger will be more compact and less likely to contain errors because it will contain _____ entries. Also, because we have separate journals for different categories of transactions, we can _____ the recording duties among employees.

B. Posting

1. Using Exhibit D-4, do we post the sales amount in the sales journal twice? ____ . Explain. _____
_____
_____
_____

Special Journals and Accounting Systems   421

B1. Yes; We post them to the customer accounts in the accounts receivable subsidiary ledger and to the general ledger.

B2. No; Individual postings to the accounts receivable subsidiary ledger are made daily, but postings to the general ledger are made monthly.

B3. Yes; Cash receipts journal.

B4. On June 7, 1997, the date we made the sale.

B5. On June 30, 1997, when we post the total.

B6. Yes.

B7. On June 30 when all posting is up to date.

B8. June 17.

B9. Yes.

2. Do we make both postings at the same time? _____ . Explain. _____
_____
_____
_____

3. Is the same relationship true for collections of accounts receivable? _____ . From what journal do we post such collections? _____
_____

4. When is the $400 sale to W. Houston posted to her account in the subsidiary ledger? _____
_____

5. When do we post this sale to Accounts Receivable in the general ledger?
_____
_____

6. Won't the controlling account and the subsidiary ledger be out of balance during June? _____

7. When will they be in balance? _____
_____
_____

8. Following W. Houston's account, refer to Exhibit D-6. When did she pay for her purchase of June 7? _____

9. Since her payment involved a cash receipt, we enter it in the cash receipts journal. Did she pay early enough to qualify for the 2% cash discount? _____

10. Exhibit D-6 shows seven transactions entered in the cash receipts journal. Of these, _____ required posting to a subsidiary ledger.

422   Appendix D

B10. three

B11. No; Special account columns involve posting of totals. We posted them on June 30.

B12. Cash, Sales Discounts, Accounts Receivable, and Sales.

B13. June 30, 1997.

B14. J. Max, Capital; Notes Payable; and Notes Receivable.

B15. We show the date of the transaction.

B16. Yes.

B17. 3,300. ($2,500 + $600 + $200)

11. These three transactions were the payments by G. Harrison, W. Houston, and L. Ronstadt. Were these three transactions also posted to the general ledger on the dates they occurred? _____ . Explain. _____
_____
_____

12. From the cash receipts journal in Exhibit D-6, which accounts do we post with total amounts? _____
_____
_____
_____

13. In these accounts, what date did we use for the posting of totals? _____
_____

14. What accounts do we post individually from the cash receipts journal (Exhibit D-6)? _____
_____
_____

15. When we made these postings, what date did we show in the account? _____
_____
_____

16. Have we posted every dollar amount entered in the cash receipts journal to the general ledger either in total or individually? _____

17. What is the total dollar amount of postings made individually? $_____ .

18. How many individual postings did we eliminate by posting to Cash in total?
_____

Special Journals and Accounting Systems 423

B18. Six. *(Seven entries posted with one total.)*

19. Post from Exhibits D-6 and D-8 to the Cash account for Max Clothing.

			Cash	Acct. No. 101	
					Balance
Date	Explan	PR	Dr.	Cr.	Dr. Cr.
___	___	___	___	___	___
___	___	___	___	___	___
___	___	___	___	___	___

B19.

1997
Jun. 30 CR1 6,130   6,130
     30 CP1   2,424 3,706

20. If Max Clothing had only a general journal, how many postings would it have to make to the Cash account in June?
_____

B20. Fourteen. *(Seven from the cash receipts journal and seven from the cash payments journal.)*

21. Also, collections on accounts receivable occur daily. Use of a cash receipts journal allows us to make only _____ posting(s) to Cash and _____ posting(s) to Accounts Receivable instead of many postings to each account for June.

B21. one, one

22. The same savings occur when we use other special journals. Instead of many credits to the Sales account, we make only _____ from the _____ journal for the total credit sales in June.

B22. one, sales

23. And, from the sales journal, only one debit posting to _____ is required instead of many postings.

B23. Accounts Receivable

24. By using a purchases journal, we save numerous postings to the accounts _____ and _____.

B24. Purchases, Accounts Payable

25. Since a need exists to record unusual transactions, correcting entries, and adjusting and closing entries, the accounting systems must still have a _____ journal.

424   Appendix D

B25. general

B26. No answer required.

C1. hardware, software

C2. integrated accounting system

C3. general ledger, accounts receivable, accounts payable, payroll.

C4. menu

C5. back-up

C6. Electronic spreadsheet

C7. formulas

C8. quality, timeliness, and variety

26. The accounting system illustrated in Appendix D is adequate for many small businesses. It is a model you could actually use.

C. Computerization of the General Accounting Function (Appendix DA)

1. Two segments make up a computerized accounting system: _____ and _____.

2. A series of computer programs tied together to perform accounting functions is called a(n) _____.

3. The modules contained in a typical computerized accounting system are _____, _____, _____, and _____.

4. A list of options displayed for the user to select from is called a _____.

5. We call a copy of programs and data files kept as part of internal control _____.

6. _____ programs allow users to create electronic sheets of columnar paper.

7. The user in essence programs reports with labels, numbers, and _____.

8. Primary benefits of computerization include _____, _____, and _____ of information.

LEARNING GOALS ACHIEVEMENT TEST

1. (LG 1, 3) Arrapaho Sales Company deals in household and art objects purchased from area artisans or from various national suppliers. Purchases and sales are made on credit. Payment for all purchases is made by check in time to take advantage of discounts. All incoming merchandise is inspected to ensure that the quantities conform to the amount ordered and there are no defects. Credit customers are billed monthly; the top half of the bill is returned with the customer's check. The accountant has designed a set of business documents on which various information is recorded. Some of them are described below. For each document, indicate the journal in which the transaction it represents should be recorded. Use the journal symbols that are used in Appendix D.

	Document	Journal
a.	A receiving report attached to a vendor's invoice for merchandise	_____
b.	A receiving report attached to a supplier's invoice for electrical repairs	_____
c.	A copy of a sales invoice indicating that merchandise has been shipped to a customer	_____
d.	A batch of cash sales tickets with a summary sheet showing total cash sales for the day	_____
e.	The group of returned portions of monthly bills to customers, each showing the amount and stamped "Received" by the cashier	_____
f.	Copies of checks written that day, each attached to a form that describes and shows authorization for payment	_____
g.	Copies of a form called a credit memorandum that credits a customer's account receivable for returned sales	_____
h.	The end-of-period work sheet showing adjustments and with the Income Statement and Balance Sheet columns completed (for closing entries)	_____
i.	A copy of the payroll listing showing check numbers	_____

426 Appendix D

2. (LG 4) For each letter appearing in the special journals on the following page, indicate how frequently (M = monthly; D = daily) and to what ledger (G = general; S = subsidiary) an amount appearing at that position would be posted or that it would not be posted (NP).

	Frequency	Ledger
a.	_____	_____
b.	_____	_____
c.	_____	_____
d.	_____	_____
e.	_____	_____
f.	_____	_____
g.	_____	_____
h.	_____	_____
i.	_____	_____
j.	_____	_____
k.	_____	_____
l.	_____	_____
m.	_____	_____
n.	_____	_____
o.	_____	_____
p.	_____	_____
q.	_____	_____

Cash Receipts Journal

Date	Explanation	Debits				
		Cash	Sales Discounts	Other Accounts		
				Title	PR	Amt
		a	b			
		d				e
		g				
	Totals	i	j			k

	Credits						
Accounts Credited	Accounts Receivable		Sales	Other Accounts	
	PR	Amount		PR	Amount
		c			
					f
			h		
		l	m		n

Purchases Journal

Date	Account Credited	Terms	PR	Amount
				o
				p
	Total			q

428 Appendix D

3. (LG 3, 5) General Company uses only a general journal. Special Company, in the same line of business, uses a general journal and the four special journals described in Appendix D. Assume that both companies had identical transactions in March 1997.

    a. Which company will have the greater number of postings to the Cash account? _____
    b. Which company will write the account title, Accounts Receivable, in journals more often? _____
    c. Which company will have the greater number of postings to the accounts receivable subsidiary ledger? _____
    d. Will the total postings to the Cash account be greater for Special Company? _____
    e. Must Special Company total its cash receipts and cash payments journals and record those totals in the general journal before posting? _____
    f. Which company will not total the debits and credits in its journal(s)? _____
    g. Suppose each company began the month with a balance of $10,000 in Cash and had the same transactions during the month. Which will have the larger cash amount in the end-of-month trial balance? _____

4. (LG A1-A4) Complete the following statements by filling in the blank.

    a. The two principal segments of a computerized accounting system are the _____ and _____ .
    b. A typical computerized accounting system is composed of the following four modules: _____, _____, _____, and _____ .
    c. An internal control procedure limiting access to system capabilities to those who have the proper authority uses _____ .
    d. The type of computer software ideally suited to the construction of such accounting reports as cash forecasts is called _____ .
    e. List three potential benefits of computerizing the accounting system. _____, _____, and _____ .

ANSWERS TO LEARNING GOALS ACHIEVEMENT TEST

1. a. P   d. CR   g. J
    b. J   e. CR   h. J
    c. S   f. CP   i. CP

2.

	Frequency	Ledger
a.	NP	NP
b.	NP	NP
c.	D	S
d.	NP	NP
e.	D	G
f.	D	G
g.	NP	NP
h.	NP	NP
i.	M	G
j.	M	G
k.	NP	NP
l.	M	G
m.	M	G
n.	NP	NP
o.	D	S
p.	D	S
q.	M	G

3. a. General   e. No
    b. General   f. General
    c. Neither (the same)   g. Neither (the same)
    d. No (the same)

4. a. computer hardware, computer software
    b. general ledger, accounts receivable, accounts payable, payroll
    c. passwords
    d. electronic spreadsheets
    e. quality of information, timeliness of information, variety of information

Appendix E

PAYROLL SYSTEM

EXPLANATION OF MAJOR CONCEPTS

Payrolls and Deductions LG 1, 2

Businesses pay employees on a regular basis. Some businesses compute and pay the payroll weekly, others every two weeks, and some monthly. There are many methods of determining the amount of an employees' pay. Two of the most common are an agreed upon salary per year and an hourly wage rate. Using the first method, a person with a salary of $26,000 per year would earn $500 = ($26,000 / 52 weeks) in gross pay per week. Using the second method, a person with an hourly rate of $10.50 would earn gross pay of $420 = ($10.50 x 40 hours) in a forty-hour week.

Gross pay is the amount of total pay earned before any deductions. Employees' pay checks are almost always less than gross pay because of deductions. The law requires some deductions and some deductions are voluntary. Gross pay minus deductions equals net pay. Net pay is take home pay. Note that in the journal entry to record the payroll, expense is equal to gross pay. The employer must pay the total amount to someone. The employer does not keep the deductions. Instead, the employer deducts them in order to remit them to a government agency, a union, or to some other entity.

The Fair Labor Standards Act (the Federal Wage and Hour Law) covers most employees. It defines all time worked in excess of forty hours per week as overtime. Employers must pay the employee at least time and one-half for overtime. A typical wage computation is the one for William Ford in the textbook. He worked forty-two hours in one week. Ford's wage rate is $15 per hour, and his gross pay computation is:

40 hours	x	$15.00	=	$600	=	Gross pay.
2 hours	x	15.00	=	30	=	Overtime pay.
2 hours	x	7.50	=	15	=	Overtime premium pay.
				$645	=	Total gross pay.

Note that the (2 hours x $15.00) + (2 hours x $7.50) is the same as 2 hours x $22.50, or time and one-half for the overtime that Ford worked this week. We separate the overtime premium because many companies account for it separately.

Payroll Taxes LG 2-5

Two major forms of payroll taxes paid by employees through payroll deductions are income tax and FICA (social security) tax. Employees are subject to federal income tax deductions in all states. And in many states, employees also are subject to state income tax. We base income tax on earnings for the entire year. We deduct it from employee gross pay for each of the fifty-two weeks of the year. FICA tax has an annual ceiling. After an employee has earned a certain amount, the tax ceases until the next year.

Employers do not bear any cost of employee income tax. The company simply withholds it and remits it to the proper governmental agency. Employers do, however, have to pay two major payroll taxes: a matching amount of FICA and the unemployment compensation tax. These are expenses in addition to the expense of gross pay. Their amount is debited to an account called Payroll Tax Expense.

The primary benefit of the Social Security program is the monthly retirement benefits for qualified workers. The law has expanded benefits to include disability benefits, survivors benefits, and Medicare benefits.

To illustrate payroll deductions, consider the case of James B. Skinner in Exhibit E-3. His gross pay appears in the total column. Deductions from that gross pay withheld by the Orbit Company are shown as follows:

Gross pay		$552.00
Deductions:		
FICA	$41.40	
Federal income tax	62.00	
State income tax	8.54	
Group health	19.50	131.44
Net pay to Skinner		$420.56

After Skinner has earned an FICA base amount (assumed to be the first $55,000 per calendar year in this textbook) the FICA tax withholding stops. He pays no more FICA tax until the next calendar year. Both federal and state income tax continue all year. The company periodically remits the total amounts of these three taxes withheld from Skinner's pay to the appropriate government agencies.

Employers pay payroll taxes in addition to those withheld from the employees' pay. The three most common ones are:

- A matching amount of FICA.
- State unemployment compensation tax.
- Federal unemployment compensation tax.

As in FICA withholding, the employer's share of the FICA tax also stops when a specific employee reaches the base amount in a calendar year. It is important to be able to compute the tax in a cutoff period. Assume that in a week ending in December

1997, James B. Skinner earns gross pay of $800 and has earned year-to-date cumulative pay of $54,750 up through the end of the last pay period. Only the first $250 = ($55,000 - $54,750) of the $800 gross pay is taxable for FICA both to Skinner and his employer. Neither Skinner nor his employer pay FICA during 1997 after the week in which Skinner reaches the $55,000 assumed FICA wage limit.

We compute unemployment taxes in a manner similar to FICA taxes in that they are charged only on a base amount (in this textbook, we assume $7,000). Unlike FICA, however, all unemployment taxes fall on the employer (*except in a few states*). When an employee has reached the cumulative year-to-date base, the tax ceases for that year.

Payroll Entries LG 3

There are three basic payroll entries as follows:

- Recording the payroll (made in the general journal).
- Paying the payroll (made in the cash payments or payroll journal).
- Recording payroll tax expense (made in the general journal).

The typical form for these three journal entries (using the general journal for ease of illustration) is:

1. Salaries and Wages Expense............................ Gross Pay
    FICA Taxes Payable .... 7.5 percent
    Federal Income Tax Withholding Payable Actual $
    State Income Tax Withholding Payable ... Actual $
    Other Liabilities for Deductions.................. Actual $
    Salaries and Wages Payable...................... Net Pay
    To record payroll for a specified period.

2. Salaries and Wages Payable............................ Net Pay
    Cash... Net Pay
    To record payment of employees;
    should be in Cash Payments Journal.

3. Payroll Tax Expense .... Total
    FICA Taxes Payable...................................... 7.5 percent
    Federal Unemployment Taxes Payable.... 0.8 percent
    State Unemployment Taxes Payable .... 5.4 percent
    To record employer's payroll taxes.

The sum of the expense items in entries 1 and 3 is the total expense of buying people's services.

Payroll Records LG 2, 6

We need payroll records to ensure that employees receive the proper amount of compensation. These records must also provide information required to prepare the tax reports that an entity must make to federal and state governmental agencies. A business must have at least a payroll register (illustrated in Exhibit E-3) and an individual earnings record (illustrated in Exhibit E-4) for each individual employee. A small organization may type or hand write them. Large organizations usually maintain them by computer.

From these records a business must prepare and file an Employer's Quarterly Federal Tax Return reporting the amount of income taxes withheld and the amount of FICA tax. The business must deposit these amounts withheld on a prescribed schedule. Annually, the business must provide each employee with a Wage and Tax Statement, Form W-2 (illustrated in Exhibit E-5).

Liabilities for Compensated Absences LG 7

Businesses often give their employees periods of time off with pay. They should charge the wages for these periods of absence to the periods when the employee performs services for the business. Therefore, each week that an employee works, the business should record the regular wages expense and payroll tax expense. They also should record a portion of the expense for the anticipated absence. Assuming that the compensated absence is for vacation, the company would make the following entry for each week that the employee works. It records a prorata portion of the wages to be paid during the vacation period:

Vacation Pay Expense	X	
Liability for Vacation Pay		X

Then, when the employee takes the vacation, the entry to record the payment would be as follows:

Liability for Vacation Pay	X	
FICA Taxes Payable		X
Federal Income Tax Withholding Pay		X
State Income Tax Withholding Pay		X
Cash		X
To accrue liability for vacation pay.		

A company should make similar accruals for sick pay or other forms of compensated absences.

GUIDED STUDY OF THIS APPENDIX

		A.	**Computation of Pay** As a starting point for study in Appendix E, use Exhibit E-3.
		1.	Exhibit E-3 illustrates a _____ _____ . We prepare one for each pay period.
A1.	payroll register	2.	The pay period covered by this payroll register is the _____ ended _____ .
A2.	week, 1/15/97	3.	Three employees, Skinner, Burke, and Howard, work in the _____ Department.
A3.	Sales (The code S means sales.)	4.	The total number of employees in this company is _____ .
A4.	five	5.	Is James Skinner paid a salary or an hourly rate? _____ . How much? $ _____ .
A5.	Hourly rate; 12.	6.	Skinner worked _____ hours this week at a rate of $12, for total regular and overtime earnings of $_____ .
A6.	44.0, 528.00 = (44 x $12)	7.	Skinner worked _____ hours overtime. Since overtime premium is one-half the regular hourly rate, Skinner has earned an additional $_____ for overtime premium pay.
A7.	four; 24 = (4 x $6)	8.	Note carefully that $24 is only the premium portion of Skinner's pay for overtime hours. We have already included these four overtime hours in the computation of his regular pay.
A8.	No answer required.	9.	If Skinner had worked forty hours at $12 per hour, he would have earned $_____ .
A9.	480	10.	However, Skinner's total earnings were $_____ . This means that in the four hours of overtime, he earned $_____ .

436 Appendix E

A10. 552; 72

11. The $72 is equal to "time and one-half" for overtime. In other words, four hours at $12 = $_____ of regular pay and the additional one-half for overtime premium = $_____ . This is the total of $72.

A11. 48, 24

12. Continue to examine Skinner's pay. Since this is January, he is not likely to have earned the assumed FICA taxable base of $55,000 in 1997. His FICA deduction is 7.5% of $552 = $_____ .

A12. 41.40

13. His federal income tax withheld is based on a wage bracket withholding table similar to Exhibit E-2. The company has deducted $_____ this week for Skinner's income tax.

A13. 62.00

14. Skinner has a weekly deduction of $_____ to buy group health insurance.

A14. 19.50

15. What is the total amount of Skinner's payroll deductions? $_____ .

A15. 131.44

16. Gross pay of $_____ minus deductions of $131.44 equals $_____ , which is Skinner's net pay (or take-home pay).

A16. 552.00, 420.56

17. We would follow the same procedure to obtain similar figures for each employee in the company. Total gross earnings of all employees this week are $_____ .

A17. 2,924.50

18. Total deductions from earnings are $_____ . We must compute these individually for each employee.

A18. 721.33

19. Total deductions include $_____ for FICA, $_____ for federal income tax, $_____ for state income tax and $_____ for group health.

Payroll System 437

A19. 219.34, 355.00,
49.74, 97.25

20. Total net pay for this week is $_____ .

A20. 2,203.17

21. The journal entry to record this payroll debits expenses with gross pay of $_____. Of this amount, we debit $_____ to Sales Salaries Expense.

A21. 2,924.50; 1,529.50

22. We should debit $_____ to Executive Salaries Expense, and $_____ to Office Salaries Expense. Check to be sure that total debits in this entry are $2,924.50.

A22. 750.00, 645.00

23. We should credit the FICA deductions of $_____ to FICA Taxes Payable, the federal income tax deductions of $_____ to Federal Income Tax Withholding Payable, the state income tax deductions of $_____ to State Income Tax Withholding Payable, and the group health deductions of $_____ to Group Health Insurance Premiums Payable.

A23. 219.34, 355.00, 49.74, 97.25

24. The total of all deductions is $_____ , which, when subtracted from gross pay of $2,924.50, leaves $_____ of net pay credited to Salaries and Wages Payable.

A24. 721.33, 2,203.17

25. Review the January 15 payroll entry for Orbit Company in the textbook. Was that entry made up from the foregoing amounts? _____ .

A25. Yes.

B. Employer's Payroll Taxes
Orbit Company will pay the payroll taxes shown on the payroll register in Exhibit E-3. However, Orbit deducted them from employees earnings. That tax burden falls on employees.

438   Appendix E

1. What additional taxes on this payroll must Orbit Company pay?
   _____
   _____
   _____

B1. A matching FICA amount and the federal and state unemployment tax.

2. Since Orbit Company pays an additional FICA amount equal to employee deductions, it will have $_____ more FICA taxes payable.

B2. 219.34

3. The state in which Orbit operates has an unemployment tax rate of _____ %. We credit the liability account State Unemployment Taxes Payable with $_____ this week.

B3. 5.4; 157.92 ($2,924.50 x 0.054)

4. At 0.8%, we credit the Federal Unemployment Taxes Payable with $_____ .

B4. 23.40 ($2,924.50 x 0.008)

5. The total debit to Payroll Tax Expense this week is $_____ .

B5. 400.66

6. Since both the payroll entry and the payroll tax entry record expenses and liabilities (but not payments), we enter them in the _____ journal.

B6. general

7. We applied both FICA and unemployment compensation tax rates to total gross pay this week because _____
   _____
   _____
   _____ .

B7. It is early in the year (January) and no employee has earned the base amount

8. Later in the year, say in October or November, some employees will have accumulated earnings to date equal to or greater than the base amounts. For those persons, FICA deductions and company FICA payroll taxes will cease.

B8. No answer required.

9. FICA taxes cease in any calendar year after an individual employee has earned greater than $_____ (an assumed amount in this textbook).

B9. 55,000

B10. 1,000

B11. 75.00 ($1,000 x 0.075)

B12. 0.00

C1. compensated absences

C2. 1,000 ($500 x 2), 50

C3. 20 ($1,000 / 50)

C4. Vacation Pay Expense, Liability for Vacation Pay

C5. Liability for Vacation Pay

C6. prepaid vacation pay

10. Assuming that G. Jones had earned a total of $54,000 as of the end of October. If her November gross pay was $3,000, only $ _____ of that would be subject to FICA tax.

11. Therefore, the FICA withholding from her pay in November would be $_____.

12. The FICA withholding from her December pay would be $_____.

C. Liabilities for Compensated Absences

1. Absences that a company pays employees for are called _____ _____.

2. If a worker earns $500 per week and is allowed two weeks paid vacation per year, the company should record the worker's wages for the two weeks they will be absent of $_____ over the _____ weeks they work.

3. Thus, they will record expense for vacation pay of $_____ each week.

4. When we journalize this, we debit _____ and credit _____ _____.

5. Then when the workers take their vacation, the journal entry to record the wages for that week would debit _____ _____ and credit the normal withholding accounts and cash.

6. If the account Liability for Vacation Pay has a debit balance, we would classify it as a current asset called _____ _____.

LEARNING GOALS ACHIEVEMENT TEST

1. (LG 1-3) Pedro Raul earns $16 per hour. In the week ended February 23, 1997, he worked a total of forty-five hours. Determine the following assuming time and one-half is paid for overtime:

    a. Gross pay earned.

    b. Federal income tax withheld if Raul has three exemptions. Use the table in Exhibit E-2.

    c. Amount of FICA tax withheld.

    d. Amount of federal FUTA tax on his employer.

    e. Amount of state SUTA tax on his employer, 5.4%.

2. (LG 2, 3, 5) Ando Company had a gross payroll of $25,000 for the week ended September 28, 1997. Deductions were as follows:

Federal income tax	$5,200
State income tax	600
FICA tax (no employee has yet earned the base amount of $55,000)	?
Union dues	100

The company pays the regular federal rate under FUTA. The state unemployment tax rate is 5.4%. Only $15,000 of wages are subject to unemployment tax.

Required:

(1) Record the payroll for the week ended September 28, 1997.
(2) Record the employer's payroll taxes (total payroll is taxable).

GENERAL JOURNAL

Date	Accounts and Explanations	PR	Debit	Credit

442 Appendix E

3. (LG 5) Assuming that the unemployment base is $7,000, the federal rate is 0.8%, and the state rate is 5.4%, what would be a company's journal entry to record the employer's payroll tax expense with the following earnings facts for the week ended May 11, 1997.

Employee	Prior Total Earnings	Current Earnings
Sam Jones	$5,000.00	$500.00
Dave Anjo	6,900.00	600.00
Andria Answorth	9,000.00	800.00

Computations:

FICA:

State unemployment:

Federal unemployment:

GENERAL JOURNAL

Date		Accounts and Explanations	PR	Debit	Credit

4. (LG 7) Icor Company gives its employees two weeks paid vacation each year. They conform to the practice of accruing the cost of compensated absences. Their employees total gross earnings are $25,000 for each of the 50 weeks they work. Journalize the entry to record the liability for compensated absences for the week ended January 26, 1997.

GENERAL JOURNAL

Date	Accounts and Explanations	PR	Debit	Credit

If an employee with a total gross pay of $1,600 per week took the week ending March 16, 1997, for vacation with pay, record the journal entry for the employee's pay, assuming a 7.5% FICA rate, federal income tax withholding of $300, and state income tax withholding of $50.

GENERAL JOURNAL

Date	Accounts and Explanations	PR	Debit	Credit

ANSWERS TO LEARNING GOALS ACHIEVEMENT TEST

1. a. 40 hours x $16 = $640 regular pay.
      5 hours x 16 =   80 overtime pay.
      5 hours x   8 =   40 overtime premium.
                     $760 gross pay.

   b.
	Exemptions			
Wages	0	1	2	3
$760-$770			$87	

   c. $760 x 0.075 = $57.00

   d. $760 x 0.008 = $6.08.

   e. $760 x 0.054 = $41.04.

   Note: By late February, Mr. Raul would not have earned a total of either $7,000 or $55,000.

2.

GENERAL JOURNAL

Date		Accounts and Explanations	PR	Debit	Credit
1997 Sep.	28	(1) Salaries and Wages Expense		25,000	
		FICA Taxes Payable			1,875
		Federal Income Tax Withholding Payable			5,200
		State Income Tax Withholding Payable			600
		Union Dues Payable			100
		Salaries and Wages Payable			17,225
		To record payroll for week ended September 28, 1997.			
	28	(2) Payroll Tax Expense		2,805	
		FICA Taxes Payable			1,875
		State Unemployment Tax Payable			810
		Federal Unemployment Tax Payable			120
		To record employer's payroll taxes.			

Computations:
$25,000 × 0.075 = $1,875.00
$15,000 × 0.054 = $810.00
$15,000 × 0.008 = $120.00

3. Computations:

   FICA $1,900 × 0.075 = $142.50.

   State unemployment $600 × 0.054   = $32.40.

   Federal unemployment $600 × 0.008   = $4.80.

GENERAL JOURNAL

Date		Accounts and Explanations	PR	Debit	Credit
1997 May	11	Payroll Tax Expense		179.70	
		FICA Taxes Payable			142.50
		State Unemployment Tax Payable			32.40
		Federal Unemployment Tax Payable			4.80
		To record employer's payroll tax expense.			

4.

GENERAL JOURNAL

Date		Accounts and Explanations	PR	Debit	Credit
1997 Jan.	26	Vacation Pay Expense		1,000	
		Liability for Vacation Pay			1,000
		Accrual of liability for 1/50 of vacation pay.			
Mar.	16	Liability for Vacation Pay		1,600	
		FICA Taxes Payable			120
		Federal Income Tax Withholding Payable			300
		State Income Tax Withholding Payable			50
		Cash			1,130
		Payment to an employee for one week's vacation.			

Appendix F

PARTNERSHIP ACCOUNTING

EXPLANATION OF MAJOR CONCEPTS

Characteristics of a Partnership LG 1

The three major forms of business in the United States are the single proprietorship, the partnership, and the corporation. A single proprietorship is the simplest form of business. It has one owner. Up to this point in the textbook, we have focused primarily on the single proprietorship. A partnership is a voluntary association of two or more persons to carry on a business for profit. The partnership is a popular form of business for professionals such as lawyers or accountants. In the eyes of the law, a corporation is a "fictitious person." A state creates a legal entity by issuing to a group of incorporators a certificate called a corporate charter. A large number of persons may own a corporation. They invest in the business and receive shares of capital stock.

Owners easily form a partnership by written or verbal agreement. Although there are no formal procedures (such as filing of applications with the state to form the business), there are state laws that regulate the relationships of partners with each other and with the public. The laws affecting partnerships are the same in most states because they have adopted a model law called the Uniform Partnership Act.

Because they pool financial resources and the borrowing power of more than one person, *partnerships can raise more capital than proprietorships*. They can also bring together in the same business a greater variety of talent. Against those advantages potential partners must weigh certain disadvantages. Each partner is personally liable for the debts of the firm. They must secure agreement of other partners for certain actions such as selling a portion of their interest. Also, through the concept of *mutual agency*, nonowners can hold one partner liable for the actions of any other partner.

The income tax status is similar to that for proprietorships. *Partners include their individual shares of partnership income and deductions in their personal income tax returns.*

Accounting for a Partnership LG 2

Owners form a partnership by contributing assets to the business. The assets may be cash or any other asset accepted by the business. The entry to record the formation debits the appropriate asset account for the fair market value of the asset contributed and credits the individual partner's capital account. The partnership differs from the single proprietorship in that there is a separate capital account for each of the owners. We keep each partners interest in the assets of the business in a separate account.

Division of Profits and Losses LG 3

In computing the division of partnership profits and losses, there are some common errors which students tend to make. The following points will help you to avoid them:

- The division of profits is a computation leading up to a single journal entry--closing of Income Summary to the capital accounts. The elements of the computation do not appear in any journal entry.
- Any formula that the partners agree to use to divide profits is possible. When the formula contains interest allowances or salary allowances, these items are not expenses. They are simply a way of dividing income or loss. If the partnership agreement specifies interest or salary allowances, we must include them even if there is not sufficient income to cover them. Remember they are part of a formula to divide profits and losses. They are not expenses nor are they part of the journal entry.
- Often a formula will provide that we divide the amount after allowances in some ratio. If the allowances are greater than net income, the excess of allowances over income will be a negative figure. Treat it as a negative figure--allocate it, and add it in as a negative figure.
- The withdrawals accounts have no relation to profit division. The partners' withdrawals are completely unrelated to any salary allowances. The salary allowances are not expense. Ignore the withdrawals accounts when dividing profits.
- Once we have computed the division of profits, make a compound general journal entry to close Income Summary into the capital accounts as follows:

Income Summary	XXX	
Partner A, Capital.............................		XX
Partner B, Capital.............................		XX
Partner C, Capital.............................		XX
To close the Income Summary account.		

- Finally, remember that withdrawals have no effect on income. Close the withdrawals accounts separately into the respective capital accounts.

You should take the time at this point to review the three examples of the division of profits under various situations which appear in the textbook. We will also study them in the Guided Study section.

Financial Statements LG 4

The financial statements for a partnership are very similar to those that we have studied up to this point. There is no difference in the income statement. The statement of partners' equity has basically the same structure as that of the statement of owner's equity except that it will have a column for each partner, see Exhibit F-1. The balance sheet is the same as for a proprietorship except for the owner's equity section. Instead of a single capital account, the partnership balance sheet will show a capital account for each partner.

Admission or Withdrawal of a Partner   LG 5

New partners may come into the business. Existing partners may die or withdraw. When this happens, we dissolve the existing partnership, and a new one takes its place. To an external viewer (except for a possible change in the business name), a partnership dissolution is not noticeable. To the partners, however, it may mean some reassignment of capital balances or at least the creation of new ones. As you work with the many possible ways to record admission or retirement of a partner, try this process of analytical reasoning:

> **Net assets = Total assets - Total liabilities**
> **Net assets = Total partners' equity.**

Follow these steps:

1. Determine the amount of net assets before the change.

2. Determine the amount of net assets after the change. It can be (a) any amount the partners agree it should be or (b) equal to old net assets plus assets contributed by the new partner (or minus assets removed by a retiring partner).

3. Using these data, determine the effect on each partner's capital balance (called that partner's interest).

Again, review the examples in the textbook at this point.

Liquidation of Partnership   LG 6

An entirely different type of dissolution occurs when we liquidate a partnership. In this case, we sell or collect all of the assets so that cash becomes the only asset (a process called realization). Then we pay the cash to the equity claimants. We pay the creditors in full before we distribute any cash to partners. Then we pay the remaining cash to partners, and the business ceases to operate. Again, here are some points to help you:

- There are almost always gains and losses in the realization process. Credit the gains and debit the losses to the partners' capital accounts in their profit-sharing ratio. We must share losses in the same ratio as profits.

450 Appendix F

- When we complete realization and pay creditors, the remaining cash belongs to the partners. We pay it to them in accordance with their remaining capital balances--not in accordance with profit-sharing ratios.
- A partner could develop a debit (negative) balance in their capital account in the realization process. This is a deficiency. Deficient partners must pay in the amount of any deficiency, to bring their capital balances up to zero. If a partner cannot do so, this is another loss the remaining partners share in their remaining profit-sharing ratios. It is important to grasp this last point. Suppose A, B, and C share profits on a 3:2:1 basis. This means that A takes 3/6 or 50%; B takes 2/6 or 33 1/3%; and C takes 1/6 or 16 2/3%. If B becomes deficient, A and C stand 3:1. A must absorb 3/4 or 75%, and C must absorb 1/4 or 25% of B's deficit.

GUIDED STUDY OF THIS APPENDIX

A. Formation of a Partnership

1. In the Appendix F example, Bach contributed land worth $ _____ and a building worth $ _____ and merchandise with a cost of $ _____ . The partnership assumed the mortgage on the building in the amount of $ _____ with accrued interest of $ _____ . We should credit Bach's capital account with $ _____ .

A1. 3,000, 20,000, 6,200; 10,000, 200; 19,000

2. Toven contributed only cash in the amount of $ _____ . So we should credit his capital account for $ _____ .

A2. 15,000; 15,000

3. When a partner withdraws assets in anticipation of income, we credit the asset and debit the partner's _____ account.

A3. withdrawals

4. On July 31, 1997, Bach and Toven each withdrew $ _____ .

A4. 1,000

5. We credited cash for $ _____ and debit J. Bach, Withdrawals for $ _____ .

A5. 2,000, 1,000

6. We debited the other $1,000 to _____ .

Partnership Accounting   451

A6. B. Toven, Withdrawals

7. If a partner withdraws assets in excess of the amount agreed on, we should debit their _____ account.

A7. capital

B. Division of Profits and Losses
The textbook uses the public accounting firm of Carter and Foley to illustrate division of profits.

1. In Example 1, they share profits on what basis? _____ .

B1. 3:2

2. This means that Carter should get what fraction? _____ .
And Foley what fraction? _____ .

B2. 3/5; 2/5

3. To divide a net income of $60,000, we credit Carter's capital account with
$ _____ .

B3. 36,000

4. Could Kay Carter withdraw more than her share of the profits for the year? _____
Explain. _____
_____
_____

B4. Yes; There is no relationship between profit-sharing formulas and withdrawals.

5. Suppose that Carter and Foley had a net loss of $12,500 in 1997 instead of a net income. How would this affect the capital accounts? _____

B5. It would reduce them.

6. Ann Foley began the year with less capital than Kay Carter ($30,000 compared to $70,000). Should Foley, therefore, absorb less of a $12,500 loss? _____ .
Explain. _____
_____
_____

B6. No; Losses are shared in the same ratio as profits; in this case, 3:2 or $7,500 and $5,000.

7. Move to Example 2. They have changed the formula to include an interest allowance of 20%. They agree to apply the 20% to? _____
_____

452   Appendix F

B7. Beginning-of-year capital balances.

8. Since total beginning-of-year capital balances are $100,000, total interest allowance of 20% will be $ _____ .

B8. 20,000

9. They also agreed on a salary allowance. Carter was to get $ _____ and Foley $ _____ .

B9. 10,000, 9,000

10. These amounts _____ (are/are not) considered an expense in the calculation of income.

B10. are not

11. With total interest and salary allowances of $ _____ and an assumed net income of $60,000 in 1997, the excess is _____ (positive/negative).

B11. 39,000, positive

12. We divide the excess, $21,000, on a 2:1 ratio. This means that _____ gets 2/3 and _____ gets 1/3.

B12. Carter, Foley

13. But the journal entry does not close out 2/3 and 1/3 of the Income Summary, respectively. Why? _____

B13. Because of the interest and salary allowances.

14. Move to Example 3. How much is the assumed net income for the year? $ _____ .

B14. 24,000.

15. How much do we allocate (in total) to salary allowances and interest allowances? $ _____

B15. 39,000.

16. This leaves a residual of $22,000 - $39,000 = $15,000 _____ (negative/positive).

B16. negative

17. Using the 2:1 division of the residual, we would allocate Carter $ _____ and Foley $ _____ .

B17. (10,000), (5,000)

B18. 12,000

B19. No answer required.

B20. have a separate column, total

C1. 30,000, 42,000

C2. 72,000

C3. 1/2, 18,000

C4. 15,000

C5. It is a personal gain to Allen. *(The individuals exchanged the cash.)*

18. If the ratio for the residual had been 4:1, we would allocate Kay Carter $_____ of the residual.

19. Remember that the purpose of the computation for division of net income is to make a single journal entry to close the Income Summary account. Do not try to journalize the interest allowances, salary allowances, or residuals in separate journal entries.

20. In the statement of partner's equity, each partner would _____ _____ and there would be a _____ column.

C. **Admission or Withdrawal of a Partner** Probably the most complex entries reflecting changes in capital structure are records of the admission of a new partner.

1. In the textbook example, Arthur Allen and Brian Barnes are partners, with capital balances of $ _____ and $ _____ respectively.

2. This means that net assets of the partnership are $_____.

3. They agree to admit Charles Cahn as a third partner. In the first example, Allen sells _____ of his interest to Cahn for $_____.

4. What is the net asset value of 1/2 of Allen's interest? $ _____.

5. What happens to the additional $3,000 ($18,000 - $15,000)? _____ _____

6. Does Cahn pay any money into the partnership? _____ . Explain. _____ _____

454 Appendix F

C6. No; It is a purchase of part of Allen's ownership from Allen.

7. Then why is a journal entry needed on the partnership books? _____

C7. It is still necessary to record the changes in the capital accounts.

8. Another way for a new partner to join a partnership is to invest cash or other assets in the partnership to acquire an interest (share of ownership). Does this always cause an increase in net assets? _____

C8. Yes.

9. Look at "Investment Equal to Interest." Allen and Barnes are partners. Their capital balances are $30,000 and $42,000, respectively. Total net assets before admission of Cahn are $_____.

C9. 72,000

10. Cahn desires to own 1/3 of the business. To do so, he must invest an amount equal to exactly _____ the combined capital balances of the other two partners before adding the new assets.

C10. 1/2

11. This amount is $36,000. When we add this to the present net assets, the new total net assets are $ _____.

C11. 108,000

12. And 1/3 of $108,000 (Cahn's interest) is $ _____.

C12. 36,000

13. Admission of a new partner is a time of negotiation. Sometimes the exiting partners may require the new partner to invest more or less than the exact book value of the new partners share. Two methods to account for such a situation are the goodwill method and the bonus method.

C13. No answer required.

14. "Investment Not Equal to Interest" covers the bonus methods. When Cahn invested $48,000 and the partners agreed that total capital would be $_____ , Cahn's 1/3 of new net assets was $ _____.

Partnership Accounting   455

C14. 120,000, 40,000

15. Cahn's investment was _____ (*more/less*) than his share of net assets.

C15. more

16. Thus, we must _____ each old partner's capital account.

C16. increase

17. If Cahn invested less than his share of the new agreed upon capital, there is a bonus to the _____ partner and the _____ partners have to give up some capital.

C17. new, old

18. How do the old partners divide this reduction of capital balances? _____

C18. They divide it in the profit-and-loss-sharing ratio.

19. If a partner retires either voluntarily (with permission of the other partners) or involuntarily (for example, by death), we should adjust assets to _____

C19. their current market value

20. Why is this necessary? _____

C20. Any increases or decreases in value occurred while the retiring partner was in the firm, and he or she should share in them.

21. How does a retiring partner participate in gains and losses due to changes in asset values? _____

C21. When revaluing assets, we will comparably revalue equities.

22. Before Fred Thomas retired from the firm of Rhodes, Wills, and Thomas, the land and building were appraised at $_____ more than their book value.

C22. 24,000

23. Why did we credit $8,000 to each partner? _____

456   Appendix F

C23. Because they share profits equally.

C24. 12,000

C25. 8,000, 4,000

C26. No answer required.

D1. the conversion of all noncash assets to cash

D2. 250,000, 100,000

D3. 150,000; profit-and-loss-sharing ratio

D4. 50,000

D5. creditors

D6. cash, 50,000

24. If the ratio had been 3:2:1, we would credit Kirsten Rhodes with $ _____ in her capital account.

25. And we would credit Wills and Thomas with $ _____ and $ _____ , respectively.

26. It would also be normal to close the books and update all partners' capital accounts with operating profit or loss in case of the death of a partner. In a voluntary withdrawal, we might avoid this process by negotiation.

D. Liquidation

1. Liquidation involves the process of realization, which is _____ _____ _____ _____ _____ .

2. In Example 3 of the textbook, the other assets had a book value of $ _____ and were sold for $ _____ .

3. Thus there was a loss of $ _____ . In the process of realization, we record losses and gains in capital accounts in accordance with the _____ _____ .

4. Since each partner shared equally, we charge each with a loss of $ _____ .

5. The first cash distribution is the payment to _____ .

6. When realization and payment to creditors are complete, the remaining asset is _____ of $ _____ .

7. Are there any remaining liabilities? _____

Partnership Accounting   457

D7. No. *(An exception could be a debt owed by the firm to one of partners.)*

D8. partners' equity

D9. 50,000, 10,000, (10,000)

D10. No; They reflect each partner's interest in cash

D11. Yes. *Frank's is negative.*

D12. deficiency

D13. The deficient partner should pay in that amount to the firm.

D14. The other partners must reduce their capital accounts.

D15. In their remaining profit-and-loss-sharing ratio.

D16. No.

8. Therefore, total cash = total _____ _____.

9. The partners' capital balances are now $_____ , $_____ , and $_____ respectively.

10. Since the partners' capital accounts have been debited and credited with losses and gains, do they now reflect the profit-and-loss-sharing ratio? _____ . Explain.
_____
_____
_____

11. Could some capital accounts be negative (debit balance)? _____

12. We call a debit balance in the capital account a(n) _____ .

13. What should happen to eliminate a deficiency? _____
_____
_____
_____

14. If he or she is unable to pay, how do we eliminate the deficiency? _____
_____
_____
_____

15. How do they share this capital reduction? _____
_____

16. When liquidation cash is finally paid to partners, do we pay it in the profit-and-loss-sharing ratio? _____

17. How do we pay the amount of final cash to each partner determined? _____
_____
_____

D17. Each is entitled to withdraw his or her capital balance.

LEARNING GOALS ACHIEVEMENT TEST

1. (LG 2, 4) Dave Johnson and Bob Olson formed a partnership on December 31, 1997. Johnson contributed $20,000 in cash and Olson contributed a truck worth $8,000 and cash of $5,000. The truck had an outstanding note on it which the business assumed in the amount of $3,000.

    Required:

    (a) Journalize the formation of the partnership.
    (b) Prepare a balance sheet immediately after the formation.

(a) **GENERAL JOURNAL**

Date	Accounts and Explanations	PR	Debit	Credit

(b)

2. (LG 3) Herman Sanderson and Alice Jones are partners with capital balances as follows on January 1, 1997:

    H. Sanderson, capital $80,000
    A. Jones, capital 60,000

They share profits as follows:

	Sanderson	Jones
Salary allowances..	$15,000	$30,000
Interest on beginning-of-year capital	10%	10%
Residual (remainder)	70%	30%

Required: Show computations to divide net income for 1997 under each of the following assumptions:

(a) There is a net income of $100,000.

(b) There is a net income of $50,000.

(c) There is a net loss of $10,000.

3. (LG 5) Maria Randado and Jim Hall are partners who share profits 2:1, respectively. Randado's capital balance is $60,000; Hall's is $40,000. They agree to admit Rita Guerra to their law firm. Show general journal entries to admit Guerra under each of the following independent possible agreements:

   a. She is to pay Hall $50,000 for 1/2 of his interest.
   b. She is to invest $50,000 for a 1/3 interest with total capital to be $150,000.
   c. She is to invest $65,000 for a 1/3 interest with total capital to be $165,000.
   d. She is to invest $44,000 for a 1/3 interest with total capital to be $144,000.

Appendix F

GENERAL JOURNAL

Date	Accounts and Explanations	PR	Debit	Credit

4. (LG 5) Dan Donver, Marcia Marin, and Sam Nevada are equal partners with capital balances after closing the books on December 31, 1997, as follows:

Donver	$32,600
Marin	40,000
Nevada	15,300

They agree that Nevada will leave the firm as of December 31, 1997. An appraisal finds the inventory overvalued by $5,000 and the building undervalued by $20,000. They share profits and losses equally.

Required: Record the necessary journal entries for Nevada's retirement from the firm by withdrawing cash.

GENERAL JOURNAL

Date	Accounts and Explanations	PR	Debit	Credit

464 Appendix F

5. (LG 6) Assume that the firm of Donver, Marin, and Nevada (Question 4) is to liquidate on December 31, 1997. In addition to the capital balances shown in Question 3, there are cash of $15,000, liabilities of $5,000, and other assets of $77,900. They sell the other assets for $38,900 cash during the month of December 1997.

   Required: Prepare a statement of liquidation.

ANSWERS TO LEARNING GOALS ACHIEVEMENT TEST

1. (a)

GENERAL JOURNAL

Date		Accounts and Explanations	PR	Debit	Credit
1997 Dec.	31	Cash		25,000	
		Truck		8,000	
		Note Payable			3,000
		D. Johnson, Capital			20,000
		B. Olson, Capital			10,000
		To record formation of partnership and investment of assets.			

(b)

JOHNSON & OLSON
BALANCE SHEET
DECEMBER 31, 1997

Assets

Current assets
Cash... $25,000
    Total current assets $25,000

Property, plant, and equipment
  Trucks 8,000
Total assets.. $33,000

Liabilities

Current liabilities
Notes payable... $ 3,000

Partners' Equity

D. Johnson, capital.. $20,000
B. Olson, capital 10,000
    Total partners' equity 30,000
Total liabilities and partners' equity...................... $33,000

2. (a)

	To Be Divided	Sanderson	Jones
Net income.....................................	$100,000		
Salary allowances...........................	(45,000)	$15,000	$30,000
Interest allowances.........................	(14,000)	8,000	6,000
Excess of income over allowances	$ 41,000		
70% to Sanderson	(28,700)	28,700	
30% to Jones...............................	(12,300)		12,300
Totals..	$ 0	$51,700	$48,300

(b)

	To Be Divided	Sanderson	Jones
Net income	$ 50,000		
Salary allowances	(45,000)	$15,000	$30,000
Interest allowances	(14,000)	8,000	6,000
Excess of allowances over income	$ (9,000)		
70% to Sanderson	6,300	(6,300)	
30% to Jones	2,700		(2,700)
Totals	$ 0	$16,700	$33,300

(c)

	To Be Divided	Sanderson	Jones
Net income	$(10,000)		
Salary allowances	(45,000)	$ 15,000	$ 30,000
Interest allowances	(14,000)	8,000	6,000
Excess of allowances over income	$(69,000)		
70% to Sanderson	48,300	(48,300)	
30% to Jones	20,700		(20,700)
Totals	$ 0	$(25,300)	$ 15,300

3.

GENERAL JOURNAL

Date		Accounts and Explanations	PR	Debit	Credit
1997	a	J. Hall, Capital		20,000	
		R. Guerra, Capital			20,000
		Purchase of 1/2 of Hall's interest.			
	b	Cash		50,000	
		R. Guerra, Capital			50,000
		Admission to 1/3 interest by investment of $50,000.			
	c	Cash		65,000	
		M. Randado, Capital			6,667
		J. Hall, Capital			3,333
		R. Guerra, Capital			55,000
		Admission to 1/3 interest by investment of $65,000.			

Date		Accounts and Explanations	PR	Debit	Credit
1997	d	Cash		44,000	
		M. Randado, Capital		2,667	
		J. Hall, Capital		1,333	
		R. Guerra, Capital			48,000
		Admission to 1/3 interest by			
		investment $44,000.			

4.
GENERAL JOURNAL

Date		Accounts and Explanations	PR	Debit	Credit
1997 Dec.	31	Building		20,000	
		Inventory			5,000
		D. Donver, Capital			5,000
		M. Marin, Capital			5,000
		S. Nevada, Capital			5,000
		Revaluation of assets.			
	31	S. Nevada, Capital		20,300	
		Cash			20,300
		Retirement of partner.			

5.
DONVER, MARIN, AND NEVADA
STATEMENT OF PARTNERSHIP LIQUIDATION
FOR THE MONTH OF DECEMBER 1997

	Cash	Other Assets	Liabilities
Balances before realization	$ 15,000	$ 77,900	$ 5,000
Sale of assets	38,900	(77,900)	
Balances	$ 53,900	$ 0	$ 5,000
Payment of liabilities	(5,000)		(5,000)
Balances	$ 48,900		$ 0
Cash to partners	(48,900)		

	Capital		
	Donver	Marin	Nevada
Balances before realization	$ 32,600	$ 40,000	$ 15,300
Sale of assets	(13,000)	(13,000)	(13,000)
Balances	$ 19,600	$ 27,000	$ 2,300
Payment of liabilities	0	0	0
Balances	$ 19,600	$ 27,000	$ 2,300
Cash to partners	(19,600)	(27,000)	(2,300)